# Advancing Consumer-Centric Fog Computing Architectures

Kashif Munir
*University of Hafr Al-Batin, Saudi Arabia*

A volume in the Advances
in Computer and Electrical
Engineering (ACEE) Book Series

Published in the United States of America by
    IGI Global
    Engineering Science Reference (an imprint of IGI Global)
    701 E. Chocolate Avenue
    Hershey PA, USA 17033
    Tel: 717-533-8845
    Fax:  717-533-8661
    E-mail: cust@igi-global.com
    Web site: http://www.igi-global.com

Library of Congress Cataloging-in-Publication Data

Names: Munir, Kashif, 1976- editor.
Title: Advancing consumer-centric fog computing architectures / Kashif Munir,
    editor.
Description: Hershey, PA : Engineering Science Reference, an imprint of IGI
    Global, [2019] | Includes bibliographical references and index.
Identifiers: LCCN 2018017253| ISBN 9781522571490 (hardcover) | ISBN
    9781522571506 (ebook)
Subjects: LCSH: Cloud computing.
Classification: LCC QA76.585 .A387 2019 | DDC 004.67/82--dc23 LC record available at https://
lccn.loc.gov/2018017253

This book is published in the IGI Global book series Advances in Computer and Electrical
Engineering (ACEE) (ISSN: 2327-039X; eISSN: 2327-0403)

British Cataloguing in Publication Data
A Cataloguing in Publication record for this book is available from the British Library.

All work contributed to this book is new, previously-unpublished material.
The views expressed in this book are those of the authors, but not necessarily of the publisher.

For electronic access to this publication, please contact: eresources@igi-global.com.

# Advances in Computer and Electrical Engineering (ACEE) Book Series

ISSN:2327-039X
EISSN:2327-0403

Editor-in-Chief: Srikanta Patnaik, SOA University, India

**MISSION**

The fields of computer engineering and electrical engineering encompass a broad range of interdisciplinary topics allowing for expansive research developments across multiple fields. Research in these areas continues to develop and become increasingly important as computer and electrical systems have become an integral part of everyday life.

The **Advances in Computer and Electrical Engineering (ACEE) Book Series** aims to publish research on diverse topics pertaining to computer engineering and electrical engineering. **ACEE** encourages scholarly discourse on the latest applications, tools, and methodologies being implemented in the field for the design and development of computer and electrical systems.

**COVERAGE**

- Computer science
- Qualitative Methods
- Sensor Technologies
- VLSI Design
- Electrical Power Conversion
- Microprocessor Design
- Digital Electronics
- Programming
- Circuit Analysis
- Optical Electronics

IGI Global is currently accepting manuscripts for publication within this series. To submit a proposal for a volume in this series, please contact our Acquisition Editors at Acquisitions@igi-global.com or visit: http://www.igi-global.com/publish/.

# Titles in this Series

*For a list of additional titles in this series, please visit:*
*https://www.igi-global.com/book-series/advances-computer-electrical-engineering/73675*

*Optimal Power Flow Using Evolutionary lgorithms*
Provas Kumar Roy (Kalyani Government Engineering College, India) and Susanta Dutta (Dr. B. C. Roy Engineering College, India)
Engineering Science Reference • ©2019 • 323pp • H/C (ISBN: 9781522569718) • US $195.00

*Advanced Condition Monitoring and Fault Diagnosis of Electric Machines*
Muhammad Irfan (Najran University, Saudi Arabia)
Engineering Science Reference • ©2019 • 307pp • H/C (ISBN: 9781522569893) • US $225.00

*The Rise of Fog Computing in the Digital Era*
K.G. Srinivasa (Chaudhary Brahm Prakash Government Engineering College, India) Pankaj Lathar (Chaudhary Brahm Prakash Government Engineering College, India) and G.M. Siddesh (Ramaiah Institute of Technology, India)
Engineering Science Reference • ©2019 • 286pp • H/C (ISBN: 9781522560708) • US $215.00

*Algorithms, Methods, and Applications in Mobile Computing and Communications*
Agustinus Borgy Waluyo (Monash University, Australia)
Engineering Science Reference • ©2019 • 297pp • H/C (ISBN: 9781522556930) • US $205.00

*Exploring Critical Approaches of Evolutionary Computation*
Muhammad Sarfraz (Kuwait University, Kuwait)
Engineering Science Reference • ©2019 • 390pp • H/C (ISBN: 9781522558323) • US $215.00

*Applications of Security, Mobile, Analytic, and Cloud (SMAC) Technologies for Effective ...*
P. Karthikeyan (Thiagarajar College of Engineering, India) and M. Thangavel (Thiagarajar College of Engineering, India)
Engineering Science Reference • ©2018 • 300pp • H/C (ISBN: 9781522540441) • US $215.00

*For an entire list of titles in this series, please visit:*
*https://www.igi-global.com/book-series/advances-computer-electrical-engineering/73675*

701 East Chocolate Avenue, Hershey, PA 17033, USA
Tel: 717-533-8845 x100 • Fax: 717-533-8661
E-Mail: cust@igi-global.com • www.igi-global.com

# Table of Contents

**Foreword** ................................................................................................................ xiii

**Preface** ................................................................................................................... xiv

**Acknowledgment** ................................................................................................. xvii

**Chapter 1**
An Overview of Cloud and Edge Computing Architecture and Its Current
Issues and Challenges .................................................................................................. 1
    *Guru Prasad Bhandari, Banaras Hindu University, India*
    *Ratneshwer Gupta, Jawaharlal Nehru University, India*

**Chapter 2**
Fog/Cloud Service Scalability, Composition, Security, Privacy, and SLA
Management ................................................................................................................ 38
    *Shweta Kaushik, Jaypee Institute of Information Technology, India*
    *Charu Gandhi, Jaypee Institute of Information Technology, India*

**Chapter 3**
Fog Computing and Its Role in the Internet of Things ............................................. 63
    *Nisha Angeline C. V., Thiagarajar College of Engineering, India*
    *Raja Lavanya, Thiagarajar College of Engineering, India*

**Chapter 4**
A Comprehensive Study on Internet of Things Security: Challenges and
Recommendations ...................................................................................................... 72
    *Manikandakumar Muthusamy, Thiagarajar College of Engineering,
        India*
    *Karthikeyan Periasamy, Thiagarajar College of Engineering, India*

**Chapter 5**
Fog vs. Cloud Computing Architecture ...............................................87
    *Shweta Kaushik, Jaypee Institute of Information Technology, India*
    *Charu Gandhi, Jaypee Institute of Information Technology, India*

**Chapter 6**
Comparing User Authentication Techniques for Fog Computing ...................111
    *Kashif Munir, University of Hafr Al-Batin, Saudi Arabia*
    *Lawan A. Mohammed, University of Hafr Al Batin, Saudi Arabia*

**Chapter 7**
Secure Data Integrity Protocol for Fog Computing Environment ....................126
    *Kashif Munir, University of Hafr Al-Batin, Saudi Arabia*
    *Lawan Ahmed Mohammed, University of Hafr Al Batin, Saudi Arabia*

**Chapter 8**
Unique Fog Computing Taxonomy for Evaluating Cloud Services....................145
    *Akashdeep Bhardwaj, University of Petroleum and Energy Studies, India*
    *Sam Goundar, Victoria University of Wellington, New Zealand*

**Compilation of References** .........................................................163

**Related References**................................................................183

**About the Contributors** ..........................................................213

**Index**...........................................................................215

# Detailed Table of Contents

**Foreword** ............................................................................................................... xiii

**Preface** .................................................................................................................. xiv

**Acknowledgment** ................................................................................................ xvii

**Chapter 1**
An Overview of Cloud and Edge Computing Architecture and Its Current
Issues and Challenges ................................................................................................1
>  *Guru Prasad Bhandari, Banaras Hindu University, India*
>  *Ratneshwer Gupta, Jawaharlal Nehru University, India*

Edge computing is a technique of optimizing cloud computing systems by performing data processing at the edge of the network, near the source of the data in the systems. And, cloud computing is a service that delivers on-demand self-service, broad network access, resource pooling, rapid elasticity or expansion, which is trending in today's technology-driven world. With the advantage of flexibility, storage, sharing, and easy accessibility, cloud is being used by major players in IT (information technology). This chapter highlights cloud/edge computing architecture and its current issues and challenges from technological and organizational aspects. A brief introduction of edge computing architecture with similar technologies along with its service models is discussed. A few counterexamples of cloud computing architecture are showed. Organizational aspects of cloud computing architecture, as well as IBM and Oracle reference cloud architecture, are briefly presented. Some emerging issues and challenges associated with cloud/edge computing on its utilization are also elaborated.

**Chapter 2**

Fog/Cloud Service Scalability, Composition, Security, Privacy, and SLA
Management ................................................................................................38

*Shweta Kaushik, Jaypee Institute of Information Technology, India*
*Charu Gandhi, Jaypee Institute of Information Technology, India*

Cloud computing has started a new era in the field of computing, which allows the access of remote data or services at anytime and anywhere. In today's competitive environment, the service dynamism, elasticity, and choices offered by this highly scalable technology are too attractive for enterprises to ignore. The scalability feature of cloud computing allows one to expand and contract the resources. The owner's data stored at the remote location, but he is usually afraid of sharing confidential data with cloud service provider. If the service provider is not the trusted one, there may be a chance of leakage of confidential data to external third party. Security and privacy of data require high consideration, which is resolved by storing the data in encrypted form. Data owner requires that the service provider should be trustworthy to store its confidential data without any exposure. One of the outstanding solutions for maintaining trust between different communicating parties could be the service level agreement between them.

**Chapter 3**

Fog Computing and Its Role in the Internet of Things ........................................63

*Nisha Angeline C. V., Thiagarajar College of Engineering, India*
*Raja Lavanya, Thiagarajar College of Engineering, India*

Fog computing extends the cloud computing paradigm to the edge of the network, thus enabling a new breed of applications and services. Defining characteristics of the Fog are 1) low latency and location awareness, 2) widespread geographical distribution, 3) mobility, 4) very large number of nodes, 5) predominant role of wireless access, 6) strong presence of streaming and real time applications, and 7) heterogeneity. In this chapter, the authors argue that the above characteristics make the Fog the appropriate platform for a number of critical internet of things (IoT) services and applications, namely connected vehicle, smart grid, smart cities, and in general, wireless sensors and actuators networks (WSANs).

**Chapter 4**

A Comprehensive Study on Internet of Things Security: Challenges and
Recommendations ................................................................................................72

*Manikandakumar Muthusamy, Thiagarajar College of Engineering,*
*India*
*Karthikeyan Periasamy, Thiagarajar College of Engineering, India*

Internet of things is a growing technology with many business opportunities and risks. It is strongly believed that IoT will cause a major shift in people's lives similar to how the internet transformed the way people communicate and share information. IoT is becoming popular in the various domains such as smart health, smart cities, smart transport, and smart retail. The security and privacy concerns of IoT are crucial as it connects a large number of devices. Security is a more critical issue that certainly needs to be resolved with a high level of attention, as with an increasing number of users, there would be a need to manage their requests and check authenticity on the cloud-based pattern. Recently, a series of massive distributed denial-of-service attacks have occurred in IoT organizations. Such malicious attacks have highlighted the threats resulting from not enough security in IoT devices together with their overwhelming effects on the internet. This chapter provides an overview of the security attacks with regard to IoT technologies, protocols, and applications.

**Chapter 5**

Fog vs. Cloud Computing Architecture ..............................................................87
*Shweta Kaushik, Jaypee Institute of Information Technology, India*
*Charu Gandhi, Jaypee Institute of Information Technology, India*

Cloud computing has emerged as a new technology that allows the users to acquire resources at anytime, anywhere by connecting with internet. It provides the options to users for renting of infrastructure, storage space, and services. One service issue that affects the QoS of cloud computing is network latency while dealing with real-time application. In this, the user interacts directly with application but delays in receiving the services, and jitter delay will encourage the user to think about this. In today's world, clients are moving towards the IoT techniques, enabling them to connect all things with internet and get their services from cloud. This advancement requires introduction of new technology termed as "fog computing." Fog computing is an extension of cloud computing that provides the service at the edge of the network. Its proximity to end users, mobility support, and dense distribution reduces the service latency and improves QoS. This fog model provides the prosperity for advertisement and entertainment and is well suited for distributed data model.

**Chapter 6**

Comparing User Authentication Techniques for Fog Computing .....................111
*Kashif Munir, University of Hafr Al-Batin, Saudi Arabia*
*Lawan A. Mohammed, University of Hafr Al Batin, Saudi Arabia*

In the IoT scenario, things at the edge can create significantly large amounts of data. Fog computing has recently emerged as the paradigm to address the needs of edge computing in internet of things (IoT) and industrial internet of things (IIoT) applications. Authentication is an important issue for the security of fog computing since services are offered to massive-scale end users by front fog nodes. Fog computing faces new security and privacy challenges besides those inherited from cloud computing. Authentication helps to ensure and confirms a user's identity. The existing traditional password authentication does not provide enough security for the data, and there have been instances when the password-based authentication has been manipulated to gain access to the data. Since the conventional methods such as passwords do not serve the purpose of data security, this chapter focuses on biometric user authentication in fog computing environments. In this chapter, the authors present biometric smartcard authentication to protect the fog computing environment.

**Chapter 7**

Secure Data Integrity Protocol for Fog Computing Environment ..................... 126
*Kashif Munir, University of Hafr Al-Batin, Saudi Arabia*
*Lawan Ahmed Mohammed, University of Hafr Al Batin, Saudi Arabia*

Fog computing is a distributed infrastructure in which certain application processes or services are managed at the edge of the network by a smart device. Fog systems are capable of processing large amounts of data locally, operate on-premise, are fully portable, and can be installed on heterogeneous hardware. These features make the fog platform highly suitable for time and location-sensitive applications. For example, internet of things (IoT) devices are required to quickly process a large amount of data. The significance of enterprise data and increased access rates from low-resource terminal devices demand reliable and low-cost authentication protocols. Lots of researchers have proposed authentication protocols with varied efficiencies. As a part of this chapter, the authors propose a secure authentication protocol that is strongly secure and best suited for the fog computing environment.

**Chapter 8**

Unique Fog Computing Taxonomy for Evaluating Cloud Services................... 145
*Akashdeep Bhardwaj, University of Petroleum and Energy Studies, India*
*Sam Goundar, Victoria University of Wellington, New Zealand*

Fog computing has the potential to resolve cloud computing issues by extending the cloud service provider's reach to the edge of the cloud network model, right up to the cloud service consumer. This enables a whole new state of applications and services which increases the security, enhances the cloud experience, and keeps the data close to the user. This chapter presents a review on the academic literature research work on fog computing, introduces a novel taxonomy to classify cloud products based on fog computing elements, and then determines the best fit fog computing product to choose for the cloud service consumer.

**Compilation of References** ............................................................................... 163

**Related References** ............................................................................................ 183

**About the Contributors** .................................................................................. 213

**Index** ................................................................................................................... 215

# Foreword

Fog computing is an architecture that uses edge devices to carry out substantial amounts of computation, storage, communication locally and routed over the internet backbone, and most definitively has input/output from the physical world, known as transduction. The rapid growth of mobile and IoT applications has placed heavy demands on cloud infrastructure, which has led to moving computing and data services towards the edge of the cloud. There terms "fog computing" and "multi-access edge computing" are used to describe this trend.

Fog computing is an extension of cloud computing into its edge and physical world to meet the data volume and decision speed requirements in many emerging applications such as augmented and virtual realities (AR/VR), cyber-physical systems (CPS), intelligent and autonomous systems, and mission-critical systems. The boundary between centralized, powerful computing cloud and massively distributed, Internet connected sensors, actuators, and things is rather blurred in this new computing paradigm.

Fog computing consists of Edge nodes that perform physical input/output via sensor input, display output, and full closed loop process control. The processing power needed in advanced Edge Clouds like those that control autonomous vehicles can be considerable compared to traditional Edge personal devices such as mobile phones and personal computers.

This book addresses Fog Computing technologies that underpin associated developments, and discusses the state of the art in terms of frameworks, methodologies, current practices, and future directions. It will be a useful source of information for enterprise architects, managers and directors of organizations, as well as students and researchers in the field of Fog Computing. It provides a timely and thorough discussion of convergence of Fog/Edge related technologies. It will be a useful addition to the existing body of knowledge in these fields and new emerging technologies.

Sincerely yours,

*Sellappan Palaniappan*
*Malaysia University of Science and Technology, Malaysia*

# Preface

If anyone in the past thought that cloud computing is the pinnacle of infrastructure designs, they should surely think again. The current cloud model would not be able to handle billions of devices and instant communication. Fog computing has presented itself as a viable option, and possibly, the only real option available to us at the present moment.

Fog computing is a paradigm that extends Cloud Computing and services to the edge of the network. Similar to cloud, Fog provides data, compute, storage, and application services to end-users. The distinguishing characteristics of Fog are its proximity to end-users, its dense geographical distribution, and its support for mobility.

Fog computing present a new architecture vision where distributed edge and user devices collaborate with each other and with the clouds to carry out computing, control, networking, and data management tasks. Realizing fog computing imposes many new challenges. For example, how should the fog interact with the cloud, and how to enable users to control their fog services provided by fog operators? Addressing these challenges necessitates rethinking of the end-to-end network and computing architecture.

Companies have begun to look for solutions that would help reduce their infrastructures costs and improve profitability. Fog computing is becoming a foundation for benefits well beyond IT cost savings. Yet, many business leaders are concerned about fog computing security, privacy, availability, and data protection. To discuss and address these issues, we invite researches who focus on Fog computing to shed more light on this emerging field.

This book aims to bring together researchers and practitioners who focus on recent advanced techniques relevant to the convergence of fog Computing. This book project is set up to provide a platform for the researchers in mobile cloud computing community to publish and report the recent advances in Fog computing and services.

# OBJECTIVES

The major objectives include the followings:

- Providing comprehensive coverage and understanding in its technological, business, and organizational dimensions.
- Disseminate the evolving theory and practice related to fog computing.
- Thorough examination of Fog Computing with respect to issues of management, governance, trust and privacy, and interoperability.

# TARGET AUDIENCE

Policy makers, academicians, researchers, advanced-level students, technology developers, and government officials will find this text useful in furthering their research exposure to pertinent topics in Fog Computing and assisting in furthering their own research efforts in this field.

# APPROACH

This book incorporates the concepts of fog computing technologies as well as design techniques, architecture and application areas. It also addresses advanced security issues such as digital forensic, big data, access control and fault tolerance etc. The chapters are organized as follows:

## Chapter 1: An Overview of Edge/Cloud Computing Architecture With Its Issues and Challenges

This chapter presents brief introduction of edge computing architecture with similar technologies is discussed. Some challenges on edge/cloud computing to its utilization in cloud are also elaborated in this chapter.

## Chapter 2: Fog/Cloud Service Scalability, Composition, Security, Privacy, and SLA Management

This chapter explained Scalability, Composition, Security, Privacy and SLA management.

## Chapter 3: Fog Computing and Its Role in the Internet of Things

This work presents a fog computing and emerging wave of Internet deployments, most notably the Internet of Things (IoTs).

## Chapter 4: A Comprehensive Study on Internet of Things Security – Challenges and Recommendations

This chapter forecast the key security challenges and remedial actions associated with the development of IoT.

## Chapter 5: Fog vs. Cloud Computing Architecture

This chapter discussed interaction between Fog and Cloud Computing Architecture. The chapter also explains key features of Fog Computer and Challenges in Fog Computing.

## Chapter 6: Comparing User Authentication Techniques for Fog Computing

This chapter presents present biometric smartcard authentication to protect the fog computing environment.

## Chapter 7: Secure Data Integrity Protocol for Fog Computing Environment

This chapter discusses a mechanism to secure authentication protocol which is strongly secure and best suited for fog computing environment.

## Chapter 8: Unique Fog Computing Taxonomy for Evaluating Cloud Services

This chapter presents a survey of the academic literature on Fog Computing. A new Fog computing taxonomy model is proposed to determine the best fit cloud Fog product evaluation for the cloud service consumers.

# Acknowledgment

I extend my thanks to the many people who contributed to the preparation of this book. In particular, I heartily thank all the contributing authors. I greatly appreciate reviewers for their helpful and insightful comments, thorough technical reviews, constructive criticisms, and many valuable suggestions.

I am indebted to the management and staff of IGI Global for their valuable contribution, suggestions, recommendations, and encouragements from inception of initial ideas to the final publication of the book. And most importantly, I am grateful to Maria Rohde for the great help received from her throughout the final stages.

Deep appreciation goes to Prof. Dr. Sellappan Palaniappan for providing us with constructive and comprehensive foreword.

The editor wishes to acknowledge University of Hafr Al-Batin, Saudi Arabia for their support in providing the various facilities utilized in the process of production of this book.

This work was supported by Deanship of Scientific Research program of University of Hafr Al-Batin, Saudi Arabia.

*Kashif Munir*
*University of Hafr Al-Batin, Saudi Arabia*

Chapter 1

# An Overview of Cloud and Edge Computing Architecture and Its Current Issues and Challenges

**Guru Prasad Bhandari**
*Banaras Hindu University, India*

**Ratneshwer Gupta**
*Jawaharlal Nehru University, India*

## ABSTRACT

*Edge computing is a technique of optimizing cloud computing systems by performing data processing at the edge of the network, near the source of the data in the systems. And, cloud computing is a service that delivers on-demand self-service, broad network access, resource pooling, rapid elasticity or expansion, which is trending in today's technology-driven world. With the advantage of flexibility, storage, sharing, and easy accessibility, cloud is being used by major players in IT (information technology). This chapter highlights cloud/edge computing architecture and its current issues and challenges from technological and organizational aspects. A brief introduction of edge computing architecture with similar technologies along with its service models is discussed. A few counterexamples of cloud computing architecture are showed. Organizational aspects of cloud computing architecture, as well as IBM and Oracle reference cloud architecture, are briefly presented. Some emerging issues and challenges associated with cloud/edge computing on its utilization are also elaborated.*

DOI: 10.4018/978-1-5225-7149-0.ch001

## INTRODUCTION

Edge computing is a method of optimizing cloud computing systems by performing data processing at the edge of the network, near the source of the data (Lopez et al., 2015). Edge computing refers to the enabling technologies allowing computation to be performed at the edge of the network, on downstream data on behalf of cloud services and upstream data on behalf of IoT services (Shi et al., 2016). Here we define "edge" as any computing and network resources along the path between data sources and cloud data centers (Shi, et al., 2016). For example, a smart phone is the edge between body things and cloud, a gateway in a smart home is the edge between home things and cloud, a micro data center and a cloudlet (Satyanarayanan et al., 2009) is the edge between a mobile device and cloud.

Cloud computing is trending in today's technology driven world. With the advantage of flexibility, storage, sharing and easy accessibility, cloud is being used by major players in IT. Apart from companies, individuals also use cloud technologies for various daily activities. From using Google drive to store, to Skype, to chat and Picasa web albums, we use cloud computing platforms extensively. Cloud computing is a service provided via virtual networks, especially the World Wide Web (Chandana, 2013). According to the National Institute of Standards and Technology (NIST), these are the fine specific qualities that define cloud computing-on demand self-service, broad network access, resource pooling, rapid elasticity or expansion, measured service (Liu, et al., 2011).

In a cloud computing architecture, all applications are controlled, managed and served by a cloud server. Its data is replicated and preserved remotely as part of the cloud configuration (Seshachala, 2015). Cloud computing architecture refers to the various components and sub components of cloud that constitute the structure of the system. Broadly, this architecture can be classified in to two sections: front end, back end. The front end and back end are connected to each other via a virtual network on the internet. There are other components like middleware, cloud resources etc. that are parts of cloud computing architecture. Front end is the side that is visible to the client, customer or the user. It includes the client's computer system or network that is used for accessing the cloud system. Back end is used by the service provider. It includes the various servers, computers, data storage systems and virtual machines that together constitute the cloud of computing services (Chandana, 2013).

The cloud computing architecture consists of major actors, their activities, their relationships and functions in cloud computing environment. Application built on cloud architectures are such that the underlying computing infrastructure is used only when it is needed, draw the necessary resources on demand, perform a specific job, then relinquish the unneeded resources and often dispose them after the job is done. The various cloud-based services have their own distinct and unique cloud architectures: Software as a Service (SaaS) involves software hosted and maintained on internet. With SaaS, users do not have to install the software locally, Development as a Service (DaaS) involves web based development tools shared across communities, Platform as a Service (PaaS) provides users with application platforms and databases, equivalent to middleware services, Infrastructure as a Service (IaaS) provides for infrastructure and hardware such as servers, networks, storage devices, etc. running in the cloud, available to users against a pay per usage basis (HCL, 2016).

The remaining of the chapter is organized as follows: Section 2 gives brief introduction about Cloud Computing Architecture. Section 3 describes the classification of Cloud Computing Architecture: public, private, hybrid and community cloud. Types of Cloud Architecture like Infrastructure as a Service, Platform as a Service and Software as a Service are presented in Section 4. Organizational aspects of Cloud Computing Architecture are described in Section 5. Finally, Section 6 associates with some relevant issues and challenges in Cloud Computing Architecture.

*Figure 1. Edge devices and edge nodes in relation to the cloud (Varghese, et al., 2016)*

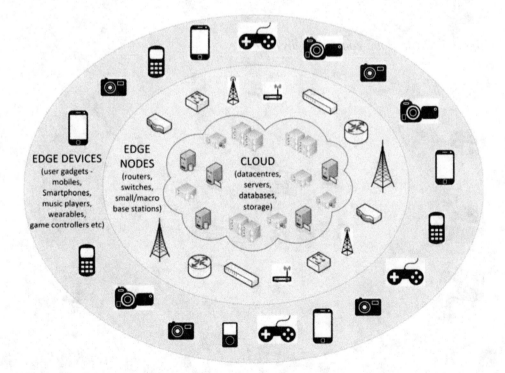

## CLOUD COMPUTING ARCHITECTURE

The term Cloud refers to a Network or Internet. In other words, we can say that Cloud is something, which is present at remote location. Cloud can provide services over public and private networks, i.e., WAN (World Area Network), LAN (Local Area Network) or VPN (Virtual Private Network). Applications such as e-mail, web conferencing, customer relationship management (CRM) execute on cloud. Cloud Computing refers to manipulating, configuring, and accessing the hardware and software resources remotely. It offers online data storage, infrastructure, and application. Cloud computing offers platform independency, as the software is not required to be installed locally on the PC. Hence, the Cloud Computing is making our business applications mobile and collaborative. Figure 2 shows a basic Cloud Computing Architecture.

Cloud Computing is often described as a stack, as a response to the broad range of services built on top of one another under the moniker "Cloud". The generally accepted definition of Cloud Computing comes from the National Institute of Standards and Technology (NIST) (NIST, 2016). According to the NIST fundamental definition (Mell, et al., 2011), cloud computing is a model for enabling convenient, on-demand network access to a shared pool of configurable computing resources (e.g., networks, servers, storage, applications, and services) that can be rapidly

*Figure 2. Basic cloud computing architecture*

provisioned and released with minimal management effort or service provider interaction. What this means in plain terms is the ability for end users to utilize parts of bulk resources and that these resources can be acquired quickly and easily. NIST also offers up several characteristics that it realizes as essential for a service to be considered "Cloud".

Some of the characteristics are;

- On-demand self-service. The ability for an end user to sign up and receive services without the long delays that have characterized traditional IT
- Broad network access. Ability to access the service via standard platforms (desktop, laptop, mobile etc)
- Resource pooling. Resources are pooled across multiple customers (Kepes, 2011b)
- Rapid elasticity. Capability can scale to cope with demand peaks (Kepes, 2011a)
- Measured Service. Billing is metered and delivered as a utility service

There are certain services and models working behind the scene making the cloud computing feasible and accessible to end users. There are two working models for cloud computing such as deployment models and service models. *Deployment models* define the type of access to the cloud, i.e., how the cloud is located? Cloud can have any of the four types of access: Public, Private, Hybrid, and Community. Cloud computing is based on *service models* which are categorized into three basic service models which are Infrastructure-as-a-Service (IaaS), Platform-as-a-Service (PaaS) and Software-as-a-Service (SaaS).

Cloud Computing architecture comprises of many cloud components, which are loosely coupled. We can broadly divide the cloud architecture into two parts: Front End and Back End. Each of the ends is connected through a network, usually Internet. Figure 3 shows the graphical view of cloud computing architecture.

The *front end* refers to the client part of cloud computing system that consists of interfaces and applications that are required to access the cloud computing platforms, for example; Internet Browser, Communication Apps etc. The *back end* refers to the cloud itself. It consists of all the resources required to provide cloud computing services. It comprises of huge data storage, virtual machines, security mechanism, services, deployment models, servers, etc. The responsibility of the back end is to provide built-in security mechanism, traffic control and protocols. The server employs certain protocols known as middleware, which help the connected devices to communicate with each other (Kim, 2013). Figure 4 shows the Oracle Browser Interface of Cloud Computing.

*Figure 3. Cloud computing architectural view*

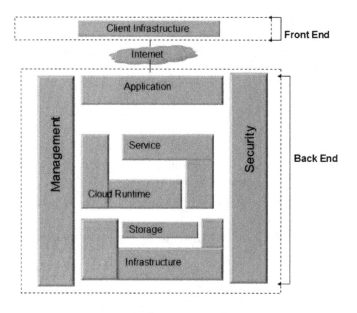

*Figure 4. Oracle browser interface of cloud computing*

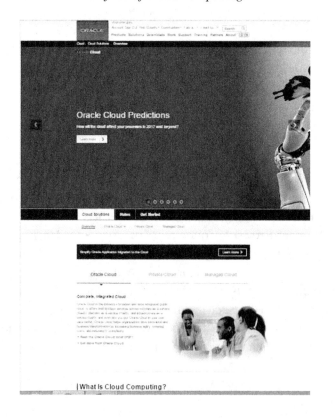

## CLASSIFICATION OF CLOUD COMPUTING ARCHITECTURE: PUBLIC, PRIVATE, HYBRID AND COMMUNITY CLOUD

In this section, four classes of cloud computing architecture are covered. Cloud can have any of the four types of access: Public, Private, Hybrid, and Community. The public cloud allows systems and services to be easily accessible to the general public. Public cloud may be less secure because of its openness. Deployment models define the type of access to the cloud, i.e., how the cloud is located?

The *public cloud* allows systems and services to be easily accessible to the general public. It may be less secure because of its openness. The *private cloud* allows systems and services to be accessible within an organization. It is more secured because of its private nature. The *community cloud* allows systems and services to be accessible by a group of organizations. The hybrid cloud is a mixture of public and private cloud, in which the critical activities are performed using private cloud while the non-critical activities are performed using public cloud.

### Public Cloud

A public cloud is one in which the cloud infrastructure and computing resources are made available to the general public over a public network. A public cloud is owned by an organization selling cloud services, and serves a diverse pool of clients. (Liu, et al., 2011). Figure 6 depicts a simple view of a public cloud and its customers

*Figure 5. Deployment models*

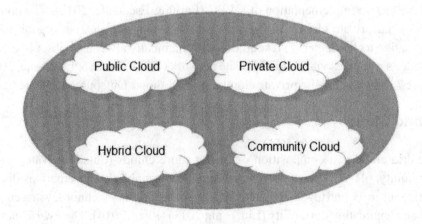

*Figure 6. Public cloud (Liu, et al., 2011)*

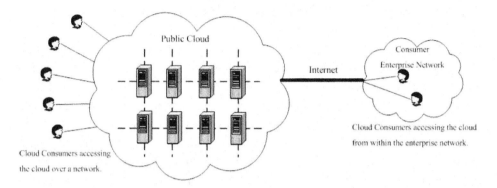

## Private Cloud

The *private cloud* allows systems and services to be accessible within an organization. It is more secured because of its private nature. A private cloud gives a single Cloud Consumer's organization the exclusive access to and usage of the infrastructure and computational resources. It may be managed either by the Cloud Consumer organization or by a third party, and may be hosted on the organization's premises (i.e. on-site private clouds) or outsourced to a hosting company (i.e. outsourced private clouds) (Liu, et al., 2011). The concept of a *virtual private cloud* (VPC) has emerged recently as a way of managing information technology resources so that they appear to be operated for a single organization from a logical point of view, but may be built from underlying physical resources that belong to the organization, an external service provider, or a combination of both. Several technologies are essential to the effective implementation of a VPC (Furht & Escalante, 2010). The concept of a virtual private cloud (VPC) is an approach that connects an organization's information technology (IT) resources to a dynamically allocated subset of a cloud provider's resources via a virtual private network (VPN) (Furht & Escalante, 2010). Figure 7 shows an on-site private cloud. Figure 8 shows Outsourced Private Cloud.

## Hybrid Cloud

A hybrid cloud is a composition of two or more clouds (on-site private, on-site community, off-site private, off-site community or public) that remain as distinct entities but are bound together by standardized or proprietary technology that enables data and application portability (Liu, et al., 2011) (Raza, 2014). The *hybrid cloud* is

*Figure 7. On-site private cloud (Liu, et al., 2011)*

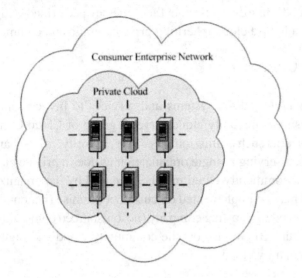

*Figure 8. Outsourced private cloud (Liu, et al., 2011)*

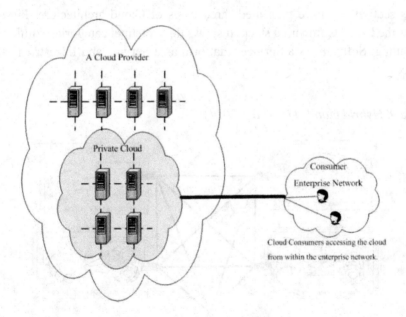

a mixture of public and private cloud, in which the critical activities are performed using private cloud while the non-critical activities are performed using public cloud. Figure 9 shows a hybrid cloud inheriting private, public and community cloud.

## Community Cloud

The *community cloud* allows systems and services to be accessible by a group of organizations. A community cloud serves a group of Cloud Consumers which have shared concerns such as mission objectives, security, privacy and compliance policy, rather than serving a single organization as does a private cloud. Similar to private clouds, a community cloud may be managed by the organizations or by a third party, and may be implemented on customer premise (i.e. on-site community cloud) or outsourced to a hosting company (i.e. outsourced community cloud) (Liu, et al., 2011). Figure 10 presents on-site community cloud and Figure 11 presents outsourced community cloud.

## TYPES OF CLOUD ARCHITECTURE

In this section, we have presented three types of Cloud architecture. Figure 12 depicts the Cloud Computing stack. It shows three distinct categories within Cloud Computing: Software as a Service, Platform as a Service and Infrastructure as a Service.

*Figure 9. Hybrid cloud (Liu, et al., 2011)*

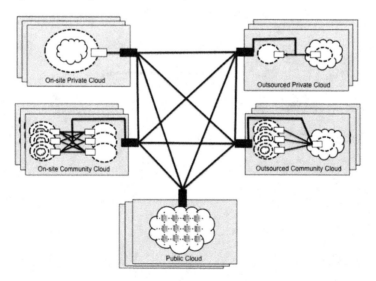

*Figure 10. On-site community cloud (Liu, et al., 2011)*

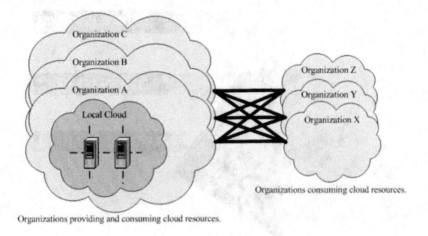

*Figure 11. Outsourced community cloud (Liu, et al., 2011)*

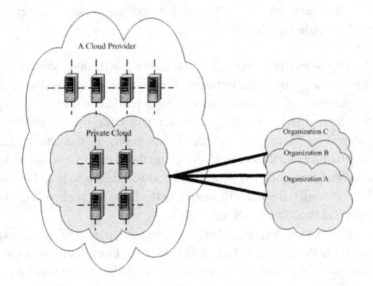

In this section we look at all three categories in detail however a very simplified way of differentiating these flavors of Cloud Computing (Kepes, 2013) is as follows;

- SaaS applications are designed for end-users, delivered over the web
- PaaS is the set of tools and services designed to make coding and deploying those applications quick and efficient

*Figure 12. Cloud computing stack (Kepes, 2013)*

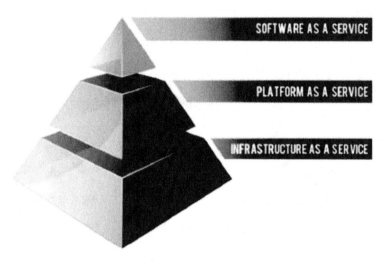

- IaaS is the hardware and software that powers it all – servers, storage, networks, operating systems

To help understand how these 3 components are related, some have used a transportation analogy; by itself, infrastructure isn't useful - it just sits there waiting for someone to make it productive in solving a particular problem. Imagine the Railway System of India even with all these tracks built, they wouldn't be useful without cars and trucks to transport people and goods. In this analogy, the roads are the infrastructure and the cars and trucks are the platform that sits on top of the infrastructure and transports the people and goods. These goods and people might be considered the software and information in the technical realm ("The difference between IaaS and PaaS," n.d.) (Kepes, 2013).

It is significant to differentiate between these categories of cloud computing; SaaS, PaaS and IaaS, especially PaaS and IaaS, have blurred in recent months and will continue to do so ("IaaS," n.d.), nevertheless, with a general understanding of how these components interact with each other. There are three models incorporated with cloud architecture which are as follows.

- Infrastructure-as-a-Service (IaaS) provides access to fundamental resources such as physical machines, virtual machines, virtual storage, etc.
- Platform-as-a-Service (PaaS) provides the runtime environment for applications, development and deployment tools, etc.

- Software-as-a-Service (SaaS) model allows to use software applications as a service to end-users.
- Anything-as-a-Service (XaaS) is yet another service model, which includes Network-as-a-Service, Business-as-a-Service, Identity-as-a-Service, Database-as-a-Service or Strategy-as-a-Service.

## Infrastructure as a Service

Infrastructure-as-a-Service provides access to fundamental resources such as physical machines, virtual machines, virtual storage, etc. Apart from these resources, the IaaS also offers: virtual machine disk storage, virtual local area network (VLANs), load balancers, IP addresses and software bundles. All of the above resources are made available to end user via server virtualization. Moreover, these resources are accessed by the customers as if they own them. The Infrastructure-as-a-Service (IaaS) is the most basic level of service. Each of the service models inherit the security and management mechanism from the underlying model. Figure 14 shows common infrastructure Services based on Oracle Cloud Architecture (Oracle, et al., 2012).

IaaS allows the cloud provider to freely locate the infrastructure over the Internet in a cost-effective manner. Some of the key benefits (Kepes, 2013) of IaaS are listed below:

- Portability, interoperability with legacy applications.
- Virtual machines with pre-installed softw are.
- Virtual machines with pre-installed operating systems such as Windows, Linux, and Solaris.
- Full control of the computing resources through administrative access to VMs.
- Flexible and efficient renting of computer hardware.

*Figure 13. Cloud architecture model (Alturki & Mehmood, 2012)*

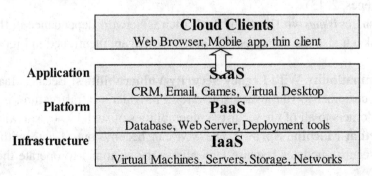

*Figure 14. Common infrastructure services based on oracle cloud architecture (Oracle, et al., 2012)*

- On-demand availability of resources.
- Allows to store copies of particular data at different locations.
- The computing resources can be easily scaled up and down.

IaaS allows the customer to access computing resources through administrative access to virtual machines. Firstly, the customer issues administrative command to cloud provider to run the virtual machine or to save data on cloud server. Next, customer issues administrative command to virtual machines they owned to start web server or to install new applications. Finally, Flexible and efficient renting of computer hardware is granted to the client. IaaS resources such as virtual machines, storage devices, bandwidth, IP addresses, monitoring services, firewalls, etc. are made available to the customers on rent. The payment is based upon the amount of time the customer retains a resource. Also, with administrative access to virtual machines, the customer can run any software, even a custom operating system.

In cloud computing ensures portability, interoperability with legacy applications. It is possible to maintain legacy between applications and workloads between IaaS clouds. For example, network applications such as web server or e-mail server that normally runs on customer-owned server hardware can also run from VMs in IaaS cloud (Kepes, 2013).

IaaS shares *issues* with PaaS and SaaS, such as Network dependence and browser-based risks. It also has some specific issues, which are mentioned in Figure 16.

- **Compatibility With Legacy Security Vulnerabilities:** Because IaaS offers the customer to run legacy software in provider's infrastructure, it exposes customers to all of the security vulnerabilities of such legacy software.
- **Virtual Machine Sprawl:** The VM can become out-of-date with respect to security updates because IaaS allows the customer to operate the virtual

*Figure 15. Infrastructure as a service*

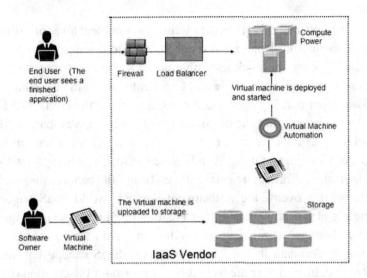

*Figure 16. IaaS Issues*

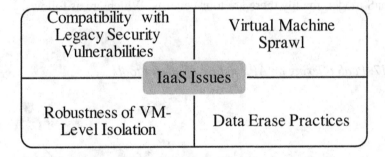

machines in running, suspended and off state (Tripathi, 2015). However, the provider can automatically update such VMs, but this mechanism is hard and complex.

- **Robustness of VM-Level Isolation:** IaaS offers an isolated environment to individual customers through hypervisor. Hypervisor is a software layer that includes hardware support for virtualization to split a physical computer into multiple virtual machines (Tripathi, 2015).
- **Data Erase Practices:** The customer uses virtual machines that in turn use the common disk resources provided by the cloud provider. When the customer releases the resource, the cloud provider must ensure that next customer to rent the resource does not observe data residue from previous customer (Tripathi, 2015).

## Platform as a Service

Platform-as-a-Service(PaaS) offers the runtime environment for applications. It also offers development and deployment tools required to develop applications. PaaS has a feature of point-and-click tools that enables non-developers to create web applications. App Engine of Google and Force.com are examples of PaaS offering vendors. Developer may log on to these websites and use the built-in API to create web-based applications. But the disadvantage of using PaaS is that, the developer locks-in with a particular vendor. For example, an application written in Python against API of Google, and using App Engine of Google is likely to work only in that environment. Platform as a Service (PaaS) brings the benefits that SaaS bought for applications, but over to the software development world. PaaS can be defined as a computing platform that allows the creation of web applications quickly and easily and without the complexity of buying and maintaining the software and infrastructure underneath it. PaaS is analogous to SaaS except that, rather than being software delivered over the web, it is a platform for the creation of software, delivered over the web. Figure 17 shows how PaaS offers an API and development tools to the developers and how it helps the end user to access business applications.

In PaaS model, mainly there are four benefits. Which are as follows.

*Figure 17. PaaS offering an API and development tools*

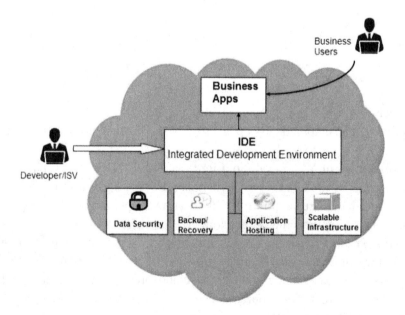

1. **Lower Administrative Overhead:** Customer need not bother about the administration because it is the responsibility of cloud provider.
2. **Lower Total Cost of Ownership:** Customer need not purchase expensive hardware, servers, power, and data storage.
3. **Scalable Solutions:** It is very easy to scale the resources up or down automatically, based on their demand.
4. **More Current System Software:** It is the responsibility of the cloud provider to maintain software versions and patch installations.

PaaS also places significant burdens on customer's browsers to maintain reliable and secure connections to the provider's systems. Therefore, PaaS shares many of the issues of SaaS. However, there are some *specific issues* associated with PaaS as follows:

1. **Lack of Portability Between PaaS Clouds:** Although standard languages are used, yet the implementations of platform services may vary. For example, file, queue, or hash table interfaces of one platform may differ from another, making it difficult to transfer the workloads from one platform to another.
2. **Event Based Processor Scheduling:** The PaaS applications are event-oriented which poses resource constraints on applications, i.e., they have to answer a request in a given interval of time.
3. **Security Engineering of PaaS Applications:** Since PaaS applications are dependent on network, they must explicitly use cryptography and manage security exposures.

*Figure 18. PaaS benefits*

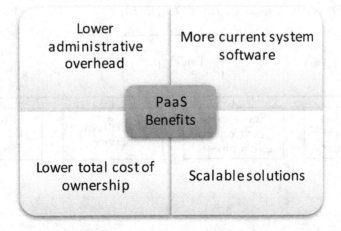

## Characteristics of PaaS Service Model

1.  PaaS offers browser-based development environment. It allows the developer to create database and edit the application code either via Application Programming Interface or point-and-click tools.
2.  PaaS provides built-in security, scalability, and web service interfaces.
3.  PaaS provides built-in tools for defining workflow, approval processes, and business rules.
4.  It is easy to integrate PaaS with other applications on the same platform.
5.  PaaS also provides web services interfaces that allow us to connect the applications outside the platform.

## PaaS Types

Based on the functions, PaaS can be classified into four types (Kepes, 2013) which are as follows (also shown in Figure 19)

1.  **Stand-Alone Development Environments:** The stand-alone PaaS works as an independent entity for a specific function. It does not include licensing or technical dependencies on specific SaaS applications.
2.  **Application Delivery-Only Environments:** The application delivery PaaS includes on-demand scaling and application security.
3.  **Open Platform as a Service:** Open PaaS offers an open source software that helps a PaaS provider to run applications.
4.  **Add-on Development Facilities:** The add-on PaaS allows to customize the existing SaaS platform.

*Figure 19. PaaS types (Kepes, 2013) (NIST, 2016)*

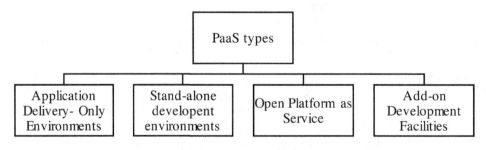

## Software as a Service

Software-as–a-Service (SaaS) model allows to provide software application as a service to the end users. It refers to a software that is deployed on a host service and is accessible via Internet. SaaS is a rapidly growing market as indicated in recent reports that predict ongoing double digit growth (Tan, et al., 2013). This rapid growth indicates that SaaS will soon become commonplace within every organization and hence it is important that buyers and users of technology understand what SaaS is and where it is suitable. There are several SaaS applications as: Billing and invoicing system, Customer Relationship Management (CRM) applications, Help desk applications, Human Resource (HR) solutions etc. Some of the SaaS applications are not customizable such as Microsoft Office Suite. But SaaS provides us Application Programming Interface (API), which allows the developer to develop a customized application (Kepes, 2013).

### Characteristics

Here are the characteristics of SaaS service model:

1. SaaS makes the software available over the Internet.
2. The software applications are maintained by the vendor.
3. The license to the software may be subscription based or usage based. And it is billed on recurring basis.
4. SaaS applications are cost-effective since they do not require any maintenance at end user side.
5. They are available on demand.
6. They can be scaled up or down on demand.
7. They are automatically upgraded and updated.
8. SaaS offers shared data model. Therefore, multiple users can share single instance of infrastructure. It is not required to hard code the functionality for individual users.
9. All users run the same version of the software.

Using SaaS has proved to be beneficial in terms of scalability, efficiency and performance. Some of the benefits are listed below:

1.   Modest software tools
2.   Efficient use of software licenses
3.   Centralized management and data
4.   Platform responsibilities managed by provider
5.   Multitenant solutions
6.   Modest software tools

The SaaS application deployment requires a little or no client-side software installation, which results in the following benefits:

1.   No requirement for complex software packages at client side
2.   Little or no risk of configuration at client side
3.   Low distribution cost
4.   Efficient use of software licenses

The customer can have single license for multiple computers running at different locations which reduces the licensing cost. Also, there is no requirement for license servers because the software runs in the provider's infrastructure. *Centralized management and data* means cloud provider stores data centrally. However, the cloud providers may store data in a decentralized manner for the sake of redundancy and reliability. *Platform responsibilities managed by providers* denotes that all platform responsibilities such as backups, system maintenance, security, hardware refresh, power management, etc. are performed by the cloud provider. The customer does not need to bother about them. *Multitenant solutions* allow multiple users to share single instance of different resources in virtual isolation. Customers can customize their application without affecting the core functionality (Kepes, 2013).

There are **several issues** associated with SaaS, some of them are: *Browser based risks, Network dependence, Lack of portability between SaaS clouds and Browser based risks* etc. If the customer visits malicious website and browser becomes infected, the subsequent access to SaaS application might compromise the customer's data. To avoid such risks, the customer can use multiple browsers and dedicate a specific browser to access SaaS applications or can use virtual desktop while accessing the SaaS applications. The SaaS application can be delivered only when network is continuously available. Also, network should be reliable but the network reliability cannot be guaranteed either by cloud provider or by the customer. Transferring workloads from one SaaS cloud to another is not so easy because work flow, business logics, user interfaces, support scripts can be provider specific (Kepes, 2013).

## SaaS on SOA (Service Oriented Architecture)

Open SaaS uses those SaaS applications, which are developed using open source programming language. These SaaS applications can run on any open source operating system and database. Open SaaS has several benefits such as No License Required, Low Deployment Cost, Less Vendor Lock-in, more portable applications, More Robust Solution (Barillaud, 2015). Many SOA applications are now migrating to cloud servers due to cloud's low cost provision elasticity for growth, and better availability (Huang, et al., 2013). The Figure 20 shows the SaaS implementation based on SOA:

## ORGANIZATIONAL ASPECTS OF CLOUD COMPUTING ARCHITECTURE

CLOUD COMPUTING is about technology changing the way we do business, but this cannot be done without changing the organization. Successful adoption of cloud services is about a cohesive triangle of technology, business and organization. Cloud services deliver managed functionality; therefore, less technical roles are required. And new roles will emerge, like technical engineers for PaaS services and functional

*Figure 20. SaaS on SOA (Barillaud, 2015)*

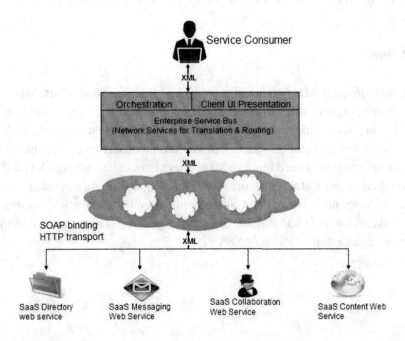

21

managers for SaaS services. This will slowly decrease the gap between business and IT, with service architects in the middle (Rhodes & Collins, 2015). Cloud computing is one of the most discussed and promising IT innovations in today's technological market. It is very attractive for organizations thanks to the potential it brings such as increased efficiency and cost savings. It constitutes a fundamental shift in the way organizations are provided with computing resources (Khajeh-Hosseini, et al., 2012). Cloud computing has changed the way organizations use computers and the Internet. This change relates mainly to how the information is stored and the applications are used. In cloud computing they are stored in the "cloud" instead of on desktop computers. The cloud is "a nebulous assemblage of computers and servers accessed via the Internet". It provides users with access to all of their data, documents and applications when they are connected to the Internet. The users are no longer tied to their desktop computers and it is easier for them to collaborate from different locations (Miller, 2009). Cloud computing allows organizations to use their hardware and software investments in more efficient ways. This is achieved by overcoming the physical barriers of the isolated systems and automated managing a group of systems as a single unit. This technology is seen as a virtualized system which constitutes a natural evolution of data centres (Boss, et al., 2008).

Therefore, for organizations aiming to move into cloud computing, an understanding of the cloud models and the security tradeoffs between them is a must. Organizations also have to be aware of the benefits and risks of cloud computing in cost and security aspect.

Some important organizational concerns of Cloud Computing Architecture are as follows:

## Cost Benefits

Cloud computing enables organizations to reduce their hardware costs. When using cloud services, organizations no longer need high-powered and high-priced computers to run applications within the cloud. This comes from the decreased needs for a processing power and storage space. Unlike traditional software, for running cloud applications computers need less memory. They also can be with smaller hard disks because there is not installation software. Thus, organizations can reduce costs by purchasing lower-priced computers. Since employing cloud computing, organizations do not have to do high investments in IT infrastructure. This especially concerns the larger organizations (Miller, 2009).

## Security Risks

According to Pearson (Pearson, 2013), security of cloud computing is the biggest concern for the organizations. The security problems associated with cloud computing come from the abstraction of infrastructure, which results in "lack of visibility and capability to integrate many familiar security controls - especially at the network layer." (CSA, 1999). On the other hand, it is argued (Pearson, 2013) that these problems come from the ambiguity regarding which parties are responsible for which aspects of security as cloud APIs are yet to be standardized. The security risks may be different according to the deployment and delivery models employed by organizations. That`s why it is critical for organizations` risk management to understand the relationships and differences between deployment and delivery models, and security trade-offs.

## Clear Outline of Service Offering and Responsibility

Having unclear Service Level Agreements (SLA) can lead to confusion as to who is responsible for data security when a data breach happens. This can delay the response to a breach as well as the investigation that follows. So, before signing a cloud service agreement, companies must first research potential cloud service providers.

Experienced providers understand the data security needs of its customers' industry, with good security measures in place that are independently audited to confirm their environment is secure. However, they usually won't come forward and accept liability for data breaches, as the cost can be huge. With data breaches on this rise, and cloud service providers unable to provide 100% protection, Global Data Sentinel ensures that even if there is a breach, data secured in the cloud will remain encrypted and safe from being viewed, wherever it resides ("Cloud Computing Issues Organizations Must Consider," n.d.)

## Clear Definition of the "Cloud" and Its Use in Individual Business

Until a company understands what is involved in cloud computing as a whole, deciding the best approach is pointless. Unfortunately, despite being almost part of everyday business, many chief executives and business owners still have an unclear idea of cloud computing and how best to adapt to the changing landscape. Depending on the company's requirements, one delivery method may be a better option than the others. Thus, it is essential the company starts with a clear set of definitions before embarking on cloud adoption ("Cloud Computing Issues Organizations Must Consider," n.d.).

## Internal Audit

In order to accommodate the move to cloud computing, cloud service providers will need to modify, upgrade, or replace systems to process, measure, and control use. This will also be critical for billing. Providers should have the right SLAs in place, and a process to monitor those SLAs. Buyers of cloud services must give themselves the same control and monitoring environment in the cloud that they did on internal networks and servers. This is much more challenging, as your organization no longer controls hardware. Methods of application management may change significantly (Beston, 2015).

## REFERENCE CLOUD ARCHITECTURE OF IBM AND ORACLE

The conceptual view of the architecture, shown in Figure 15, brings together three key Cloud perspectives - the provider, consumer, and the broker. The role of the Cloud provider is the most important and most complex of all. Infrastructure for the Cloud is usually of unprecedented scale and stringent requirements. Implementing the Cloud and maintaining it to satisfy the SLAs of the consumers requires extensive planning and precise execution (Oracle, et al., 2012).

A Cloud provider can spread the costs of facilities, across consumers to achieve economies of scale. Facilities expense may include the cost of real estate, cooling, utilities, and rack space among other things. The physical infrastructure components may include blades, networks, engineered systems, and storage disks. These resources must be pooled and provisioned through grid technologies in order to support the elasticity and scalability demands of Cloud infrastructure (Oracle, et al., 2012).

The physical resources need to be logically partitioned and secured in order to support multi-tenancy. Rapid elasticity requires the resources to be quickly deployed and undeployed at granular levels. Traditional deployments require downtime for scaling and maintenance but Cloud infrastructure does not have that luxury. The approach is to create and deploy new instances on the fly to grow, shrink, or fix the existing deployments. The resource abstraction layer provides the capabilities to logically abstract the physical resources (Oracle, et al., 2012). Figure 21 shows the conceptual view of cloud computing architecture.

## Oracle Reference Architecture

The role of the Cloud provider is the most important and most complex of all. Infrastructure for the Cloud is usually of unprecedented scale and stringent

*Figure 21. Conceptual view of the cloud architecture (Oracle, et al., 2012)*

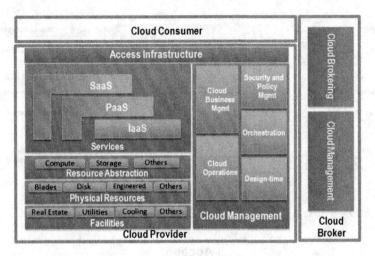

requirements. Implementing the Cloud and maintaining it to satisfy the SLAs of the consumers requires extensive planning and precise execution.

A Cloud provider can spread the costs of facilities, across consumers to achieve economies of scale. Facilities expense may include the cost of real estate, cooling, utilities, and rack space among other things. The physical infrastructure components may include blades, networks, engineered systems, and storage disks. These resources must be pooled and provisioned through grid technologies in order to support the elasticity and scalability demands of Cloud infrastructure. The physical resources need to be logically partitioned and secured in order to support multi-tenancy. Rapid elasticity requires the resources to be quickly deployed and undeployed at granular levels. Traditional deployments require downtime for scaling and maintenance but Cloud infrastructure does not have that luxury. The approach is to create and deploy new instances on the fly to grow, shrink, or fix the existing deployments. The resource abstraction layer provides the capabilities to logically abstract the physical resources (Oracle, et al., 2012). Figure 22 presents Oracle Reference Architecture Figure 23 shows logical view of Oracle Reference Architecture.

## IBM Reference Model Architecture

The IBM Cloud Computing Reference Architecture (CCRA) (Amanatullah, et al., 2011) is a blueprint to guide IBM development teams and field practitioners in the design of public and private clouds. It has been created from the collective experiences of hundreds of cloud client engagements and implementation of IBM-hosted clouds.

*Figure 22. Oracle reference architecture (Oracle, et al., 2012)*

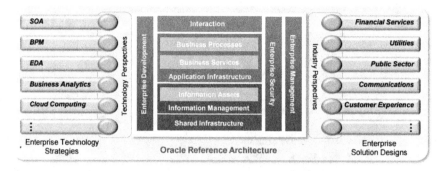

*Figure 23. Logical view (Oracle, et al., 2012)*

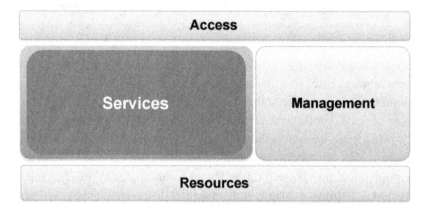

A Reference Architecture (RA) provides a blueprint of a 'to-be' model with a well-defined scope, requirements it satisfies and the architectural decisions it realizes. It includes prescriptive architecture and product recommendations in the form of cloud adoption patterns. By delivering best practices in a standardized, methodical way, an RA ensures globally consistent delivery and high quality project results (Liu, et al., 2011).

The IBM architecture introduces three main roles: The Cloud Service Provider, Cloud Service Consumer, and Cloud Service Creator. For each of them, the high-level diagram in the following picture shows the main components; additional diagrams explode each of the actor functions. The NIST architecture, in the following picture, introduces three new actors: Cloud Broker, Cloud Auditor, and Cloud Carrier. This is an important addendum and serves to better model the actors and relationships between them that we are seeing in the real market.

The Cloud Service Creator is not mentioned at all and we have to think it as embedded in the Cloud Service Provider role, even if I think it is important to distinguish it because, for example, a cloud service provider can have multiple external ISVs or suppliers playing this role and creating new services.

## RESEARCH ISSUES AND CHALLENGES IN EDGE COMPUTING ARCHITECTURE

The diverse devices in Cloud Computing environment forms with heterogeneous technologies. Some of the major key challenges on Cloud Computing are interoperability, adaptation, reliability, reusability, performance, management, scalability, mobility and security and privacy. Following paragraphs gives brief discussion about key challenges on Cloud Computing in development of Cloud Computing Architecture and identified reasons and models/projects.

Some major challenges like security and interoperability have gained a lot of attention, where others like interoperability, availability, performance and scalability also require more attention. Consistency and robustness (Wang, et al., 2013) are also noticed as challenges of the service in cloud. Some other challenges are there in consumer side like user interface, mapping from high-level to low level description and the poor observability and controllability (Tahir, et al., 2013). Some hybrid cloud accountability challenges (Huang, et al., 2013) is also highlight as follows;

*Figure 24. IBM cloud architecture (Amanatullah, et al., 2011)*

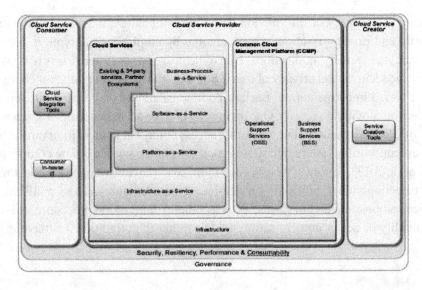

*Figure 25. IBM cloud computing reference model (Amanatullah, et al., 2011)*

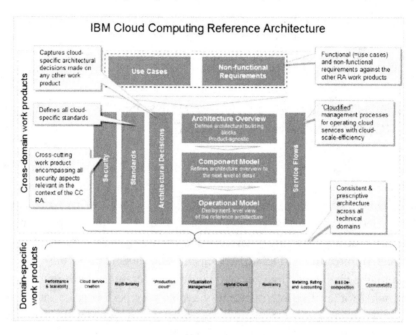

Heterogeneous, instability, scalability and end-to-end auto-scaling. Figure 26 presents major cloud computing challenges.

Major issues and challenges in cloud computing are as follows.

## Security and Privacy

Security and Privacy of information is the biggest challenge to cloud computing. Security and privacy issues can be overcome by employing encryption, security hardware and security applications. Due to heterogeneous systems, it is not easy to ensure the security and privacy of users. So, the security is its significant challenge for the Cloud implementation. Lack of common standard and architecture creates problem on providing security. One approach could be access control on application layer of Cloud Computing but validating access control at composition time results high execution-time failure rate so it is good to validate service before composition (She, et al., 2013). Antunes (Antunes & Vieira, 2013) have developed a model to deal with detecting vulnerabilities in service-based infrastructures. Cross-platform and service composition architectures needs a complex integration procedure and limit adoptability of newer authentication models rather than traditional authentication

*Figure 26. Cloud Computing Challenges*

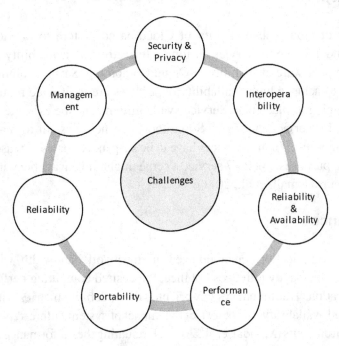

model. So, Khan et al. (Khan & Hasan, 2015) have presented a model with fuzzy authentication using past interactions and linguistic policies.Casola et al. (Casola, et al., 2016)have presented a security SLA model by security SLA life cycle management with a framework. Metrics can be enforced and monitored via the activation of security mechanisms automatically on the basis of standard security control framework.

## Reliability

It is necessary for cloud systems to be reliable and robust because most of the businesses are now becoming dependent on services provided by third-party.In general, reliability is the probability that a system functions correctly for a given time period. Overall system reliability increases with service redundancy. Reliability increases the rate of service delivery to the customer. Reliability of Cloud Computing services is related with security and service availability. Infrastructures like software, hardware and network channel should be trust worthy to enrich reliability throughout all the layers of Cloud Computing Architecture. Unreliable communication may lead system failures, data loss, and long delays.

## Availability

Availability of cloud means ability of Cloud-based system to provide services anywhere and anytime for service customer. Infrastructure availability refers 24*7 hardware and software availability of Cloud Computing. Several solutions (Wu & Chu, 2013) to achieve high availability of services are to provide redundancy for services, logging, replacement Service availability means the existence of service all the time for service customer. Some tools can help system to maximize the service availability., If some services have to be suspended for a few reasons such as maintenance purposes, not 24/7 services, some might only available within certain operating hours (Ismail, et al., 2011).

## Performance

Data intensive applications on cloud needs high network bandwidth, which results in high cost. Low bandwidth does not meet the desired computing performance of cloud application. Traditional system-oriented dependability metrics with identical reliability and availability do not reflect the impact of system failure-repair behavior in cloud environments (Mondal, et al., 2015). Evaluating the performance depends on the type of strategy used and components and faults underlying technologies,Cloud needs to be correct, reliable and affordable with the best performance. Evaluating performance of fault handling model is always a big issue. Two algorithms FTCloud1 and FTCloud2(Applications, et al., 2012) are proposed for significant component ranking and hybrid component ranking. FTCloud1 concerns about some components which are frequently invoked by a lot of other components called significant components are considered to be more importance since their failures will have greater impact in comparison with other components. FTCloud2 considers some components fulfil critical tasks like payment and other components realize noncritical tasks like providing advertisements to display in the web page. So, failures of the critical components have great impact that non-critical component.

## Scalability

Scalability is another challenge on handling faults for Cloud system. The scalability of the Cloud Computing means the ability to add new services, components and functions for the consumers without negatively affecting the quality of existing services. Increasing the functionality is always a difficult task in case of heterogeneous SOA platforms and communication protocols. Eg: vertical service delivery. SOA must provide scalable mechanisms for registration, discovery of service faults as well as services interoperability.

## Interoperability

In Cloud Computing, interoperability always gets high concern as a challenge. It means the application on one platform should be able to incorporate services from the other platforms. It is made possible via web services, but developing such web services is very complex. Interoperability becomes challenge as it needs to handle a large number of heterogeneous services that may belong to different diversified platforms. Service developers and service providers are responsible stakeholders to consider this interoperability issue to ensure the proper delivery of services for all service customers no matter on what the hardware/software specifications are.

## Management

Cloud Computing system management is very discouraging issue to manage the fault. The fault management effort needs development of new management protocols to ensure all times functioning on demand services. Maintaining compatibility across the Cloud Computing Architecture layers also necessities to be managed to enhance the performance and to ensure service delivery with no fault. Mohamed et al. (Mohamed, et al., 2016) have also developed rSLA framework to address the issues of monitoring and configuring complex and heterogeneous SLAs.

## Mobility

Mobility is another challenge for Cloud Computing realization because most of the services are expected to be delivered to mobile users. Mobile users can move one place to another place that may lead temporary service unavailability of service due to the devices transfer from gateway to gateway. For e.g. Internet of Vehicles (Chanak, et al., 2016; Ghazizadeh, et al., 2015; Zhai, et al., 2014), Ad-hoc etc.

## Portability

This is another challenge to cloud computing that applications should easily be migrated from one cloud provider to another. There must not be vendor lock-in. However, it is not yet made possible because each of the cloud provider uses different standard languages for their platforms. Cloud computing, an emergent technology, has placed many challenges in different aspects of data and information handling.

## CONCLUSION

In this chapter, a brief introduction of edge computing architecture with similar technologies is discussed. Few examples of edge computing architecture with the help of cloud computing architecture are showed. Some challenges on edge computing in its utilization in cloud are also elaborated in this chapter. It has been observed that there has a lot to do for the realization of edge computing architecture in cloud computing architecture.

# REFERENCES

Alturki, R., & Mehmood, R. (2012). *Using Cross-Layer Techniques for Communication Systems. Using Cross-Layer Techniques for Communication Systems.* Information Science Reference; doi:10.4018/978-1-4666-0960-0

Amanatullah, Y., Lim, C., Ipung, H., & Juliandri, A. (2011). *Toward Cloud Computing Reference Architecture.* Academic Press.

Antunes, N., & Vieira, M. (2013). SOA-scanner: An integrated tool to detect vulnerabilities in service-based infrastructures. *Proceedings - IEEE 10th International Conference on Services Computing, SCC 2013*, 280–287. 10.1109/SCC.2013.28

Applications, F. C., Zheng, Z., Zhou, T. C., Member, S., Lyu, M. R., King, I., & Member, S. (2012). Component Ranking for. *IEEE Transactions on Services Computing, 5*(4), 540–550.

Barillaud, F. (2015). *IBM cloud technologies : How they all fit together.* Retrieved April 3, 2017, from https://www.ibm.com/developerworks/cloud/library/cl-cloud-technology-basics/

Beston, C. (2015). *What are the business impacts of cloud computing?* Retrieved April 3, 2017, from http://www.pwc.com/us/en/issues/cloud-computing/functional-changes.html

Boss, G. P., & Hall, H. (2008). Cloud Computing. IBM Corporation.

Casola, V., De Benedictis, A., Erascu, M., Modic, J., & Rak, M. (2016). Automatically Enforcing Security SLAs in the Cloud. *IEEE Transactions on Services Computing, 1374*, 1–15.

Chanak, P., Banerjee, I., & Sherratt, R. S. (2016). Mobile sink based fault diagnosis scheme for wireless sensor networks. *Journal of Systems and Software, 119*, 45–57. doi:10.1016/j.jss.2016.05.041

Chandana. (2013). *Cloud Computing Architecture.* Author.

Cloud Computing Issues Organizations Must Consider. (n.d.). Retrieved April 3, 2017, from https://www.globaldatasentinel.com/the-latest/data-security-news/cloud-computing-issues-organizations-must-consider/

CSA. (1999). Security research alliance to promote network security. *Network Security*, (2): 3–4. doi:10.1016/S1353-4858(99)90042-9

Furht, B., & Escalante, A. (2010). *Handbook of Cloud Computing*. Springer; doi:10.1007/978-1-4419-6524-0

Ghazizadeh, P., Olariu, S., Zadeh, A. G., & El-Tawab, S. (2015). Towards Fault-Tolerant Job Assignment in Vehicular Cloud. *Proceedings - 2015 IEEE International Conference on Services Computing, SCC 2015*, 17–24. 10.1109/SCC.2015.13

HCL. (2016). *Cloud architecture: What is cloud computing technology architecture?* HCL.

Huang, Z., Lin, K. J., Zhang, J., Nie, W., & Han, L. (2013). Performance diagnosis for SOA on hybrid cloud using the Markov network model. *Proceedings - IEEE 6th International Conference on Service-Oriented Computing and Applications, SOCA 2013*, 17–24. 10.1109/SOCA.2013.55

Ismail, A., Yan, J., & Shen, J. (2011). Analyzing fault-impact region of composite service for supporting fault handling process. *Proceedings - 2011 IEEE International Conference on Services Computing, SCC 2011*, 290–297. 10.1109/SCC.2011.51

Kepes, B. (2011a). A Primer for "The Cloud.". *Cloud University, 53*(11), 43.

Kepes, B. (2011b). Revoution Not Evolution How Cloud computing differs from traditional IT and why it matters. *Diversity Limited*. Retrieved from https://docs.google.com/viewer?a=v&q=cache:2Y0nj1_GULMJ:broadcast.rackspace.com/hosting_knowledge/whitepapers/Revolution_Not_Evolution-Whitepaper.pdf+revolution+not+evolution+how+cloud+computing+differs+from+traditional+it+and+why+it+matters&hl=en&gl=us&p

Kepes, B. (2013). *Understanding the Cloud Computing Stack SaaS, Paas, IaaS*. Retrieved April 3, 2017, from https://www.rackspace.com/knowledge_center/sites/default/files/whitepaper_pdf/Understanding-the-Cloud-Computing-Stack.pdf

Khajeh-Hosseini, A., Greenwood, D., Smith, J. W., & Sommerville, I. (2012). The Cloud Adoption Toolkit: Supporting cloud adoption decisions in the enterprise. *Software, Practice & Experience, 42*(4), 447–465. doi:10.1002pe.1072

Khan, R., & Hasan, R. (2015). Fuzzy Authentication Using Interaction Provenance in Service Oriented Computing. *Proceedings - 2015 IEEE International Conference on Services Computing, SCC 2015*, 170–177. 10.1109/SCC.2015.32

Kim, W. (2013). *Cloud computing architecture.* Academic Press. doi:10.1504/IJWGS.2013.055724

Liu, F., Tong, J., Mao, J., Bohn, R., Messina, J., Badger, L., & Leaf, D. (2011). NIST Cloud Computing Reference Architecture. *National Institute of Standards and Technology Special Publication*, *500*(292), 35.

Lopez, P. G., Montresor, A., Epema, D., Iamnitchi, A., & Felber, P. (2015). Edge-centric Computing : Vision and Challenges. *Computer Communication Review*, *45*(5), 37–42. doi:10.1145/2831347.2831354

Mell, P., Grance, T., & Grance, T. (2011). The NIST Definition of Cloud Computing Recommendations of the National Institute of Standards and Technology. *National Institute of Standards and Technology Special Publication 800-145*, *2*, 7. Retrieved from http://scholar.google.com/scholar?hl=en&btnG=Search&q=intitle:The+NIST+Definition+of+Cloud+Computing+Recommendations+of+the+National+Institute+of+Standards+and+Technology#6

Miller, M. (2009). *Cloud Computing: Web-Based Applications That Change the Way You Work and Collaborate Online.* Que Publishing Company; doi:10.1109/CLOUD.2009.53

Mohamed, M., Anya, O., Sakairi, T., Tata, S., Mandagere, N., & Ludwig, H. (2016). The rSLA framework: Monitoring and enforcement of service level agreements for cloud services. *Proceedings - 2016 IEEE International Conference on Services Computing, SCC 2016*, 625–632. 10.1109/SCC.2016.87

Mondal, S. K., Yin, X., Muppala, J. K., Alonso Lopez, J., & Trivedi, K. S. (2015). Defects per million computation in service-oriented environments. *IEEE Transactions on Services Computing*, *8*(1), 32–46. doi:10.1109/TSC.2013.52

NIST. (2016). *Cloud Computing.* NIST.

Oracle, A., Paper, W., Enterprise, O., & Solutions, T. (2012). *Cloud Reference Architecture.* Oracle Enterprise Transformation Solutions Series Cloud- An Oracle White Paper.

Pearson, S. (2013). *Privacy and Security for Cloud Computing.* Academic Press. doi:10.1007/978-1-4471-4189-1

Raza, M. (2014). Article. *Analysis of Cloud Computing and Security Challenges*, *1*(6), 104–107.

Rhodes, S. M., & Collins, S. K. (2015). *The organizational impact of presenteeism.* Retrieved April 3, 2017, from https://www.wired.com/insights/2012/11/the-organizational-impact-of-the-cloud/

Satyanarayanan, M., Bahl, P., Cáceres, R., & Davies, N. (2009). The case for VM-based cloudlets in mobile computing. *IEEE Pervasive Computing*, *8*(4), 14–23. doi:10.1109/MPRV.2009.82

Seshachala, S. (2015). *Cloud Computing Architecture: an overview.* Academic Press.

She, W., Yen, I. L., Thuraisingham, B., & Bertino, E. (2013). Security-aware service composition with fine-grained information flow control. *IEEE Transactions on Services Computing*, *6*(3), 330–343. doi:10.1109/TSC.2012.3

Shi, W., Cao, J., Zhang, Q., Li, Y., & Xu, L. (2016). Edge Computing: Vision and Challenges. *IEEE Internet of Things Journal*, *3*(5), 637–646. doi:10.1109/JIOT.2016.2579198

Tahir, A., Tosi, D., & Morasca, S. (2013). A systematic review on the functional testing of semantic web services. *Journal of Systems and Software*, *86*(11), 2877–2889. doi:10.1016/j.jss.2013.06.064

Tan, C., Liu, K., & Sun, L. (2013). A design of evaluation method for SaaS in cloud computing. *Journal of Industrial Engineering and Management, 6*(1), 50–72. doi:10.3926/jiem.661

The difference between IaaS and PaaS. (n.d.). Retrieved April 3, 2017, from http://www.qrimp.com/blog/blog.The-Difference-between-IaaS-and-PaaS.html

Tripathi, M. (2015). *Cloud Computing Concepts: IaaS.* Retrieved April 2, 2017, from https://www.mindstick.com/Blog/799/cloud-computing-concepts-iaas

Varghese, B., Wang, N., Barbhuiya, S., Kilpatrick, P., & Nikolopoulos, D. S. (2016). Challenges and Opportunities in Edge Computing. *Proceedings - 2016 IEEE International Conference on Smart Cloud, SmartCloud 2016*, 20–26. 10.1109/SmartCloud.2016.18

Wang, L., Wombacher, A., Pires, L. F., Van Sinderen, M. J., & Chi, C. (2013). Robust client/server shared state interactions of collaborative process with system crash and network failures. *Proceedings - IEEE 10th International Conference on Services Computing, SCC 2013*, 192–199. 10.1109/SCC.2013.39

Wu, Z., & Chu, N. (2013). Efficient service re-composition using semantic augmentation for fast cloud fault recovery. *Proceedings - IEEE 10th International Conference on Services Computing, SCC 2013*, 176–183. 10.1109/SCC.2013.78

Zhai, K., Jiang, B., & Chan, W. K. (2014). Prioritizing test cases for regression testing of location-based services: Metrics, techniques, and case study. *IEEE Transactions on Services Computing*, 7(1), 54–67. doi:10.1109/TSC.2012.40

# Chapter 2
# Fog/Cloud Service Scalability, Composition, Security, Privacy, and SLA Management

**Shweta Kaushik**
*Jaypee Institute of Information Technology, India*

**Charu Gandhi**
*Jaypee Institute of Information Technology, India*

## ABSTRACT

*Cloud computing has started a new era in the field of computing, which allows the access of remote data or services at anytime and anywhere. In today's competitive environment, the service dynamism, elasticity, and choices offered by this highly scalable technology are too attractive for enterprises to ignore. The scalability feature of cloud computing allows one to expand and contract the resources. The owner's data stored at the remote location, but he is usually afraid of sharing confidential data with cloud service provider. If the service provider is not the trusted one, there may be a chance of leakage of confidential data to external third party. Security and privacy of data require high consideration, which is resolved by storing the data in encrypted form. Data owner requires that the service provider should be trustworthy to store its confidential data without any exposure. One of the outstanding solutions for maintaining trust between different communicating parties could be the service level agreement between them.*

DOI: 10.4018/978-1-5225-7149-0.ch002

# INTRODUCTION

## Cloud Computing

Cloud computing can be defined as on-demand delivery of computer resources such as database storage, computer power, applications and other IT services over the internet by cloud service provider with pay-as-you-go pricing technique. A user can acquire the resources as per the needs at anytime and anywhere (24x7) by just connecting with the internet. It enables the various companies to consume the required resources such as storage, application and virtual machines as utility, like electricity, without its computing infrastructure construction and maintenance in house.

## Need of Cloud Computing

1.  **Flexibility:** Cloud-based services are perfect for organizations with developing or fluctuating data transfer capacity requests. In the event that your needs increment it's easy to scale up your cloud limit. In like manner, on the off chance that you have to downsize once more, the adaptability is prepared into the administration. This level of agility can give organizations utilizing cloud computing a genuine advantage over competitors.
2.  **Disaster Recovery:** Organizations of all sizes choose to put resources into strong disaster recovery, however for littler organizations that do not have the required money and ability, this is regularly more a perfect than the truth. Cloud is presently helping more associations resist that pattern. As indicated by Aberdeen Group, private companies are twice as likely as bigger organizations to have actualized cloud-based reinforcement and recovery arrangements that spare time, keep away from huge in advance venture and move up outsider skill as a feature of the arrangement.
3.  **Automatic Software Updates:** The beauty of cloud computing is that the servers are off-premise from end user. Service provider take care of them for you and roll out regular software updates – including security updates – so you don't have to worry about wasting time maintaining the system yourself. It will leave the end user free to focus on the things related to the software updates.
4.  **Capital-Expenditure Free:** Cloud computing cuts out the high cost of hardware purchase and management for any service user. You simply pay as you go and enjoy a subscription-based model that's kind to your cash flow.

5.  **Increased Collaboration:** At the point when your groups can get to, alter and share reports whenever, from anyplace, they're ready to accomplish all the more together, and improve. Cloud-based work process and document sharing applications enable them to make refreshes continuously and gives them full visibility of their joint efforts.

6.  **Work From Anywhere:** With cloud computing, in the event that you have a web association you can be grinding away. What's more, with most genuine cloud administrations offering portable applications, you're not limited by which gadget you must hand. Organizations can offer more adaptable working advantages to employees so they can appreciate the work-life adjust that suits them – without profitability enduring a shot.

7.  **Security:** Lost workstations/ laptop are a billion dollar business issue. Also, possibly more significant than the loss of a costly bit of pack is the loss of the subtle information inside it. Cloud computing gives you more significant security when this happens. Since your information is put away in the cloud, you can get to it regardless of the end result for your machine. What's more, you can even remotely wipe information from lost PCs so it doesn't get into the wrong hands

8.  **Competitiveness:** Moving to the cloud offers access to big business class innovation, for everybody. It likewise enables littler organizations to act speedier than enormous, built up contenders. Pay-as-you-go administration and cloud business applications mean little outfits can keep running with the enormous young men, and upset the mar\ket, while staying lean and deft.

*Figure 1. Need of cloud computing*

## Cloud Entities

In cloud computing the various entities according to their data usage and responsibility can be categorized as shown in figure 2:

1.  **Data Owner:** These are those entity who want to store their data on the cloud storage and further share it with other entity according to their access criteria defined by data owner. It release itself from any data storage, management, distribution and security assurance, as after storing the data over cloud storage these all task are handled by the service provider only. Data owner can also keep track of the security for its data by auditing timely and make sure that integrity of its data is either maintained or not. This entity is also responsible for updating any data or service at service provider end also, if occur. Since, service provider is an external un-trusted party; therefore, owner will always stored their data in encrypted format.
2.  **Cloud Service Provider (CSP):** This entity is responsible for handling the data which includes data storage, management, distribution, security maintenance and updating the data if suggested by the data owner. CSP is totally responsible for all the task related to data and releases the owner from any concern. CSP will provide the data to the end users only after verifying their authenticity and access capability as defined by the data owner. As data is stored in encrypted format, CSP will not be able to know exactly what data is stored. Apart from all these, CSP will also responsible for storing redundant copy of the same data in order to avoid single point of failure.
3.  **End User:** These are those entities who wants to access the data owner data or services stored at service provider end. These entity will not directly contact the owner for acquiring any service, instead they contact with service provider for accessing any data or service. Since data is encrypted format, end users are also provided with decryption key to get back the original data from the received one.

## CLOUD SERVICE SCALABILITY

Cloud computing has many advantages out of which scalability is most important. A technology is treated as scalable only if it can rapidly meet the user's data or resource requirement- increase in size, quality, volume etc. before cloud computing, all traditional techniques are restricted towards physical constraints such as memory,

*Figure 2. Cloud entities*

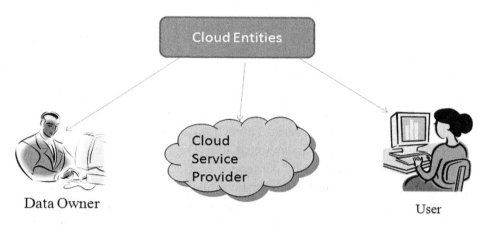

physical space, resources. Thus introduction of scalability feature provides an infrastructure to user in which the required resources can be easily scaled up or down as per the requirement. After the usage of scalability features user's still needs to pay only for the service used instead of a complete service. It unwinds the user to define all the requirements at initial stage for any service/resource. User can acquire the resources/ services whenever need arise at anytime without starting from scratch.

Cloud computing has many advantages out of which scalability is most important. A technology is treated as scalable only if it can rapidly meet the user's data or resource requirement- increase in size, quality, volume etc. without impacting the performance. Before cloud computing, all traditional techniques are restricted towards physical constraints such as memory, physical space, resources. Thus introduction of scalability feature provides an infrastructure to user in which the required resources can be easily scaled up or down as per the requirement. After the usage of scalability features user's still needs to pay only for the service used instead of a complete service. It unwinds the user to define all the requirements at initial stage for any service/resource. User can acquire the resources/services whenever need arise i.e. at anytime, without starting from scratch.

The resources required to support the scalability features are usually planned prior, with a certain amount of backup to handle peak demand, if arise. For any computing system, scalability can be applied generally to the following areas- 1) Memory 2) CPU 3) Network or I/O and 4) Disk I/O. While considering the cloud computing environment, it can be further divided into vertical scalability (scale up within the system) and horizontal scalability (scale out multiple systems). Therefore, each and every application must have a backup repository to easily scale up or scale out the resources, in-order to prevent the hindering performance due to lack of resources. There are many situations where IT person knows in advance that he/she will no longer need some particular resources. In this case he/she can scale down the computing environment to support a new smaller environment with less resources needed for proper functioning. Either increase or decrease in the requirement of resources and services is a planned static event for the worst case workload scenario.

For example:

1.  Suppose, you have a web application gets featured over a particular website. Suddenly, thousands of visitors are applied for using your app. Can the app infrastructure is able to handle that much traffic? If we have a scalable application then we can easily scale up to handle the load without any crash or losing its performance. Crashing or slow processing of any pages of app leaves users unhappy and results in bad reputation.
2.  Another situation can be a small database application supported by a server for small scale businesses. At the time passes, business will grow so will the resources, demand of database and application. If the IT manager has understood the rising demand of database or the business application, he/she may purchase extra provisioned infrastructure such as computer, storage and network in advance. It will help the database application to have a backup plan in advance and grow its business application to maximize the performance and meet expected capacity. In other words, scaling up the application performance without worrying about not meeting SLA, is a solution for pay-as-grow in a steady manner.

## Scalability Advantages

1.  Scalability features allow any computer application or product to continue its function after change in any infrastructure facility, such as size or volume, to meet user requirement. Generally, scaling is done to increase the size or volume of any application to support the raising requirement of users.
2.  Scalability features have the ability to take full advantage of any rescaled situation to larger the application program and support multiple clients simultaneously. For example, a small business application can be rescaled to move towards large business application by using new functionality such as OS and take full advantage of it to increase the number of users support and performance of business application.
3.  Generally, scalability moves upward rather than downwards to accomplish any objective. Scaling any application downwards means developer trying to achieve the same result in more constrained manner.

## Types of Scalability

As discussed earlier while talking about scalability in cloud computing, it can be further divided into two parts- 1) Horizontal scalability and 2) Vertical scalability.

1.  **Horizontal Scalability:** It is the ability of cloud environment to add more software or hardware unit such as networks or services to work as a single logical unit inorder to meet the user's demand. While applying horizontal scalability, we generally add more servers to spread the load across them. This addition of more server may also bring complexity along with it. Multiple server increases the load of administrative task as well, such as their monitoring, update, security. Synchronization of backup, data and application also require lots of effort. Horizontal scalability also provides many benefit, for example, as per the requirement by adding more server could also increase the speed of processing and performance. As after this for a single task, multiple server are available who are doing the same work in more efficient manner. It will also reduce the waiting time of user, which generally occurs whenever the server is overloaded. The horizontal scalability is also termed as scaling out.
2.  **Vertical Scalability:** It is the ability of cloud environment to increase the ability or capacity of a particular hardware or software by adding more services or resources to the same existing hardware or software, not by adding extra hardware or software support. For example, to make a server processing faster, adding more processing power to the same server. It means we can add more fast storage such as Solid State Drives (SSDs), more powerful processor (CPUs) or more memory (RAM) to existing software, so that the performance of the service or application cam be improved. It is easier operation than horizontal scalability as it requires addition of configuration to the software. The vertical scalability is also termed as scaling in.

## Cloud Service Composition

The increasing tendency of usage of cloud services by many users encourages various web service providers to include several functional and non-functional services into a single pool. A simple single service will not be able to satisfy the entire real world problem. It is essential to combine all the related atomic services into a service pool for handling the user's requirements at a single point only. Cloud service provider faces a tough competition against each other in facilitating the best quality of service to their users based on the supply and demand. It is a challenge for service provider to scrutinize and address the issues regarding the quality of different service to be provided, conquer composition limitations, rapidly change in the network and service demands, characteristics etc. Thus composition of services requires lots of effort for finalizing a fruitful application. It can be achieved by dividing the problem into different category based on intentional objectives, identifying the quality of service to be offered, statistics and beneficial outcome from this.

Nowadays, many organizations are moving towards the web services compositions by applying various AI based approach, genetic based algorithm, network awareness etc. This composition will also helps in handling and managing big data services. For example-

1.  **QoS Based Service Composition:** This composition is also referred to as NP-hardproblem. In market, various cloud services are available having their own approaches to solve a particular problem. Earlier for defining any optimal service composition local optimization techniques was utilized. In this approach, various local services which work as suitable to each other are found and finally they all are combined together into a composite service inorder to handle user's demand. Various techniques used to achieve this are- depth first search, dynamic programming, single additive weight method and linear integer programming.
2.  **Network Co-Ordinate System:** This approach is used to estimate the latency between different communicating nodes in network. The main purpose of this approach is to reduce the Round Trip Time (RTT) delay between the nodes during the packet send from one physical node to another. It can be achieved by measuring the RTT delay for a few fractionsof nodes by using the combination of techniques such as- Euclidean distance Estimation (EDE) and Matrix Factorization (MF). Here, EDE is responsible for calculating the distance between the known networks and store it into 2D matrix to find the distance between unknown network nodes. On the other hand, MF calculates the unmeasured distance by factorizing the distance matrix; contain the known and unknown RTT values, using a concept of gradient descent.

## SLA MANAGEMENT

A Service Level Agreement (SLA) in cloud environment is defined as a legal commitment prevails between a user and cloud service provider. In cloud computing, an effective cloud service is the one which delivers all the adequate resources to the user as mentioned in SLA and re-address the issues if arise. It includes all the aspect related to data or service availability, quality, controlling, allocation, management etc. The most common aspect of SLA is to deliver the services to the user as per the agreement done with service provider. The SLA must be properly followed by the service provider. To ensure this the agreements are generally designed with specified limit of enclosure and all the parties involved in SLA are required to regularly audit for verification of resource/service as per the agreement. All the rewards and penalties must be defined while drafting the agreement.

The SLA contains various generic and technical term in summarized manner as-activities and duties assigned to each party, pricing strategy, attributes of resources required to operate the services (Yeo et al., 2007), possible action and remedy against contravention, business ending etc. It has been stated in Internet Center Group's report (Wustenhoff et al., 2002), presented by Sun Microsystems, that appropriate usage of SLA while using in delivering any service provide the following advantages-

1.  **Improved Customer Acceptance Level:** A properly explained SLA attract large amount of customer, as it provides the customer with complete details of services. Also the service provider is known in advance about clients need and work accordingly, in right way to match the entire stated requirement in SLA.

2.  **Enhanced Relationship Between the Parties:** A well stated SLA contains all the information related to remuneration and retribution policies for all the service provided. The client can cross check all the services accordingly to the Service Level Objectives (SLO) defined in SLA. Apart from this, this specific contract helps the parties to solve any disagreements without any difficulties (Wu et al., 20012, Marillyet al., 2002, Alhamad et al., 2010, Sahai et al., 2003, Keller et al., 2003), if required.

3.  **Enhanced Quality of Service (QoS):** An SLO contains various information regarding any service to be delivered such as- specific period, specific target value to be achieved, service level, performance parameter for handling fault tolerance etc. The actual performance of every service to be offered is compared with stated one in the SLO to prepare a performance report for better evaluation in future (Rosa et al., 2004). The only way to get the exact QoS is to initialize and set the quality indication at the initial stage only and use them later to determine any violation. These SLA templates and mechanism can described various parameters as – fault tolerance, availability, performance, service prioritization etc.

4.  **Performance:** The performance of any service to be offered by service provider is determined by QoS which refers to maximum period taken by any request from its arrival time and storage to its final response. Whenever any client or user request for any service from service provider, then the provider depending on the client's requirement find out the response time it will take for client request. After which, the service provider acquires the required resources from the infrastructure and reserved them to that client for the complete duration of

contact. Then as a response, service provider treats the client request according to the requirement. Thus, performance of any service is guaranteed by booking the resources and shaping the client request accordingly (Freitas et al., 2012).

5.  **Fault Tolerance:** This feature of any system can be determined by its degree of dependency and reliability. This parameter is generally utilized by the service provider to find out any crash or fault during any service treatment. These faults can be treated as either job delay or job failure. Fault tolerance of any service is guaranteed by solving any job delay or its failure during its request processing (Hasselmeyer et al, 2007).

## SLA COMPONENTS

An ideal SLA contains the following components for its complete and fair description:

1.  **Purpose**: Mention why SLA is made or the service task needs to be delivered by service provider.
2.  **Parties**: Mention various parties involved with their respective roles and responsibility.
3.  **Validity or Time Period-Mention**: The time period in which the SLA needs to be exists. It is delivered by both initial and final time period.
4.  **Restrictions**: Mention various essential steps needs to be followed before actually supplying the required resources.
5.  **Penalties**: Mention the actions needs to be taken if service provider not able to achieve the goal as stated in SLA.

## SLA LIFE CYCLE

From the time SLA formation initiates for any service till the termination or decomposition, the SLA undergoes six steps, known as its life cycle. The steps, to be followed by each and every SLA can be categorized as- development of services and SLA templates, discovery and negotiation of an SLA, service provisioning and deployment, service execution, corrective or assessment action taken during service execution and both termination and decomposition of the service.

1.  **Development of Service and Templates:** This stage includes the identification of client's needs and requirements, identification of the best suitable parameter and features, the network capabilities, fault tolerance and performance parameters, various service levels, service execution environment, implementation of standard template of SLA which includes various component as defined above.

2.  **Discovery and Negotiation of SLA:** This stage includes a negotiation between the client and service provider to discover the things such as- various SLA parameters values related to any specific service, the cost gained from the client for signing the SLA, the cost incurred by the service provider in case of SLA violation, definition of various terms and at last periodicity of reports associated with services to be delivered to the client.

3.  **Service Provisioning and Deployment:** This stage concern with the service availability and preparation of various services for the user's consumption. Service activation along with the configuration management of the network which might be required to achieve specific service requirements. They are also required the reconfiguration of various resources to support the execution stage for successfully achievements of various SLA parameters (Bianco et al., 2008).

4.  **Service Execution:** This stage includes the actual processing or testing various services. It is mainly divided into three phases as- 1) service execution and their monitoring, 2) real time reporting of various services and 3) at last validating the Quality of Service (QoS). The final phase of this stage involves checking the SLA violation processing (Sen et al., 2005).

5.  **Corrective or Assessment Action Taken During Service Execution:** The SLA assessment stage comprises of two tasks- 1) assessment with the individual customer and 2) overall service assessment. The first task includes the activities as- receiving the QoS of customer services, proper enhancements achievements, customer gratification and examines all alternatives requirements for SLA. On the other hand, overall service assessment for major activities includes readjustments of service goals, modification in service operation, defining the service support problem and at last establishing different service levels.

6.  **Termination and Decomposition of Services:** This stage concern with the termination of existing services. This termination may occur due to a few reasons which may include any issue in contract violation expiation. The decommissioning of discontinued services can cause termination of the SLA (Yeo et al., 2007).

*Figure 3. SLA life cycle*

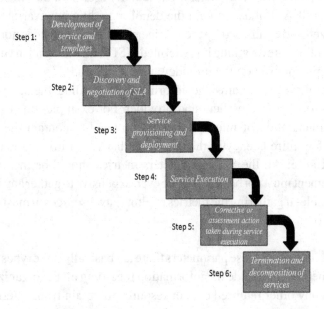

## SLA METRICS AND PARAMETERS

Metrics are utilized for monitoring the various process or procedure used in software, their environment, business policy usage &employment and any area which required gathering the information from multiple sources to confirm whether their objective are being achieved or not. Similarly, for identifying various SLA parameters required by metrics group. These metrics are utilized to get the information regarding the SLA parameters such as- reasonability, enforceability, achievability and target achievement to identify whether SLA parameters reached the required level or not. And if not, how much further information needs to be collected, for achieving this. SLA parameters are generally licensed between the provider and client. Its corresponding matrices are further utilized for verification of the negotiation done between them. The commonly used SLA parameters are as-

1.  **Reasonability:** It encourages the cloud service distributor to behave in a way that is useful for both parties i.e, user and distributor. for example- A SLA parameter will be able to compute the cost or user invoice depending on the amount of services and for how much time service is utilized by the user. It must be able to help in taking a decision regarding the revenue generation by weaken the service plan.

2.   **Enforceability:** This parameter is particularly useful for the client/users while preparing SLA. It must contain the detail regarding how various parameters are utilized and controlled by the service provider. Client does not wait for any contravention, as everything is predefined in SLA including all the measurement and equipment used on the provider and client's end.

3.   **Achievability:** It contains the information regarding the matrices outside the monitoring of both client and provider. For example- due to any kind of miscommunication of internet, there is no need to contain the information metrics for entire latency of the operation that goes through the internet.

4.   **Quantifiable:** All the SLA parameters metrics should be measurable. This measurement must not be very hard or even expensive to gather any information. For example- if gathering the metrics exploits any resources, it must not decrease any effort.

While considering all these parameters there are basically three types of matrices- 1) Resource metrics- it include the information regarding all the organized and used resources and any other required data or resource to obtain from external resource agency. 2) Composite metrics- these matrices are usually made by merging resource metrics depending upon particular algorithm. 3) Business matrices- it contains the information regarding economic expression related to the client (Alhamad et al., 2010).

## SECURITY AND PRIVACY OF CLOUD COMPUTING

## Privacy

Data privacy in cloud environment meansto kept data secret and hide from unauthorized access. Privacy of data can be obtains by encoding, encryption, translation of data, cryptographic techniques etc. which transforms the confidential data into incomprehensible form. It normally includes protection of data from any malicious activity performed by the opposition or malicious attacker. In cloud, owner's information is stored at remote location which may include some sensitive or confidential information. Users can access the data only after proper identification and authorization process as suggested by the owner. It is necessary that service provider will deliver owner's data according to access criteria defined by him in order to protect its data from unauthorized access. Since owner can not completely trust service provider for its data privacy, so owner requires high deliberation towards achieving this.

## Security Issues

Apart from privacy and trust maintenance between different communicating parties, there are other security issues such as authorization, access control, integrity, non-repudiation, network security, confidentiality etc. needs high prudence. To provide the authorization and access control for data access by different users, data owner can decide one of three mechanisms i.e. role based access control, user based access control or attribute based access control to allow the users to get required data. Owner also needs to notify service provider about access control for verification purpose before transferring the data to any user according to the request. To prove that data integrity is maintained without any vulnerabilities owner can encrypt the data with digital signature. Only the authorized users get verification key to check the integrity of received data from the service provider to ensure that retrieved data is intact.

In cloud computing, numerous security issues needs high consideration, as it encompasses many technology which include OS, database, networking, resource scheduling, virtualization, concurrency control, load balancing, memory management etc. For all these techniques security requirements are differ and applicable for proper handling of cloud computing environment. For example, memory management and resource management algorithms need to be secure and transparent to user. Owner's data security requires encryption along with appropriate policy enforcement before data sharing. Furthermore, usage of virtualization in cloud computing also requires several security concerns such as mapping between physical and virtual machine need to be carried out securely. In addition, network connecting the user with cloud also need to be secure for secure data transmission to and from cloud service provider. Finally, for detection of any malware activity data mining techniques must be applied- an approach usually adopted for intrusion detection system (Sen et al., 2006b, Sen et al., 2008, Sen et al., 2010a, Sen et al., 2010b, Sen et al., 2010c, Trusted Computing Group White Paper, 2012).

Broadly, cloud computing environment can be divided into six specific areas where any software or hardware requires high security attention before their usage (Berticon et al., 2009). The six specific areas are- 1) data at rest 2) data at transit 3) authentication and authorization of users 4) separation of data belongs to different users 5) legal and regulatory security cloud issues and 6) incident happening.

Applying cryptographic encryption scheme provides the best mechanism for securing the data at rest. Nowadays, the hard drive manufactures are also shipping self-encrypting drives which implements trusted storage paradigm for trusted computing group (Berticon et al., 2009). This drive contains encryption hardware, providing automated encryption with minimal performance impact or cost. On the other hand, if software encryption will be applied, it will slower the process and less secure as it is possible for any adversary to crack the encryption key from the machine without being detected. This encryption mechanism is also a best option during transmission. Along with encryption, authentication and integrity protection mechanism are also need to apply to make sure that data will received by only authorized users as suggested by data owner and also not allowed or modified during transmission over network.

In cloud environment, authentication and access control are prime requirements than others because owner's data stored at remote location and accessible to user or anyone over the internet. Usage of authentication and access control provides a mechanism to restrict the user access on data and only authorized user satisfying the access criteria can access the data. The real time communication between cloud service provider and users are managed by the Trusted Computing Group's (TCG's) IF- MAP standard. Whenever any revocation of user or reassignment of access control happens than service provider will be notify as soon as that service provider can take necessary action within very short period of time. On the other hand, it is very important to check and verify the integrity of received data as well as policies and practices of service provider. To check that service provider's policy and practices for legal and regulatory issues, an expert system/person is required by data owners to ensure their adequacy. Apart from these, owners must also be prepared for any security breaches or unexpected behavior of the service provider or user. To handle this, Trusted Computing Group's (TCG's) IF- MAP standard provides standards for real time notification of any misbehavior or unexpected incident. Thus, while adopting any cloud organization for accessing the services, the following security challenges needs to be examined very carefully either through designing and implementing security control mechanism in privately owned cloud or by accessing the activity on public or vendor cloud.

## Attacks in Cloud Computing

Each of the cloud computing model is attached or threatened by the attacker, who tries to access the data for which they are not eligible. These attackers in cloud computing can be classified into two category- internal and external attacker. Both the attackers are different from each other on the basis of successful execution of attack which threatens the vendor and owners alike.

1.  **Internal Attack:** An internal attack involves those entities who have some access on the internal data, application or infrastructure, depending ontheir role under the organization and access control possessed by them. They are generally employed by owner, service provider or third party organization which supports the cloud services. The internal attackers use their own privilege to further gain access on the other services out of their access control. They also

support the external third parties in breaching the security of internal data by attacking against the Confidentiality, Integrity and Availability (CIA) of data available in cloud service.

2.  **External Attack:** An external attack involves those entities who don't have any access on data, application or services provided by the cloud. They arealso not employed by anyone in cloud scenario such as owner, service provider or other third party. Their target is to acquire other sensitive or confidential data stored at cloud service provider's end. They generally exploits the process, operational, technical and social engineering vulnerabilities to access the data from service provider, or the third party organization supporting the cloud service for financial and economical benefit. The external attacker also attack against CIA to gain further access.

In cloud environment, based on the ability to initiate an attack, rather than type of threat they present, cloud attacker can be categorized into four categories as-

1.  **Random:** These are the simplest attack employed by randomly scanning the internet to find out the vulnerable components and expressed it by deploying a very simple tools and techniques, which are easily detected.
2.  **Weak:** These attackers are semi- skilled in nature and targeting the specific cloud provider/server by applying the tools publically available. They use the advance method for attacking as they are using already available exploit tool for customization.
3.  **Strong:** These attacks are better defined, organized and skilled in nature and try to exploit particular user or application of cloud. These groups are well organized in nature and specialize in large scale attack.
4.  **Substantial:** They are highly motivated and strong attacker which are not easily detected or recognized by the organization they attack. Even the organization specializing in cyber security or crime, well known for law enforcement and investigation, are unable to detect them.

## Cloud Security Risks

While accessing the data over cloud environment various security risks are associated with cloud delivery model. All the cloud risks are dependent upon the number of features including the cloud architecture, data sensitivity and security measures utilized by various cloud environment. The various risks in cloud environment can be categorized as-

1. **Privileged User Access:** Once the data is stored over cloud environment, cloud provider has complete access to the data and also responsible for controlling its access control from external entities, which may include either third party supplier or cloud users. Maintaining the access control of privileged user and confidentiality of owner's data are prime requirement which can be achieved by applying any of two approaches by data owner as- 1) By applying the encryption technique over the data before storing it over cloud environment and share the decryption key only with authorized users. 2) By enforcing the cloud provider to make sure that all the legal contract and standard are maintained properly. Various access control mechanism used in cloud environment are Role Based Access Control (RBAC), Identity Based Access Control (IBAC) and Attribute Based Access Control (ABAC). Applying encryption of data prior to its storage on cloud provider require another security challenge. For monitoring data confidentiality, decryption key must be shared securely in-order to ensure that only authorized user will be able to access the data. Secondly, enable the auditing of user actions to find the malicious attacker inside or outside by segregation of duties of privileged user access control.

2. **Data Location and Segregation:** Owner's data shared at cloud service provider with no physical access. If cloud environment use the central storage mechanism then it helps the attacker to get rich information from a single place. In a single attack, attacker will be enriched with lots of confidential data shared by single or multiple data owner at that service provider. Therefore, applying adequate segregation of owner's data will relief the user from various securities breach incident. This can be achieved by virtualization technologies.

3. **Data Disposal:** Deletion and disposal of cloud data are high risk concern where hardware or resources are issued dynamically to the customer. Cloud administration, that offer information capacity ordinarily gives either assurance or service level objectives around the availability of data to user. Cloud service provider achieves this by keeping multiple duplicate copies of the data. Whenever the cloud client has a necessity to erase information, cloud storage may be inappropriate for that particular information from all its replicated point. Depending upon the sort of information facilitated in the cloud, customer may required service provider to erase information in accordance with industry standards. Until then cloud environment particularly limit the media on which data may be situated and data owner can mandate use of media fresher technique, the risk of data not being erased from data backup, stores and physical media during transition is enhanced within cloud environment.

4.  **E-Investigation and Protective Monitoring:** The capacity of cloud owner to apply their own electric investigation strategies inside the cloud can be restricted by the delivery or deployment model usage. Owner cannot effectively deploy its own data on the cloud infrastructure; they must depend on the framework it utilize by the cloud provider to support investigation. There is a high chance of risk of inside attack or threats, which require expertise in e-investigation and protective monitoring.

## Good Security Practices in Cloud Computing

While using cloud computing environment to store and process any confidential data, various security practices needs to be taken care for securing the data from any occurrence of attacks or risk are as follows-

1.  **Protection Against Internal and External Threats:** Security hacking administration offer assistance to progress the adequacy of security framework of a user by effectively analyzing logs and alarms from framework devices around the clock an in real time. Observing team correlate data from different security gadgets to provide security analyst with the information they require to dispense with wrong positives and react to genuine dangers against the enterprise. Usually the services altitude required to preserve the level of benefit and security of an organization is very high. The data security group can evaluate framework execution on a periodically recurring premise and give suggestion for changes as required.
2.  **Early Detection:** An early detection or discovery of services identifies and reports new security vulnerabilities without further delay after they appear. Generally, the security dangers and threats are connected with third party sources and an alert or report is issued to data owner regarding this. These security vulnerabilities reports incorporate a point by point description of the vulnerabilities and the platform influenced, along with affected data. The exploitation of these vulnerabilities would have on the frameworks or applications already chosen by the company accepting the report. Most frequently, the report to demonstrate particular action to be taken to minimize the impact of the vulnerabilities.
3.  **Intelligent Log Centralization:** Intelligent log centralization and examination is a checking arrangement, basically based on the correlation and coordinating of log entries. Such examination makes a difference to set up a standard of operational performance and gives or index of security threats or risks. Alert can be raised in the occasion of an incident move the built up standard

parameters beyond a predefined threshold limit. These types of sophisticated tools are utilized by a group of security specialist who are responsible for handling these incidents. Once such an edge has been reused and the risk has created, a caution or warning picked up by security analyst who is responsible for monitoring the system.

4.   **Vulnerabilities Detection and Management:** Vulnerabilities recognition and administration empower mechanized confirmation and administration of the security level of data framework. The administration intermittently plays out a progression of mechanized test to identify the framework shortcomings that might be uncovered over the internet, count the likelihood of unauthorized access to regulatory administration, the process of administrations that have not been refreshed and the discover vulnerabilities. For example phishing and so forth. The administration performs occasional follow-up of undertaking performed by security experts overseeing data framework security and gives reports that can be utilized to execute an arrangement for ceaseless change of the framework's security level.

5.   **Intervention, Forensics, and Help Desk Services:** Immediate or rapid interpretation when a risk is identified is most important to moderate the impact of this risk. This requires a team of security engineers with adequate knowledge of different technologies and innovations, along with the capacity to strengthen application and infrastructure on (24x7) premise. At any point of time when a distinguished risk is identified, it is necessary to frequently examine the issue to find out what it is, how much exertion it will take to settle the issue and what impacts are probably going to be seen. At the point when owner or user figured out the problem, the first thing they do is to pick up the phone and call helpdesk. Helpdesk administration is responsible for helping with inquiries or issues about the operation of running frameworks. It includes composing disappointment reports, overseeing issues and so on.

## EMERGING TRENDS IN SECURITY AND PRIVACY IN CLOUD COMPUTING

Nowadays, cloud computing is utilized in various domain and each domain have their own requirements regarding the security, privacy and trust, they employ their own mechanisms, semantics and interface. While applying any new technology, some critical issues regarding security and privacy requires immediate attention for the adoption as-

1. **Authentication and Identity Management:** Cloud services allow the users to access their services and/or data to make it available to other users across the internet. An identity management mechanism can help authenticate users and services based on the characteristics and credentials (Bertino et al., 2009). Identity management will also helps in protecting the sensitive and private information of owner from attacker using authentication techniques. While users are interacting with any front–end service, that service must ensure the users that their identity is kept secret from other services with which it interacts (Bertino et al., 2009; Ko et al., 2009). The usage of authentication techniques helps to ensure that only the authorized user for a service is able to access the data.

2. **Access Control and Accounting:** Heterogeneity and decent variety of data or services, and prerequisite in distributed computing conditions, request fine-grained access control strategies. In specific, access control should be sufficiently adoptable to catch dynamic setting, attribute or credential based access prerequisite and to uphold the guidelines of least privilege. Such access control services may need to coordinate security insurance requirements communicated through complex guidelines. It should be ensured that cloud delivery model provide generic access control interface for proper interoperability and address cross-domain access issues as well (Joshi et al., 2004).

3. **Trust Management and Policy Integration:** There are multiple service providers coexist in cloud environment, collaborate to provide various services from a single place only. Each collaborative service may have their own security and privacy policies. Hence, we must address heterogeneity among their policies (ENISA, 2009; Blaze et al., 2009; Zhang & Joshi, 2009). Security provider should be very careful, while managing access control policies, to make sure that integration of policy doesn't breach any security or privacy policy. Thus a trust framework should be developed to efficiently capture a generic set of parameters required for trust management (Zhang & Joshi, 2009; Shin &Ahn, 2005). In addition, while going for integration of cloud policies, various security challenges regarding semantic heterogeneity service interoperability and policy evaluation needs to address very carefully.

## Security Requirements in Cloud Based Services

See Table 1.

*Table 1. Security requirements*

| Security Requirement | Description with solution |
|---|---|
| Authentication and access control | To provide the owner's data to authorized user according to user's access criteria. Service provider must differentiate between the authorized and unauthorized users and allow only authorized users to access the required data according to their role, capability, identity etc. |
| Confidentiality& Privacy | To guarantee the confidentiality and privacy, thedataneeds tobe transmitted and stored in encrypted form rather than original. Only the authorized users are able to get the original data after decryption, service provider must be unaware of this decryption process. |
| Integrity | Data owner must sign its data and only the authorized users has its verification key to check that the received data is intact without any alteration done by malicious attacker during transmission. |
| Auditing | To maintain the interoperability feature in cloud based system, any malicious activity will be monitored by auditor and auditing reports are sent to alert the owner. Owner will take necessary action as required. |
| Trust | To assure that the data is stored at right place and retrieved correctly without introducing any vulnerability. It can be achieved by a contract signed between the different communicating parties such as Service Level Agreement. |

## Strategic Approval for Cloud Services

1. Understand the owner's information sensitivity and its importance before moving towards cloud computing.
2. Security concerns depending on the type of data should be discussed along with the type of access criteria depending upon the user's capability.
3. Explore different cloud models according to the information storage and composition to facilitate user specific need.
4. Users will acquire their requisite data from cloud environment and also verify it to ensure its integrity.
5. Scalability of data is prime concern as more data can be feed into the system according to its popularity and also existing data can be removed as per the requirement.
6. Auditing of data is required to ensure the data is intact and deliver to the users as specified in access criteria without any modification or alteration while transition from one party to another.
7. Portability of data is required to allow the authorized users to get the information at any place without struggling so hard.

## CONCLUSION

The introduction of cloud computing gave new direction to the way user communicate, store and manage the data from anywhere at any time to improve the service provided by the user and the work performed by the user. The major impact is on the fields such as healthcare, banking etc. But it has also introduced many security concerns which must be handled carefully. In this chapter, we are dealing with the trust, privacy and various security issues in cloud based services and also provide the various solutions to deal with any of these problems. In addition to this, we have also provided a brief description related to the benefit and strategic approval of cloud based services. Since owner's sensitive data is stored at service provider end, it requires high security concerns and care along with scalability feature. In future, we will provide a complete secure framework which will provide a composite framework and handle all these security concern wisely and maturity will be improved.

# REFERENCES

Alhamad, M., Dillon, T., & Chang, E. (2010, April). Conceptual SLA framework for cloud computing. In *Digital Ecosystems and Technologies (DEST), 2010 4th IEEE International Conference on* (pp. 606-610). IEEE. 10.1109/DEST.2010.5610586

Bertion, E., Paci, F., & Ferrini, R. (2009, March). Privacy-Preserving Digital Identity Management for Cloud Computing. IEEE Computer Society Data Engineering Bulletin, 1-4.

Bianco, P., Lewis, G. A., & Merson, P. (2008). *Service level agreements in service-oriented architecture environments (No. CMU/SEI-2008-TN-021)*. Carnegie-Mellon Univ Software Engineering Inst. doi:10.21236/ADA528751

Blaze, M., Kannan, S., Lee, I., Sokolsky, O., Smith, J. M., Keromytis, A. D., & Lee, W. (2009). Dynamic Trust Management. *IEEE Computer, 42*(2), 44–52. doi:10.1109/MC.2009.51

European Network and Information Security Agency (ENISA). (2009). *Cloud Computing: Cloud Computing: Benefits, Risks and recommendations for Information Security*. Report No: 2009. Author.

Freitas, A. L., Parlavantzas, N., & Pazat, J. L. (2012, June). An integrated approach for specifying and enforcing slas for cloud services. In *Cloud Computing (CLOUD), 2012 IEEE 5th International Conference on* (pp. 376-383). IEEE.

Hasselmeyer, P., Mersch, H., Koller, B., Quyen, H. N., Schubert, L., & Wieder, P. (2007, October). Implementing an SLA negotiation framework. In *Proceedings of the eChallenges Conference (e-2007)* (Vol. 4, pp. 154-161). Academic Press.

Joshi, J. B. D., Bhatti, R., Bertino, E., & Ghafoor, A. (2004). Access Control Language for Multi-domain Environments. *IEEE Internet Computing, 8*(6), 40–50. doi:10.1109/MIC.2004.53

Keller, A., & Ludwig, H. (2003). The WSLA framework: Specifying and monitoring service level agreements for web services. *Journal of Network and Systems Management, 11*(1), 57–81. doi:10.1023/A:1022445108617

Ko, M., Ahn, G.-J., & Shehab, M. (2009). Privacy-Enhanced User-Centric Identity Management. *Proceedings of IEEE International Conference on Communications*, 998-1002.

Marilly, E., Martinot, O., Betgé-Brezetz, S., & Delègue, G. (2002). Requirements for service level agreement management. In *IP Operations and Management, 2002 IEEE Workshop on* (pp. 57-62). IEEE. 10.1109/IPOM.2002.1045756

Rosa, N. S., Cunha, P. R. F., & Justo, G. R. R. (2004). An approach for reasoning and refining non-functional requirements. *Journal of the Brazilian Computer Society*, *10*(1), 59–81. doi:10.1590/S0104-65002004000200006

Sahai, A., Graupner, S., Machiraju, V., & van Moorsel, A. (2003, May). Specifying and monitoring guarantees in commercial grids through SLA. In *Cluster Computing and the Grid, 2003. Proceedings. CCGrid 2003. 3rd IEEE/ACM International Symposium on* (pp. 292-299). IEEE.

Sen, J. (2010a, August). An Agent-Based Intrusion Detection System for Local Area Networks. *International Journal of Communication Networks and Information Security*, *2*(2), 128–140.

Sen, J. (2010b). An Intrusion Detection Architecture for Clustered Wireless Ad Hoc Networks. *Proceedings of the 2nd IEEE International Conference on Intelligence in Communication Systems and Networks (CICSyN'10)*, 202-207.

Sen, J. (2010c). A Robust and Fault-Tolerant Distributed Intrusion Detection System. *Proceedings of the 1st International Conference on Parallel, Distributed and Grid Computing (PDGC'10)*, 123-128.

Sen, J., & Sengupta, I. (2005). Autonomous Agent-Based Distributed Fault-Tolerant Intrusion Detection System. In *Proceedings of the 2nd International Conference on Distributed Computing and Internet Technology (ICDCIT'05)* (pp. 125-131). Springer. 10.1007/11604655_16

Sen, J., Sengupta, I., & Chowdhury, P. R. (2006b). An Architecture of a Distributed Intrusion Detection System Using Cooperating Agents. *Proceedings of the International Conference on Computing and Informatics (ICOCI'06)*, 1-6.

Sen, J., Ukil, A., Bera, D., & Pal, A. (2008). A Distributed Intrusion Detection System for Wireless Ad Hoc Networks. *Proceedings of the 16th IEEE International Conference on Networking (ICON'08)*, 1-5.

Shin, D., & Ahn, G.-J. (2005). Role-Based Privilege and Trust Management. *Computer Systems Science and Engineering*, *20*(6), 401–410.

Trusted Computing Group (TCG)'s White Paper. (2010). *Cloud Computing and Security- A Natural Match*. Available online at: http://www.trustedcomputinggroup. org

Wu, L., & Buyya, R. (2012). Service level agreement (SLA) in utility computing systems. IGI Global.

Wustenhoff, E., & BluePrints, S. (2002). *Service level agreement in the data center.* Sun Microsystems Professional.

Yeo, C. S., Buyya, R., de Assuncao, M. D., Yu, J., Sulistio, A., Venugopal, S., & Placek, M. (2007). Utility computing on global grids. *Handbook of Computer Networks*, 110-130.

Zhang, Y., & Joshi, J. (2009). *Access Control and Trust Management for Emerging Multidomain Environments.* In S. Upadhyay & R. O. Rao (Eds.), *Annals of Emerging Research in Information Assurance, Security and Privacy Services* (pp. 421–452). Emerald Group Publishing.

# Chapter 3
# Fog Computing and Its Role in the Internet of Things

**Nisha Angeline C. V.**
*Thiagarajar College of Engineering, India*

**Raja Lavanya**
*Thiagarajar College of Engineering, India*

## ABSTRACT

*Fog computing extends the cloud computing paradigm to the edge of the network, thus enabling a new breed of applications and services. Defining characteristics of the Fog are 1) low latency and location awareness, 2) widespread geographical distribution, 3) mobility, 4) very large number of nodes, 5) predominant role of wireless access, 6) strong presence of streaming and real time applications, and 7) heterogeneity. In this chapter, the authors argue that the above characteristics make the Fog the appropriate platform for a number of critical internet of things (IoT) services and applications, namely connected vehicle, smart grid, smart cities, and in general, wireless sensors and actuators networks (WSANs).*

DOI: 10.4018/978-1-5225-7149-0.ch003

## INTRODUCTION

An emerging wave of Internet deployments, most notably the Internet of Things (IoTs), requires mobility support and geo-distribution in addition to location awareness and low latency. We argue that a new platform is needed to meet these requirements; a platform we call Fog Computing or Fog because the fog is a cloud close to the ground. We also claim that rather than cannibalizing Cloud Computing, (Bonomi, 2011). Fog Computing enables a new breed of applications and services, and that there is a fruitful interplay between the Cloud and the Fog, particularly when it comes to data management and analytics. The Internet of Things (IoT) is generating an unprecedented volume and variety of data. But by the time the data makes its way to the cloud for analysis, the opportunity to act on it might be gone.

## Fog Computing

Fog computing also known as edge computing which provides elastic resources and services to the end users at the edge of network. Fog computing is an extension of cloud computing not its replacement. As the number of devices connected to internet has been increasing. In future the world would be full of sensor, it would provide the massive amount of data and storing these data in the cloud and retrieving is difficult. Hence fog can be used. Fog computing is an effective replacement of cloud computing for Internet of Things. It reduces the latency and overcomes the security issues in sending data to the cloud.

## Cloud, Fog, and Edge: Overview

Fog Computing extends a substantial amount of data storage, computing, communication, and networking of cloud computing near to the end devices. Due to close integration with the front-end intelligence enabled end devices, fog computing enhances the overall system efficiency, after that improving the performance of critical cyber-physical systems. An important key difference is that cloud computing tries to optimize resource in a global view, whereas fog computing organizes and manages the local virtual cluster. Edge computing and fog computing terms are interchangeably used in both academia and industry. Although the main objectives of edge computing and fog computing are same, i.e., to reduce end-to-end delay and lower network congestion, however, they differ how they process and handle the data and where the intelligence and computing power are placed. The main idea of

Edge computing is to push computation facility towards data sources, e.g., sensors, actuators, and mobile devices. In Edge computing, each individual edge component plays its role to process data locally rather than sending them towards the cloud, whereas, fog node decides whether to process the data from multiple data sources using its own resource or send to the cloud. Also, several services like Infrastructure-as-a-Service (IaaS), Software-as-a-Service (SaaS), Platform-as-a-Service (PaaS), and other cloud-related services are not supported in Edge computing, however, these services can be extended with fog computing. To summary, Edge computing is totally edge localized, however, fog computing extends the computing and communication resources towards edge of the network.

## FOG COMPUTING: AN EFFECTIVE REPLACEMENT OF CLOUD FOR IOT DEVICES

Though cloud computing offers on demand service and scalable storage and processing capabilities for IoT devices, for monitoring health, emergency applications and other latency sensitive applications, the time or delay caused by the applications for transferring data to the cloud and then processing it, is unacceptable. On the other hand, sending large amount big data collected by the devices to the cloud will saturate the network bandwidth sometimes. To overcome these issues, edge computing was introduced which provides the computing capabilities within the edge of the network near the IoT sensors. This also has some drawbacks like the edge computing resources can't handle multiple applications competing for the same limited resources. This again increases the latency or delay time for processing the application requests.

Fog computing has the following characteristics: multiple application support, simple, fast and standardized protocols, strong security, fault tolerance, versatile operating environment, supports multiple operating platforms such as unix, linux, mac, windows etc..,

Fog computing came as a solution for these problems and overcomes its limitations by providing faster processing at the network level where the IoT devices are located. In fog computing, the data collected from the IoT devices like sensors and other devices, are processed and data analytics is done by the fog devices present in the network. The network includes the nearby gateways and private clouds which analyses the data collected. Fog computing architecture consists of components that integrate the various activities in the fog environment.

Fog computing applications provide data for processing, since large amount of data generated by the sensors, stream processing is done on the collected data. The application programming interfaces are used to identify and adopt to various applications and the data is received and processed from the authorized devices. Resource management is used to identify or track the state of available fog, cloud or other network resources and find the best suited one for processing the data. In multi-tenant applications, the tasks are prioritized based on the users. The edge and cloud computing resources communicates with the fog layer using software defined networks and Machine to machine communication. M2M standards includes Constraint Application Protocol (CoAP) and MQ Telemetry Transport (MQTT). SDN provides an efficient management of fog computing to interact with heterogeneous environment.

Fog Computing is the platform that brings modern, cloud-inspired computing, storage, and networking functions closer to the data-producing sources, while also integrating real-time and safety capabilities.

Fog Computing provides a unified solution at the edge for communications, device management, data harvesting, analysis and control. Fog Computing enables the deployment of a highly distributed but centrally managed infrastructure.

## Fog Computing and the Internet of Things

Capitalizing on the IoT requires a new kind of infrastructure. Today's cloud models are not designed for the volume, variety, and velocity of data that the IoT generates. Billions of previously unconnected devices are generating more than two exabytes of data each day. An estimated 50 billion "things" will be connected to the Internet by 2020 (Aazam, 2015). Moving all data from these things to the cloud for analysis would require vast amounts of bandwidth. These billions of new things also represent countless new types of things. Some are machines that connect to a controller using industrial protocols, not IP. Before this information can be sent to the cloud for analysis or storage, it must be translated to IP.

### Connected Vehicle

The Connected Vehicle deployment displays a rich scenario of connectivity and interactions: cars to cars, cars to access points (Wi-Fi, 3G, LTE, roadside units (RSUs), smart traffic lights), and access points to access points (Bonomi, 2012). The Fog has a number of attributes that make it the ideal platform to deliver a rich menu safety, traffic support, and analytics: geo-distribution (throughout cities and along roads), mobility and location awareness, low latency, heterogeneity, and support for real-time interactions.

## Smart Traffic Light

A smart traffic light system illustrates the latter. The smart traffic light node interacts locally with a number of sensors, which detect the presence of pedestrians and bikers, and measures the distance and speed of approaching vehicles. It also interacts with neighboring lights to coordinate the green traffic wave. Based on this information the smart light sends warning signals to approaching vehicles, and even modifies its own cycle to prevent accidents.

The data from clusters of smart traffic lights is sent to the Cloud for global, long term analytics.

## Smart Grid

Smart Grid is another rich Fog use case. We defer to the next section, a discussion of the interplay of Fog and Cloud in the context of Smart Grid.

## Wireless Sensors and Actuators Networks

The original Wireless Sensor Nodes (WSNs) were designed to operate at extremely low power to extend battery life or even to make energy harvesting feasible. Most of these WSNs involve a large number of low bandwidth, low energy, low processing power, small memory motes, operating as sources of a sink (collector), in a unidirectional fashion (Bowman, 1993). Sensing the environment, simple processing, and forwarding data to the static sink are the duties of this class of sensor networks, for which the open source TinyOS2 is the de-facto standard operating system. Motes have proven useful in a variety of scenarios to collect environmental data (humidity, temperature, amount of rainfall, light intensity, etc).

Energy constrained WSNs advanced in several directions: multiple sinks, mobile sinks, multiple mobile sinks, and mobile sensors were proposed in successive incarnations to meet the requirements of new applications. Yet, they fall short in applications that go beyond sensing and tracking, but re-quire actuators to exert physical actions (open, close, move, focus, target, even carry and deploy sensors). Actuators, which can control either a system or the measurement process itself, bring new dimensions to sensor networks.

## Augumented Reality

Augmented Reality (AR) and Real-time video analytics Augment reality applications are popular on smart-phone, tablet and smart glasses by overlaying an informative view on the real world (viewed on the device display system). Recent popular products or projects include Google Glass, Sony SmartEyeglass and Microsoft HoloLens. AR applications usually need high computation power to process video streaming and high bandwidth for data transmission. For example, a normal AR application needs to process real time video frame using computer vision algorithm and at the same time process other inputs such as voice, sensor and _nally output timely informational content on displays. However, human are very sensitive to delays in a series of consecutive interactions. A processing delay of more than tens of milliseconds will ruin the user experience and leads to negative user feedback. AR system supported by fog computing can maximize throughput and reduce latency in both processing and transmission, design and implement a wearable cognitive assistance spanning on Google Glass and Cloudlet, which can offer the wearer hints for social interaction via real-time scene analysis. The system achieves tight end-to-end latency constraint by offering computation-intensive task to nearby Cloudlet. Network failure and unavailability of distant Cloudlets are also considered and provided automatic degrade services. Largely-deployed camera sensors in city or along the road are important component of smart city and smart connected vehicle to support surveillance, traffic management etc. Fog computing can provide sufficient resource of computation and storage to store captured video streams, transcode and process video frame for tasks such as object recognition, object tracking and data mining etc. After that we can just send out notification, events, description or video summary to end users, central servers or databases. With the help of fog, we can achieve real-time processing and feedback of high-volume video streaming and scalability of service on low-bandwidth output data. Privacy-preserving techniques can also be applied at the fog side, to ease the concern of personal privacy leakage in public surveillance systems.

## Medical Field

Edge computing is currently used in several other medical closed-loop systems besides diabetes systems, where the sensor input is designed to affect the actuator output, including cardiac pacemakers; cardiac defibrillators; investigational closed-loop mechanical ventilation systems which are not yet on the market; the Sedasys closed-loop anesthesia delivery system that was approved by FDA but taken off the market because of poor sales and brain function which can be modulated with closed-loop stimulation. Edge computing is suited for closed-loop systems that use smart sensors to maintain physiologic homeostasis, but the approach is adopted only to a limited extent currently because few autonomous closed-loop systems have been developed and approved by the FDA. This approach would be suitable for an intensive care unit or an emergency medical department where acutely ill patients can require immediate responses to changes in their condition. Edge computing is achieved by connecting a system's sensors to small, local control systems that handle processing, and communication. The result of edge computing can be rapid machine-to machine communication or machine-to-human interaction. This paradigm (compared to fog computing) takes localized processing farther away from the network right down to the sensor by pushing the computing processes even closer to the data sources. The sensor can then either send information directly to another edge device, up to a fog node, or to the cloud. By using edge computing, instead of doing the bulk of processing in a centralized server or a distributed local server, each device on the network would play its own role in processing the information.

## Benefits of Fog Computing

Extending the cloud closer to the things that generate and act on data benefits the business in the following ways:

- **Greater Business Agility:** With the right tools, developers can quickly develop fog applications and deploy them where needed. Machine manufacturers can offer MaaS to their customers. Fog applications program the machine to operate in the way each customer needs.
- **Better Security:** Protect your fog nodes using the same policy, controls, and procedures you use in other parts of your IT environment. Use the same physical security and cybersecurity solutions.
- **Deeper Insights, With Privacy Control:** Analyze sensitive data locally instead of sending it to the cloud for analysis. Your IT team can monitor and control the devices that collect, analyze, and store data.
- **Lower Operating Expense:** Conserve network bandwidth by processing selected data locally instead of sending it to the cloud for analysis.

## Security in Fog Computing

In cloud computing there occurs various security issues such as man in middle attack and insider attack. Cloud computing provides various services for storing and accessing data but they did not gave much importance for security of data. It is very difficult to build a secured cloud because there occurs continuous attack to the cloud. This might leads to loss in data. Hence fog computing is used for storage of data which is considered as secured storage.

## CONCLUSION

Hence the vision and defined key characteristics of Fog Computing are define. A platform of new services and applications at the edge of the network. The motivating examples given in the discussion range from conceptual visions to existing prototypes. The Fog will be a platform, rich enough to deliver new breed of emerging services and enable the development of new applications. The following are expected to come up in the future Architecture of this massive infrastructure of compute, storage, and networking devices; Orchestration and resource management of the Fog nodes; Innovative services and applications to be supported by the Fog.

# REFERENCES

Aazam, M., & Huh, E.-N. (2015). Fog computing micro datacenter based dynamic resource estimation and pricing model for IoT. *IEEE 29th International Conference on Advanced Information Networking and Applications*, 687–694.

Bonomi. (2012). *Fog Computing and Its Role in the Internet of Things*. ACM.

Bonomi. (2011). Connected vehicles, the internet of things, and fog computing. *VANET 2011*.

Bowman, M., Debray, S. K., & Peterson, L. L. (1993). Reasoning about naming systems. *ACM Transactions on Programming Languages and Systems*, *15*(5), 795–825. doi:10.1145/161468.161471

# Chapter 4
# A Comprehensive Study on Internet of Things Security:
## Challenges and Recommendations

**Manikandakumar Muthusamy**
*Thiagarajar College of Engineering, India*

**Karthikeyan Periasamy**
*Thiagarajar College of Engineering, India*

## ABSTRACT

*Internet of things is a growing technology with many business opportunities and risks. It is strongly believed that IoT will cause a major shift in people's lives similar to how the internet transformed the way people communicate and share information. IoT is becoming popular in the various domains such as smart health, smart cities, smart transport, and smart retail. The security and privacy concerns of IoT are crucial as it connects a large number of devices. Security is a more critical issue that certainly needs to be resolved with a high level of attention, as with an increasing number of users, there would be a need to manage their requests and check authenticity on the cloud-based pattern. Recently, a series of massive distributed denial-of-service attacks have occurred in IoT organizations. Such malicious attacks have highlighted the threats resulting from not enough security in IoT devices together with their overwhelming effects on the internet. This chapter provides an overview of the security attacks with regard to IoT technologies, protocols, and applications.*

DOI: 10.4018/978-1-5225-7149-0.ch004

# INTRODUCTION

The Internet of Things is enchanting industries and society due to its possibility to quickly renovate businesses and people's lives. IoT comprises sensors that interacting and communicating with other machines, objects and environments by providing connectivity to each and every one and everything. IoT connects the physical objects like buildings, vehicles and other devices with embedded sensors and enables those objects to collect and transport data. IoT is a convergence of wireless nodes, internet and computing. IoT can be recognized as a next generation of the Internet that focuses on machine to machine learning. The IoT embeds some code in network connected objects to collect, communicate, exchange data, make decisions, invoke events and offer many services (Gubbi, Buyya, Marusic, & Palaniswami, 2013). The increase in interaction between sensor devices and systems, large volume of data are likely to be generated and moved across information management systems. These gathered big data will be processed and analyzed to generate meaningful form and to perform actionable decision making(Manikandakumar, & Ramanujam, 2018). The variety of services being planned using IoT means no one company can develop a full end-to-end solution and support IoT-based innovations. The IoT is getting increased for educational institutions, industrial sectors as well as in government agencies that have the possibility to bring major personal, professional and economic benefits. At the mean time security challenges respect to each and every layer of the IoT architecture need to be identified, analyzed and resolved to the maximum possible extent. The overall security needs of the Internet of Things encompass security of physical nodes, information acquisition security, information transmission security and information processing security, in order to achieve the authenticity, confidentiality and integrity of information. This chapter forecast the key security challenges and remedial actions associated with the development of IoT.

# IoT ARCHITECTURE

The architecture of IoT is included with the recent technologies of communication protocols, sensors and RFID like devices. The architecture can be typically represented by four interconnected layers or entities namely Acquisition layer, Network layer, Support layer or Middleware layer and Application layer as represented in Figure 1.

*Figure 1. IoT security architecture*

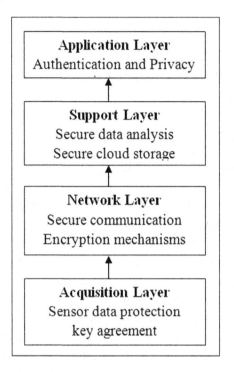

## Acquisition Layer

In the information acquisition or perception layer of IoT, a large number of low cost sensors are deployed. Many connectivity options are necessarily needed to connect them with internet. Even connectivity also needs interoperability among diverse kinds of information. Hence the IoT architecture must be open in nature, should be scalable, layered in order to support heterogeneous upcoming applications.

Perception layer also represented as sensing layer, which resembles the physical layer of ISO-OSI model. The major role of this layer is to acquiring the information from the physical world.

In general sensors are used to acquire information from the environment with the help of advanced built in sensing and recognition technologies. Wireless Sensor Network (WSN) is deployed to gather, analyze and process the information. Sensors like soil, temperature, moisture, humidity, sound, smoke sensors and vibration sensors etc., are presented to collect the information. Identification of physical objects can be done through the recognition technology. RFID tags, bar codes and two dimensional codes can be used to identify the objects. The data collected in perception layer is may be in the form of pH level, humidity, temperature, location and vibration etc. The sensed data is transmitted through network to reach the information processing and management system.

Basically there are three types of devices based on the capacity and processing power:

- The devices have 8-bit system on a chip (SoC) controllers like Arduino boards.
- The next higher level devices are based on Atheros or ARM chips with 32-bit structure.

Familiar examples of this type are OpenWRT and the most capable are 32-bit/64-bit versions of Raspberry Pi or BeagleBone. Such kind of devices can execute a full Linux OS or Android based operating systems. In most of the cases these devices are based on mobile phone technology. Some of the most widely used technologies and standards that the devices connected with the external world are,

- Ethernet
- Bluetooth
- Wi-Fi
- Zigbee
- Near field communication

## Network Layer

IoT technology basically consists of sensors and communication network nodes. Sensor network acts as peripheral network which mainly uses short distance communication technologies. The technologies used with sensor networks are Bluetooth, RFID, Zigbee, Infrared light communication technology etc. Telecommunication network acts as core host network which communicates between sensor and transmission network such as Wi-Fi, WiMAX technologies and with core telecommunication network such as 2G, 3G and 4G etc.

To uniquely identify the deployed network devices an IP addressing mechanism like IPV6 is essential. For transferring or exchanging data across the network, secure and an advanced data aggregation scheme is required. Network gateways are the intermediary systems that connect IoT sensor devices via the Internet and provide required supportive functions such as manageability and security. Gateways are highly required in environmental situations in which the deployed sensory devices can not directly connect to existing systems on the Internet. From an IoT point of view about 85% of existing devices are in use were not designed to connect to the Internet and gateways are the key systems to connect these existing things to the IoT domain.

## Support Layer

Support layer or Middleware layer lies between the application layer and network layers. It offers services to end users by storing physical layer data in database or in the cloud storage infrastructure. The cloud infrastructure affords necessary means in terms of hardware capacity, storage and processing power required for processing the larger amounts of data expected to be generated from IoT.

As IoT produces enormous volumes of data and concentrates providing information to user data storage and analytics, visualization techniques gained importance. A network is the current Internet with connected Internet Protocol (IP) systems, such as routers, repeaters and gateways, which control data flow and connect to telecommunication and cable networks such as 3G, 4G and LTE.

## Application Layer

Application layer is the topmost layer in the IoT architecture which involves the user interaction by having application management system based on the information gained from lower layers. The applications can be of various fields such as agriculture, environment monitoring, healthcare, smart home, smart business, smart transportation, logistics, media, mobile, utilities etc. This layer consists of middleware interfaces to perform data massaging and presenting activities for user level consumption through various mediums such as desktop, browser and mobile applications.

## PROTOCOLS

Protocol or standard is a set of rules and regulations for effective communication within the networks (Sheng, Yang, Yu & Vasilakos, 2014). The existing protocols like

HTTP and TCP/IP are cannot be used for IoT communication due to the existence of smart devices and other constraints. For machine to machine communication, the protocols such as Message Queue Telemetry Transport (MQTT) protocol and Constraint Application Protocol (CoAP) are can be used. MQTT protocol has the features of publish message pattern, messaging transport. CoAP is a web transfer protocol for constrained nodes and constrained networks. The protocol stack provides three classes. Class 1 shows protocol stack for traditional environment (TE1, TE2). Class 2 shows protocol stack for routing device. Class 3 shows protocol stack for constrained environment (CE1, CE2). As IoT consists of huge number of devices, the management of network becomes difficult. To enable the proper network management the protocols like LNMP, SNMP protocols are used. LNMP is LoW PAN network management 6LoWPAN networks, SNMP is Simple Network Management Protocol is a protocol used to control and manage IP network devices. SNMP can also be used for various devices like routers, switches, workstations, servers, etc.

## SECURITY AND PRIVACY CHALLENGES

Security and privacy is the biggest issue in IoT industry. When data is transmitted through the internet, private networks, and VPNs security aspects are crucial. Ineffective cyber security in IoT infrastructure cost will rise to several trillions in near future. As long as more number of devices is connected, security issues need to be addressed. The data stored in IoT can be personal, social, home, industrial, enterprise, historical, healthcare, smart city, agriculture, academic, transportation, inventory and consumer etc (Manikandakumar, & Ramanujam, 2018). Due to the heterogeneity of IoT devices conventional security mechanisms does not directly suit with IoT framework. The security constraints based on hardware can be memory constraints, Computational and energy constraint, Tamper resistant packaging. Limitations of security based on software include, embedded software constraint, Dynamic security patch. Based on network the security constrains are mobility, scalability, multiplicity of devices, and multiplicity of communication channel, networking protocols and dynamic network topology (Maple, 2017). The IoT security should be provided early from the physical objects level, while acquiring information and during information transmission and the requirements such as availability, confidentiality, integrity authentication and authorization, access control, exception handling, resiliency, self organization, anonymity, non-repudiation, freshness need to be provided (Zhang et al, 2014 & Li, 2012). Sensors are the important equipment in collecting information of IoT objects and sent for processing. They were generally deployed in the absence of monitoring system. This sensed information can be attacked and programmed in such a way so that the information is sent to intruders. The possible threats to this sensed information can be eavesdropping, unauthorized access and denial of service attack.

IoT agrees to provide dynamic access to the devices that create everything from health and wellness devices, and transportation systems to weather sensors (Kamalinejad et al, 2015).

Such strict less access to that much data poses major security and privacy challenges that includes,

- **Lack of Authorization:** A large number of users and IoT devices might rely on weak and simple passwords and authorizations.
- **Lack in Data Encryption:** Most of the deployed devices failed to encrypt the data that are being transmitted, even the devices are being uses the public internet.
- **Insecure Programming Strategy:** Business logics, services and applications would be programmed without stick on with secure code practices.
- **Insecure Interfaces**: Many IoT-based applications have the interface as a mobile or web sources for device management and for consumption of aggregated data. This mobile or web interfaces are found to be weak in relate with the Open Web Application Security Project (OWASP) top 10 vulnerabilities.
- **Default Prompts:** Many IoT devices and sensors are set to use the default usernames and passwords. Many devices acknowledge the default passwords such as "12345."
- **Privacy Issues:** Devices and sensors used in the health care field collect at least one piece of personal data of the patient; most of the devices in internet collect details such as username and date of birth. But the fact is in many cases more devices transmit information across networks without doing encryption which poses even more privacy risk.

## VULNERABLE DEVICES

IoT infrastructure comprises of many embedded devices that are designed to be plugged in often and usually forgotten to unplug after the initial configuration setup. In general almost all IoT devices are internet accessible and hence malwares taking advantages to target such non-PC embedded sensors and devices due to the limitations of their operating system. Several users do not have frequent firmware updates and the sensors tend to be replaced only at the time of their final lifecycle. So any malware threat on the devices may not be noticed by the user and it leads to open more possibilities to other remote attackers.

## DENIAL OF SERVICE ATTACK

By definition, Denial of Service (DoS) attacks are organized electronic incursions. Their purpose is to disrupt an organization's network operations by denying the access to its users. In our scenario, the attacks were designed to severely limit the access and use of online games and e-mail, but they can affect any online activity. Making matters worse, the culprit, or attacker, can take control of our IoT environment or terminal and use it to infect thousands of other computers and devices, referred to as zombies. Zombies are nodes that are infected and taken over by the attacker. The attacker then uses these zombies to generate millions of data packets, or requests for service, which eventually overload e-mail, web, and network servers. In this scenario, because more than one computer was involved and infected zombies were used, this type of attack is considered a distributed attack.

## DISTRIBUTED DENIAL-OF-SERVICE (DDOS) ATTACK

IoT is a network of sensors, actuators, mobile and wearable devices, simply things that have processing and communication modules and can connect to the Internet. In a few years time, billions of such things will start serving in many fields within the concept of IoT. Self configuration, device addition and Internet connectivity features of IoT creates it to be prone to security attacks. Denial of Service attacks will be the dangerous threats to IoT networks. A DoS attack launched by the unauthorized installation of malicious code to take control of multiple computers or other devices forming a botnet or zombies to coordinate a concerted DoS attack on other computer resources or networks. Distributed denial of service attack is one of the major threats to the current Internet. It is challenging to detect DDoS attacks accurately and quickly. A DDoS attack exploits the vulnerabilities of the infected nodes and internet connected devices to create a distributed attack that has a effect on the target than that of a single attacking device.

IoT is becoming a new backdoor for DDoS attacks. Large numbers of attackers are turning to perform DDoS attacks to steal the organization's sensitive data. It leads to many impacts an organization by denying the customers, stakeholders and partners from utilizing their organization's resources thereby impacting daily business activities. It can cause a break in organizations supply chain by disrupting the facets of the operations. About fifty percent of the IoT attacks are originate from United States and China. Number of attacks also increased in Russia, Germany, Ukraine and the Netherlands. Poor security implementations on IoT infrastructure makes them easier targets and the victims may not even noticed that they have been infected.

## RANSOM DENIAL OF SERVICE ATTACKS (RDOS)

In RDoS attack, the attacker send a threatening letter to attack an organization rendering its business, services or capability would be unavailable unless a ransom is paid with in the specified deadline. Such kinds of attacks are being increasing in number every year from 2010 and typically known in the form of a volumetric distributed denial-of-service attack. The most advanced attacks combine both RDoS attacks, as well as the more commonly known ransom ware attacks.

### Mirai Attack

One of the mass attacks targeted IoT held in United States is called Mirai, which works by making use of the weak security on many IoT devices. It operates by continuously analyzing for IoT devices that are accessible over the internet and are protected by factory default or hardcoded user names and passwords. Mirai malware infects the devices and forces them to report a central server, making those devices become a bot that can be used in DDoS attacks. Mirai exploited a huge DDoS attack against the website of popular journalist Brian Krebs, which reached upto 620 Gbps. Another larger attack was on the Dyn server. Web cameras and CCTV cameras are the primary devices used to exploit in the Dyn attack. IoT devices are increasingly affected by Distributed Denial of Service attack. Due to this, the client cannot get access to the server. This reduces or degrades the performance of the IoT devices and affects the valuable information collected by those devices.

The source code of Mirai attacks are made public by the attacker after the successful attack on the Krebbs Web site. Since the source code has been used and further developed to built and used by many others to launch attacks on internet infrastructure. The device often uses default username and password and other unsecure internet devices can easily be infected with the Mirai botnet source code.

# MITIGATING SECURITY AND PRIVACY CHALLENGES

Network layers in IoT environment also plays main role in transmission of data in secure way and in maintaining the quality of information. Since huge information is transmitted through networked nodes there may be a possibility of denial of service attack in machine to machine communication. Sensor collected data and transmitted data should be backed up at back end data store for potential analysis and management process of data. This data needs to be supported with various security services like authentication, confidentiality, access control and integrity etc. Different kinds of security protocols and structures like IPSec, DTLS and 6LoWPAN have been proposed to perfectly suit with IoT framework. In addition to that embedded IoT environments must be available with security measures[9]. IoT objects should have internal fault recovery options as well as external security measures.

## Protecting IoT Devices

IoT devices become secure only when security implementations are embedded within the device at product design itself. Each layers of IoT framework should processed for security vulnerabilities. The following countermeasures can be taken to mitigate the security challenges:

1.  **Naming and Identity:** IoT connects more number of objects to offer efficient services. Each sensor deployed in the IoT infrastructure need to be named with a unique identification over the Internet. Hence, to manage the specific device or sensor dynamically among the large collection of objects an intelligent naming and identification management scheme is necessary.
2.  **Interoperability:** Different vendors provide devices based on their own dependent technologies and services that may not be suitable to other consumers. The standardization and policy regulations for IoT architecture are most important to offer best interoperability to access all things and sensor devices.
3.  **Origin Platform Analysis:** Poor configuration of the platform setup may results many compromises such as privilege provision. Device operating system, its security policies, configurations and other characters should be regularly verified against the basic information security requirements (Gou et al, 2013).
4.  **Information Privacy:** In order to prevent from the illegal or unauthorized access it is mandatory to provide proper privacy concerns. Due to the nature of IoT which is being uses various types of object identification methods such as RFID, barcodes, QR code etc., the proper information privacy is highly needed. Necessary policies have to be implemented to protect the information from external interference.

5. **Security:** IoT includes large number of sensor devices that are widely spread over on the application area hence it is required to restrict the unauthorized and intruders attack. The data collected from sensor devices are transmitted over wired or wireless communication nodes. The communication system must possess adequate intelligence to handle large volume of sensor data without any data loss. It should ensure the security provisions for the transmitted data. Network congestion, flow control and access control mechanisms are should be implemented.

6. **Authentication:** Authentication ensures devices are connected to legal parties. Most of the Telnet based implementations do not authenticate at all. Secure Shell (SSH) and Secure Socket Layer (SSL) are the two important authentication protocols that rely on public private key authentication schemes to authorize all clients and servers. When the Mirai botnet attacked the IoT devices, the devices themselves cannot be checked to make ensure the commands they received were coming from the right resource.

7. **Encryption:** Encryption secures the message content of both sender and the receiver. It prevents message from being accessed or edited at the time of transit. The widely used protocol is TLS / SSL which effectively protects the data at the time of transmission by converting the plain text into cipher text (Shahzad, Kim, & Elgamoudi, 2017).

8. **Firewalls:** Firewall is the majorly used security mechanism to protect the internal private network from the open public internet. These firewalls isolate the malicious data so that a compromised system will not give attacker access. Huge numbers of various kinds of smart firewalls are available to protect the organizational and stand alone home networks. These firewall devices perform as a temporary cache between IoT devices and outside internet world, and perform in-out packet flow monitoring, packet analysis etc.

9. **Traffic Analysis:** Both wired and wireless network traffic should be analyzed for any unencrypted or intruder data flow. Encryption algorithms can be used to achieve the expected performance. There is a trade-off between security and performance when encryption is needed. Verification needs to be done periodically to ensure that no malware is transported over the allowed network.

10. **Turn off Plug and Play:** Universal plug and play option makes devices easily connected and set up with other devices over the local network by allowing them to discover one another. But at the same time vulnerabilities in the protocol structure may allow the attackers to detect devices from outside of the network.

11. **End-to-end Penetration Test:** To identify and isolate the vulnerability in physical level, web interface level, mobile network and cloud store level there is a need of end-to-end penetration testing. Side channel protection can be

implemented both in software and hardware, further they should be checked with penetration testing. It assists to reduce the advanced threats.

12.  **Electromagnetic Spectrum:** The Iot devices and sensors will need separate dedicated electromagnetic spread spectrum to exchange the data over wireless communication medium. In near future billions of sensors may need to communicate over the air medium, thus dynamic spectrum allocation approach is required.

13.  **Data Encryption:** Sensor devises used to collects data independently from perception layer and exchange them to data processing layer. Proper data encryption at the sender or transport layer and decryption at the data processing layer is needed to ensure security and provide the guarantee that the integrity is maintained at all layers.

14.  **Green IoT:** Energy utilization is growing at high rate due to increase in data rates, increase in the number of Internet services and rapid growth connected devices. So green IoT solutions need to be invented and adopted to enable the IoT devices consume less energy resources.

15.  **Create Separate IoT Network:** In general, networks used to permit the users to connect with our own network without getting access to distributed data and devices. In such cases it is necessary to form the separated IoT network.

16.  **Keep Updated Firmware:** Device hardware and software need to be updated with the current version. Always look the product vendors for updates on the firmware.

## Defense Against Ransom

Compromising with ransom always leads to repeated attack again and again. Instead for paying the ransom developing and practicing a proper security system makes the IoT infrastructure as less targeted one. It can be achieved by using the following steps.

- **Defense Against Availability Attacks:** Correlation between downtime and loss of revenue can be calculated often and steps need to be taken to reduce the downtime by defending the availability attack. But with the increase in frequency and severity of DDoS and RDoS attacks, efficient practical protection is a must.

- **Prepare for Encrypted Attacks:** Execution of attacks in encrypted traffics is on the growing face. Small scale businesses should ensure they can address the needs of high level mitigation, support all common versions of SSL and TLS, and separate suspicious encrypted traffic using behavioral analysis to limit legitimate user impact.

- **Implement IP Protection:** Malicious actors have turned IP address spoofing into an art form with the goal of masquerading as seemingly legitimate users based on geo-location or positive reputational information about IP addresses they are able to compromise. Businesses should look for solutions that use device fingerprinting technology to gather IP-agnostic information about the source.
- Security audit can be conducted on IoT devices at the time of purchase and at the time of deploying on the network.
- Good encryption and decryption mechanisms need to be implemented while setting up the Access Points (AP). Make use of SSH for login purpose and disable the remote login through Telnet whenever applicable. Most of the time the devices are available with many of the user services. Disable the services and features which are not required.
- Update IoT device's default security and privacy settings as per the requirements rather using the default one. Modify the default user name and passwords of the devices. Avoid common passwords such as your name, date of birth, "12345" or any other guessable credentials. Often change the default credentials and implement password policies that give alert about the passwords needs to be updated regularly.
- Use the wire networked connections instead of wireless where ever applicable.
- Often audit the hardware and software expiry in order to avoid the unsecure state of the device.
- Regularly explore with the device or service owner's website for firmware and related updates

## Security Assessment of an IoT Solution

Threat modeling like the STRIDE software approach has to be conducted periodically to identify the threat scenarios and mitigation plans have to be formulated for each of the IoT components. The STRIDE approach assess the components with the following,

- Spoofing
- Tampering
- Repudiation
- Information disclosure
- Denial of service
- Elevation of privilege

## CONCLUSION

This chapter suggests the need for implementing security and privacy mechanism at the initial development of the IoT environment that can build the mitigation process much easier. Developing secure IoT architecture in its each layer, secure protocols design for communication and application level security are needs to be designed carefully. The default user name and passwords of the IoT devices need to be changed often. Mirai infected devices can be cleaned by performing periodical scanning and restarts. Devices have to build to with the capability of facing the future attacks. It must focus on the physical hardware security, privacy of data being collected, processed and transmitted across the network.

# REFERENCES

AL-Hawawreh, M., Moustafa, N., & Sitnikova, E. (2018). Identification of malicious activities in industrial internet of things based on deep learning models. *Journal of Information Security and Applications*, *41*, 1–11. doi:10.1016/j.jisa.2018.05.002

Gou, Q., Yan, L., Liu, Y., & Li, Y. (2013). Construction and Strategies in IoT Security System. *IEEE International Conference on Green Computing and Communications and IEEE Internet of Things and IEEE Cyber*, 1129-1132. 10.1109/GreenCom-iThings-CPSCom.2013.195

Gubbi, J., Buyya, R., Marusic, S., & Palaniswami, M. (2013). Internet of Things (IoT): A Vision, Architectural Elements, and Future Directions. *Future Generation Computer Systems*, *29*(7), 1645-1660.

Kamalinejad, P., Mahapatra, C., Sheng, Z., Mirabbasi, S., Leung, V. C., & Guan, Y. L. (2015). Wireless energy harvesting for the Internet of Things. *IEEE Communications Magazine*, *53*(6), 102–108. doi:10.1109/MCOM.2015.7120024

Li, L. (2012). Study on Security Architecture in the Internet of Things. *International Conference on Measurement Information and Control*, *1*, 374–377.

Manikandakumar, M., & Ramanujam, E. (2018). Security and Privacy Challenges in Big Data Environment. In *Handbook of Research on Network Forensics and Analysis Techniques* (pp. 315–325). IGI Global. doi:10.4018/978-1-5225-4100-4.ch017

Maple, C. (2017). Security and privacy in the internet of things. *Journal of Cyber Policy*, *2*(2), 155–184. doi:10.1080/23738871.2017.1366536

Shahzad, A., Kim, Y. G., & Elgamoudi, A. (2017). Secure IoT Platform for Industrial Control Systems. In *International Conference on Platform Technology and Service (PlatCon)* (pp. 1-6). IEEE.

Sheng, Yang, Yu, & Vasilakos. (2014). A Survey on the IETF Protocol Suite for the Internet of Things: Standards, Challenges, and Opportunities. *Wireless Communications, IEEE*, *20*(6), 91-98.

Zhang, Z. K., Cho, M. C. Y., Wang, C. W., Hsu, C. W., Chen, C. K., & Shieh, S. (2014). IoT security: ongoing challenges and research opportunities. In *Service-Oriented Computing and Applications (SOCA), IEEE 7th International Conference on* (pp. 230-234). IEEE.

# Chapter 5
# Fog vs. Cloud Computing Architecture

**Shweta Kaushik**
*Jaypee Institute of Information Technology, India*

**Charu Gandhi**
*Jaypee Institute of Information Technology, India*

## ABSTRACT

*Cloud computing has emerged as a new technology that allows the users to acquire resources at anytime, anywhere by connecting with internet. It provides the options to users for renting of infrastructure, storage space, and services. One service issue that affects the QoS of cloud computing is network latency while dealing with real-time application. In this, the user interacts directly with application but delays in receiving the services, and jitter delay will encourage the user to think about this. In today's world, clients are moving towards the IoT techniques, enabling them to connect all things with internet and get their services from cloud. This advancement requires introduction of new technology termed as "fog computing." Fog computing is an extension of cloud computing that provides the service at the edge of the network. Its proximity to end users, mobility support, and dense distribution reduces the service latency and improves QoS. This fog model provides the prosperity for advertisement and entertainment and is well suited for distributed data model.*

DOI: 10.4018/978-1-5225-7149-0.ch005

# INTRODUCTION

## Cloud Architecture

Cloud computing enables the user to access their required resources on demand with lower cost at anytime by just connecting with internet. Depending upon the types of services it offered and its existence, along with different entities involvement, cloud architecture is defined under two categories as – 1) Deployment model and 2) Development model, as shown in Figure 1.

## Deployment Model

In deployment model, cloud can be categorized into public, private, hybrid and community cloud. These all deployment model are differing on the basis of availability of the resources to the user.

1.  **Public Cloud:** This cloud is one which allows the general public to access the cloud computing data or resources and infrastructure over a public network. It is generally owned by the organization which serves a diverse pool of clients by selling their cloud services. A public cloud allows all the users to access the data provided by it without any firewall implementation. For example- Amazon Elastic Compute Cloud (EC2), Windows Azure etc. for end users, the public cloud provide best economic of scale i.e., inexpensive as all the hardware, bandwidth costs and application are covered by the provider.
2.  **Private Cloud:** A private cloud is owned by a particular organization and only the users belong to that organization is allowed to access the resources under the firewall maintenance. It is generally managed either by a third party or the cloud consumer organization. It can be hosted either outside organization (outsourced private cloud) or under the organization's premises (on- site private cloud). These can be little expensive which includes moderate economic scale. Thus, it is not usually a good option for small to medium scale organization, only applicable for large organization.
3.  **Community Cloud:** A community cloud provide resources to a group of users which share a common features such as their policy, mission, security requirement etc. a user is allowed to access the resources situated at local cloud as well as other participating organization through the connection established between them. As similar to the private cloud, a community cloud may be managed either by a third party or organization itself, and can be implemented on customer premises (i.e., on site community cloud) or outsources to a hosting company (i.e., outsourced community cloud) (Charlton, 2008).

4. **Hybrid Cloud:** A hybrid cloud is a combination of two or more distinct cloud community which is bound together based on some proprietary technology or standardization for enable the data application portability.

## Development Model

In development model, the cloud resources are categorized on the basis of the types of services they delivered to users as- Infrastructure as a Service (IaaS), Platform as a Service (PaaS), Software as a Service (SaaS).

1. In SaaS, users are provided by the various services/ application hosted by service provider over a network. Here, service provider is totally responsible for up gradation, maintenance, security aspect and installation of the application. User have no administrative control, they can just use the services as defined.
2. In PaaS, service provider provides an environment in such a way that the cloud user can deploy and develop its own applications, create IDE, SDK etc. Users are totally responsible for controlling and managing the application parameter.
3. IaaS provide the end user with resources such as storage space, hardware, servers OS etc. Here, service provider manages the virtual server and network interface only. All other services are managed by the user itself.

*Figure 1. Cloud Computing Reference Architecture*

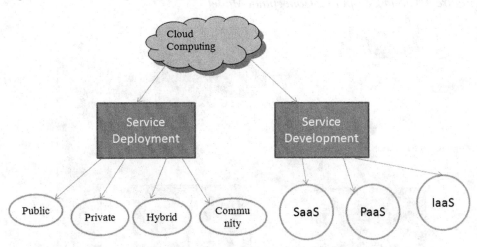

Apart from all the above deployment and development model, cloud computing architecture also comprises two other main components termed as front end and back end. Front end comprises all the components visible to the user such as desktop, I-pad, mobile phone etc. the remaining part, hidden from cloud users come under back end category which comprises of various software, application, storage devices etc.

## Cloud Computing Conceptual Model

A cloud computing conceptual model generally describe the various entities involve in cloud data processing. These entities can be described as shown in Figure 2.

1.  **Cloud Consumer:** It is also termed as end user. It is one of the principal stakeholders for cloud computing, which may be a person or organization who will utilize the services from cloud service provider and maintain a business relationship with it. Whenever, a cloud consumer requires to access any cloud service, it first browse the service provider catalogue, select and request the appropriate service as per requirement, set up the agreement with service provider and uses the acquired services. Service provider prepared the bill according to the service provisioned by the consumer, and consumer needs to pay accordingly.

*Figure 2. Cloud Computing Conceptual Model*

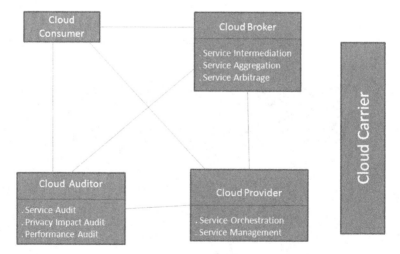

Cloud provider also provide the consumer with a SLA, which specify all the technical requirements regarding the security measures, quality of services and any remedies in case of occurrence of any performance failure, pricing policies etc. Generally a cloud provider's SLA and pricing policies are non- negotiable, unless the customer expects heavy usage and might be able to negotiate for better contracts (Badger et al, 2012). Depending upon the service request, usage and activities, scenario can be different among cloud consumer, as shown in Figure 3.

Various cloud consumer comes under the SaaS can be an end user who will directly use the end service provided by the provider, any organization which provide their end user with the access to software applications and configure more new applications for them. The SaaS consumers are billed according to the end user network bandwidth consumption, the time of their usage, no. of users etc.

In case of PaaS, cloud consumer can use the tools and resources as provided by the cloud provider to deploy, develop, test and manage its own application in a cloud environment. The PaaS consumers can be billed according to the duration of platform usage, network resources and database usage by the consumer.

On the other hand, in IaaS, cloud consumer can be IT manager, system developer and system administration who are interested in controlling, managing, monitoring and installing any new service in different IT infrastructure. The IaaS consumer can be billed according to CPU usage, resource usage, duration of data stored and number of IP addresses used for that interval.

*Figure 3. Service Availability to cloud consumer*

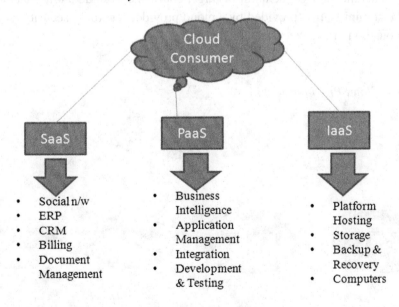

2.  **Cloud Provider:** A cloud provider may be an organizations or a person. This entity responsible for making the service availability to any interested party or end user. It will be responsible for collecting and managing the cloud infrastructure for providing the various services to the users, run the different cloud software and make possible arrangement for network accessibility to deliver the required service or software to the intended cloud consumer. For SaaS, the cloud provider will configure, deploy, maintain and update the software, required for providing the services to the intended user efficiently. For Paas, the cloud provider will manage the computing infrastructure, for the cloud platform. Cloud provider also maintain the various software which supports the platform such as database, middleware component, network bandwidth and software execution stack etc. In IaaS, the cloud provider will responsible for maintaining the underline physical computing resources for providing the best service such as- network storage, servers and hosting infrastructure, as shown in Figure 4.

A cloud provider's different activities can be categorized under the four major areas, as shown in Figure 4, as service deployment, service management, security and privacy.

3.  **Cloud Auditor:** A cloud auditor is a gathering that can play out an autonomous examination of cloud benefit controls with the expectation to express an assessment consequently. Reviews are performed to check conformance to benchmark through the audit of target confirms. A cloud auditor can access the administration provided by a cloud provider regarding security controls, protection offset execution and so forth.

*Figure 4. Cloud Provider activities*

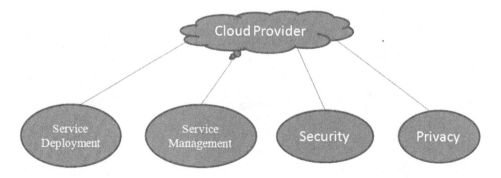

Auditing is especially important for government agencies as "agencies should include a contractual clause enabling third parties to assess security controls of cloud provider" (Kundra, 2011). Security Controls (DRAFT, 2009) are the administration, operational and specialized shields or countermeasures utilized inside an authoritative data framework to ensure the classification, trustworthiness and accessibility of the framework and its data. For security reviewing, a cloud auditor can make an appraisal of the security controls in the data framework to decide the degree planned, and delivering the accurate result as for the security necessities for the framework. A security affect review can enable government offices to agree to appropriate protection laws and directions administering an individual's security, and to generate secrecy integrity and accessibility of an individual's personal data at each phase of improvement and activity (Mell et al, 2011).

4.  **Cloud Broker:** A cloud carrier goes about as a mediator that gives network and transport of cloud benefits between cloud consumers and cloud providers. Cloud carriers give access to carriers through system, media transmission and different access gadgets. For instance, cloud consumer can get cloud benefits through network access devices, such as computers, laptops, mobile phones, mobile Internet devices (MIDs), etc. Note that a cloud provider will set up SLAs with a cloud carrier to give administrations predictable the level of SLAs offered to cloud consumers, and may require the cloud carrier to give devoted and secure associations between cloud consumers and cloud providers.

5.  **Cloud Carrier:** As cloud computing develops, the combination of cloud administrations can be excessively mind boggling for cloud consumers, making it impossible to oversee. Cloud consumers may ask for cloud administrations from a cloud broker, instead of contacting a cloud provider directly. A cloud broker is an entity that deals with the utilization, execution and delivery of cloud benefits and arranges connections between cloud providers and cloud consumers.

In general, a cloud broker can provide services in three categories (Aazam et al., 2015).

•   **Service Intermediation:** A cloud broker upgrades a given Service by enhancing some particular ability and offering some value-added services to cloud customers. This change can be overseeing access to cloud Service, personality administration, execution revealing, improved security, and so on.

- **Service Aggregation:** A cloud broker joins and coordinates different cloud brokers into at least one new administration. The merchant gives information incorporation and guarantees the protected information development between the cloud customer and different cloud suppliers.
- **Service Arbitrage:** Service arbitrage is like Service Intermediation aside from that the administrations being cumulative are not settled. Administration arbitrage implies a merchant has the adaptability to pick administrations from different offices. The cloud broker, for instance, can utilize a credit-scoring administration to quantify and select an organization with the best score.

## Fog Computing

Fog computing is complementary to cloud computing and provide the services by the cloud at the edge of network. It reduces the data transmission time and faster the processing. It includes many component reside both at cloud and at edge, between sensor and cloud. Fog model provides various benefits to user in terms of entertainment, computing, advertising and other application, which are well situated for distributed data collection points and data analytics. Configuration of any end service like set up boxes and access point can be done easily using this technology with reduction in latency and improvements in QoS.

## Advantages

- With the reduction in data movement while moving across the network will result in the reduction of cost, congestion and latency.
- Security of encrypted data is also improved due to its closeness to the end users which reduces the data exposure to any malicious attacker. Scalability features is also improved because of virtualized systems.
- Reduction in bandwidth consumption.
- Eliminates the core central computing environment, result in reduction for point of failures.

According to the availability of sensors and services the fog computing architecture can be categorized into many layers, as shown in Figure 5. The bottom layer, closet to the user, contains all the end device includes sensor, gateway, edge devices etc. apart from this, this layer also holds apps which can be installed at end devices to increase the services functionality. The second layer above this, the network layer, is utilized by the end devices for the communication between them and with the

*Figure 5. Fog Computing Architecture*

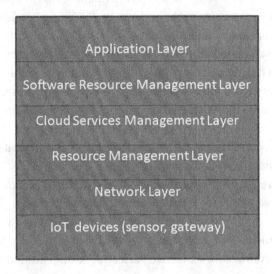

cloud for requesting or receiving any service from cloud service provider. The next layer contains all the resources and cloud services which are required by the fog computing for IoT task processing.

These entire IoT task provided to users acquire their resources and services from the cloud through this layer only. This layer is also responsible for resource management handling. On the top of cloud layer, there is a software defined resource management layer. This layer manages the QoS and complete infrastructure for fog computing application. It includes the various services related to cost reduction for usage of cloud, resource provisioning, flow and task placement, raw data management, profiling etc. Finally, the topmost layer contains all the application which allows the fog computing to facilitate end user with intelligent and innovation application to attract crowd of users.

Apart from all the above stated layer, the various component which also require high concentration in defining the architecture are – authentication & Authorization, service location monitoring, offloading management, VM scheduling, resource management etc.

## KEY FEATURES OF FOG COMPUTING

1.   **Heterogeneity:** Fog processing is a virtualized stage that offers computational, systems administration and capacity benefits between distributed computing

and end gadgets. Its heterogeneity features include fills in as a building obstruct as it exists in various structures and can be sent in far reaching situations as it cover wide distributed area.

2.  **Edge Location, Location Awareness and Low Latency:** The rise of fog processing is mostly because of the absence of help for endpoints with quality administrations at the edge of the system. Cases of utilizations with low latency prerequisites are video streaming in progressively closed circuit TV observing and gaming.

3.  **Support for Versatility:** Mobility support is fundamental for some, fog figuring applications to empower coordinate correspondence with cell phones utilizing conventions, for example, Cisco's Locator/ID Separation Protocol that decouples host character from area personality utilizing a circulated catalog framework.

4.  **Interoperability:** Fog computing must have the capacity to interoperate to guarantee encourage for extensive variety of administrations like information conversational.

5.  **Large-Scale Sensor Networks:** This is pertinent when checking the environment or in keen framework utilizing naturally circulated frameworks that require distributed processing and storage resources.

6.  **Geographical Distribution:** Fog computing has a widely dispersed deployment in order to distribute high-quality services to both mobile and fixed end devices.

7.  **Real-Time Interaction:** Various fog computing applications, such as real-time traffic monitoring systems, request continuous handling abilities instead of group preparing.

## DESIGNING GOALS

For an adequate fog computing architecture following design goals needs to be consider as-

1.  **Latency:** It is the fundamental requirement of fog computing to provide end user with the low- latency services and applications. This latency is generally calculated on the basis of offloading time, task execution time, decision making speed etc.

2.  **Efficiency:** The efficiency of any system or task is generally depends upon the latency and on the efficient utilization of various resources. While designing the fog architecture, counterpart to cloud computing it may have obvious reason- 1)

mostly of fog nodes and end users are battery powered, such as wearable and wireless sensor units. 2) Not all the fog nodes are equally resource rich; they vary in terms of memory, computing power etc. Thus, for an efficient design these issues require more concentration.

3.  **Generality:** The various fog client or end users are not using the same API or protocol i.e., heterogeneous in nature. To support this heterogeneity, there is a need arise for an abstract layer at the top of fog services and end users to have same view.

## CHALLENGES IN FOG COMPUTING

Fog computing is considered as the promising expansion of Cloud processing worldview to deal with IoT related issues at the edge of system. In any case, in Fog computing, computational hubs are heterogeneous and appropriated. Furthermore, Fog based administrations need to manage distinctive parts of compelled condition. Affirmation of security is likewise prevalent in Fog computing. Breaking down the highlights of Fog processing from basic, benefit situated and security points of view, the difficulties in this field can be recorded as takes after.

## Structural Issues

1.  Distinctive segments from both edge and center system can be utilized as potential Fog computing Architecture. Ordinarily these parts are prepared with different sorts of processors yet are not utilized for broadly useful registering. Provisioning the segments with broadly useful calculation other than their conventional exercises will be extremely testing.
2.  Based on operational necessities and execution condition, the determination of appropriate hubs, relating asset design and places of organization are imperative in Fog too.
3.  In Fog computing, computational hubs are conveyed over the edge arrange also, can be virtualized or shared. For this situation, distinguishing proof of fitting procedures, measurements, and so forth for between nodal joint effort and productive asset provisioning are imperative.
4.  The auxiliary introduction of Fog figuring is perfect for IoT. In any case, competency confirmation of Fog computing in other systems administration frameworks such as Content Distribution Network (CDN), vehicular system, and so forth will be extremely testing.

## Service Oriented

1. Not all Fog hubs are asset enhanced. Consequently, substantial scale applications advancement in asset compelled hub is not exactly simple contrasted with customary data centers. For this situation, potential programming stage for appropriated applications advancement in Fog is required to be presented.
2. Policies to appropriate computational assignments and administrations among IoT gadgets/ sensors, Fog and Cloud frameworks are required to be indicated. Information perception through web-interfaces are additionally hard to configuration in Fog computing.
3. In Fog processing, the Service Level Agreement (SLA) is frequently influenced by numerous components, for example, benefit cost, vitality utilization, application qualities, information stream, arrange status and so on. Along these lines, on a specific situation, it is very hard to indicate the administration provisioning measurements and comparing Service Level Objectives (SLOs). Also, it is very required to hold the central QoS of the Fog hubs for which they are really composed.

## Security Aspects

1. Since Fog processing is planned upon conventional systems administration parts, it is exceptionally helpless against security assaults.
2. Authenticated access to administrations and support of protection into a great extent circulated worldview like Fog processing are difficult to guarantee.
3. Implementation of security instruments for information driven trustworthiness can influence the QoS of Fog processing all things considered.

## FOG NODES CONFIGURATION

While talking about fog computing we need to establish five types of nodes as discussed below

1. **Servers:** The Fog servers are geo-dispersed and are sent at exceptionally basic spots for case; transport terminals, strip malls, streets, parks, and so forth. Like light-weight Cloud servers, these Fog servers are virtualized and outfitted with capacity, process and organizing offices. There are numerous works that have considered Fog servers as primary useful part of Fog processing. In a few papers in light of the physical size, Fog servers are named as miniaturized scale servers, smaller scale datacenters (Lee et al., 2016, Aazam et al. 2015),

nano servers (Jalali et al., 2016), and so on though different works sort Fog servers in light of their functionalities like reserve servers (Zhu et al., 2013), calculation servers, stockpiling servers (Zeng et al., 2016), and so on. Server based Fog hub engineering improves the calculation what's more, stockpiling limit in Fog computing. Be that as it may, it restricts the inescapability of the execution condition.

2.  **Networking Devices:** Gadgets like portal switches, switches, set-top boxes, and so on other than their conventional organizing exercises (directing, bundle sending, simple to advanced flag changes, and so on.) can go about as potential framework for Fog computing. In some current works, the systems administration gadgets are outlined with certain framework assets including information processors, extensible essential and optional memory, programming stages, and so on. (Hong et al., 2013, Nazmudeen et al., 2016). In different works, aside from traditional systems administration gadgets, a few committed organizing gadgets like Smart portals (Aazam et al., 2014), IoT Hub (Cirani et al., 2015) have been presented as Fog hubs. Dispersed organization of systems administration gadgets encourages Fog figuring to be omnipresent albeit physical assorted variety of the gadgets altogether influences administration and asset provisioning.

3.  **Base Stations:** Base stations are essential segments in portable and remote systems for consistent correspondence and information flag handling. In late works, customary base stations furnished with certain putting away and processing abilities are considered appropriate for Fog processing (Yan et al, 2016; Gu et al., 2015). Like conventional base stations, Road Side Unit (RSU) (Truong et al., 2015) and little cell get to focuses (Oueis et al., 2015), and so forth can likewise be utilized as potential Fog hubs. Base stations are best for Fog based augmentation of Cloud Radio Access Network (CRAN), Vehicular Adhoc Network (VANET), and so forth. In any case, development of a thick Fog condition with base stations is subjected to systems administration impedance what's more, high organization cost.

4.  **Cloudlets:** Cloudlets are considered as miniaturized scale cloud and located at the center layer of end gadget, cloudlet, and Cloud chain of command. Essentially cloudlets have been intended for broadening Cloud based administrations towards cell phone clients and can supplement MCC (Mahmud et al, 2016). In a few works (Dsouza et al., 2014; Cardellini et al., 2015), cloudlets are said as Fog hubs. Cloudlet based Fog processing are exceedingly virtualized and can manage substantial number of end gadgets all the while. Now and again, because of basic imperatives, cloudlets even in the wake of sending at the edge go about as incorporated parts. In this sense, the constraints of incorporated calculation still stay critical in Fog registering which oppose to help IoT.

5.  **Vehicles:** Moving or stopped vehicles at the edge of system with calculation offices can fill in as Fog hubs (Hou et al., 2016; Ye et al., 2016). Vehicles as Fog hubs can shape an appropriated and exceedingly versatile Fog condition. Nonetheless, the confirmation of protection also, adaptation to non-critical failure alongside wanted QoS support will be extremely testing in such condition.

## FOG COMPUTING APPLICATIONS

We can sort haze processing applications into ongoing and close continuous applications, as appeared in Figure 6. Ongoing applications are low-dormancy and capacity inside a pre-characterized time span which client senses as quick or current. Close ongoing applications, then again, are those that are liable to time delay presented by information handling or system transmission between the moment an occasion happens and the utilization of the prepared information (Antonic et al, 2016). Close continuous is regularly dictated by subtracting the present time from the preparing time that is about the season of the live occasion. In this segment, we exhibit prominent utilize instances of both constant and non-continuous applications.

1.  **Video Streaming**: Transmissions of video applications and administrations are more effective in a fog computing procedure, due to the capacity of fog computing to give local computation, low latency, versatility, and ongoing

*Figure 6. Fog Computing Applications*

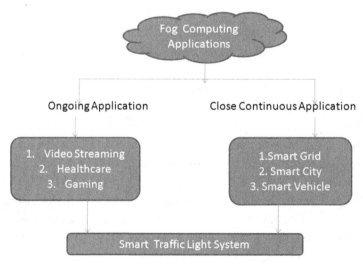

examination. A few smart gadgets strengthen shrewd investigation that can be utilized by law implementation officers to show live streams of events of interest. For instance, Hong et al. (2013) portrayed a video surveillance application that requires a three-level chain of command framework to perform movement identification with smart camera, confront acknowledgment with fog processing cases, furthermore, personality accumulation with cloud computing examples. Magurawalage et al. (2015) proposed Aqua computing, inspired from water cycle, which can appear as either fog or then again cloud computing. The proposed engineering comprises of clones set at the edge of the system that serve end clients in a video spilling situation to go about as a support. Zhu et al. (2015) utilized fog processing to change video applications and administrations to help on-request video conveyance. Such an approach improves collaborations in a virtual work area framework also, gives continuous video examination to an observation camera. Other potential advantages of deploying fog computing to enhance video spilling execution, for example, intelligent caching and adaptive streaming were also highlighted. Foerster et al. (Foerster et al, 2015) recognized key necessities of fog processing that supplements cloud computing to help an intelligent network node. This enhances the nature of transmitted video by guaranteeing a smart delicate handoff of versatile client and radio aware resource management.

2.  **Healthcare:** IoT applications have given an organized approach towards enhancing our human services administrations. This is accomplished by conveying universal observing frameworks and transmitting the information to fog devices continuously before sending the data to the cloud for facilitate investigation and finding. Gia et al. (2015) used fog processing as a keen entryway to give advanced strategies and administrations, for example, disseminated capacity and installed information mining. A contextual analysis of electrocardiogram includes extraction that assumes a fundamental part in the conclusion of heart illnesses was displayed. The test result recommended that sending fog processing accomplishes a low latency and constant reaction with over 90% transmission capacity proficiency. Appealing security observing is one of the key application zones of biomedical huge information query about for making early forecasts to help brilliant human services basic leadership. Cao et al. (2015) proposed a continuous fall recognition calculation, U-Fall, which comprises of three noteworthy modules, front-end, back-end and correspondence module. Both front-end and back-end make autonomous location results. Be that as it may, a synergistic discovery will build the precision and diminish the false alert rate. A trial exhibiting the utilization of the U-Fall calculation in haze registering that consequently identifies inescapable fall accompanied by

security checking to improve stroke was introduced. Results got recommended that a high affectability and specificity was accomplished.

3. **Smart Traffic Light System (STLS)**: Brilliant activity lights associate locally with various sensor hubs to recognize the nearness of cyclists, bikers or people on foot, and additionally evaluating the speed and separation of moving toward vehicles. This data can be utilized to avert mischances by sending early cautioning signs to moving toward vehicles. Stojmenovic and Wen (2014) depicted the utilization of camcorder that detects the nearness of a rescue vehicle blazing light amid a crisis to consequently change road lights and enable the crisis vehicle to go through activity. Bonomi et al. (Bonomi et al, 2014) distinguished three noteworthy objectives of STLS, in particular: mishap anticipation, relentless activity stream upkeep, and recovery of applicable information to assess and enhance the framework. Mischance avoidance is a continuous procedure, while movement stream and information recovery are viewed as close constant and cluster forms. Remote passageways and savvy movement light units are sent along the roadside to give correspondence, for example, vehicle-to-vehicle, vehicle to passage, passage to passage.

4. **Smart Cities:** A smart city is one key IoT application that extents from smart movement administration to vitality administration of structures, and so forth. The smart city idea has drawn awesome enthusiasm from both science and building divisions, and from both research and specialist networks, as a way to defeat challenges related with fast urban development. Kitchin (2014) depicted smart city as a city that is immensely controlled and made up of universal registering whose economy and administration are driven by advancement and innovativeness. In any case, some of these IOT applications and gadgets in a smart city require high calculation and capacity limits, and posture interoperability challenges. For instance, Byers and Wetterwald distinguished the many-sided quality related with a cloud unified design including shrewd city that comprises of street activity control, parking area administration and ecological observing over a conveyed an area. Yi et al. (2015) distinguished fog processing that is near the edge of the system as the arrangement and additionally coordinating all segments in a bound together stage to empower dedicated home applications with flexible assets. Smart city was depicted as an open space in the edge that streamlines vitality utilization and enhance the personal satisfaction of subjects. In crafted by Tang et al. (2015), a progressive disseminated fog processing that backings an immense number of infrastructural segment and administrations for future keen urban communities was exhibited. A brilliant pipeline observing framework utilize case was examined, which depends on fiber optic sensors. Successive learning calculation was utilized to distinguish occasions debilitating pipeline wellbeing.

## INTERACTION BETWEEN FOG COMPUTING, CLOUD COMPUTING AND INTERNET OF THINGS

Fog processing conveys cloud computing nearer to Internet of Things (IoT) devices (Bonomi et al, 2014). The approach of IoT has brought about an expanding number of utilization cases that create significant volume of information, aggravating the difficulties of managing enormous information from various topographically distributed information sources (Bomomi et al, 2014). To proficiently break down this time-sensitive information, fog processing was proposed. To tackle the advantages of IoT and accelerate mindfulness and reaction to occasions, we require another arrangement of frameworks as present cloud models are not intended to deal with the specifics of IoT (i.e., volume, variety and velocity of information) ("Fog Computing", 2017). In particular, billions of already detached devices are currently creating more than two Exabyte of information consistently and it has been evaluated that by 2020, 50 billion ''things'' will be associated with the Internet ("Fog Computing", 2017). In this manner, fog computing has been recognized as a reasonable arrangement.

Sehgal et al. (2015) proposed a framework that consolidates IoT, cloud computing, and fog processing for smart human security. This structure gives a wearable figuring framework by harnessing the pervasive idea of IoT, unavoidability highlight of cloud, and the expansion of fog computing to give security cover to individuals. In a comparative vein, Yannuzzi et al. (2014) coordinated fog processing and cloud computing by thinking about mobility, reliability control and actuation, and scalability to show that fog processing can be utilized as the fundamental stage for IoT applications. Suciu et al. (2015) displayed engineering for secure E-wellbeing applications utilizing huge information, IoT, and cloud merging to empower telemonitoring. This approach utilizes CloudView Exalead as a pursuit stage that offers access to data introduces in the infrastructural level for seek based application on the web and at the endeavor level. Cirani et al. (2015) proposed a fog node and IoT center point, appropriated on the edge of different systems to upgrade organize ability by executing fringe switch, cross-intermediary, store, and asset index. IoT works at both the connection layer and application layer to empower asset revelation and consistent co operations among applications.

## CLOUD COMPUTING VS. FOG COMPUTING

Both the techniques are similar to each other in providing the user with renting of services, data storage etc. but differ from each other in the following manner:-

*Table 1. Summary of fog computing, cloud computing, and IoT features (Osanaiye et al., 2017)*

| Features | Fog Computing | Cloud Computing | Internet of Things |
|---|---|---|---|
| **Target User** | Mobile users | General Internet users | Stationary and mobile devices |
| **Number of Server Nodes** | Large | Few | Large |
| **Architecture** | Distributed | Centralized | Dense and distributed |
| **Service Type** | Localized information service limited to specific deployment location | Global Information collected worldwide | Information specific to the end device |
| **Working Environment** | Outdoors (i.e, streets, fields, tracks) or Indoor (i.e, home, malls, restaurants) | Indoors with massive space and ventilation | Outdoor and Indoor |
| **Location Awareness** | Yes | No | Yes |
| **Real- time Interaction** | Supported | Supported | Supported |
| **Mobility** | Supported | Limited Supported | Supported |
| **Big data and duration of storage** | Short duration as it transmits big data | Months and years as it manages big data | Transient as it is the source of big data |
| **Major service Provider** | Close IOx | Amazon, Microsoft, IBM | ARM, Atmel, Bosch |

- In cloud computing data is located at remote location which may be far away and take some time during transition from one party to other. On the other hand fog data is situated near to the operational device, reduce transaction time.

- Cloud computing require high demand for bandwidth, latency and cost as each bit of data transmit over cloud channel. While in fog computing, demands for bandwidth, cost and latency is reduced as data is aggregated at certain access point.

- In cloud computing, data move across different nodes situated in the network which increases the chances of data theft and requires high security concern. Instead fog computing improves the security as data is encoded and situated towards the network edge.

- In cloud computing, response time is slow and scalability is also reduced because of location of depending servers are far away. While in fog computing, by situating small server, edge server near to the user, it is easier to avoid scalability issue and avoid response time delay.

- The chances of fault tolerance and reliability are also increase with the usage of fog computing, which require high consideration in cloud computing.

## CONCLUSION

To meet the today's emerging paradigm demand of technology for the faster processing of data requirement and less delay, cloud computing is not sufficient. To overcome these requirement, fog computing arise with advancement and focus towards IoT service delivery. But, fog computing can't total replace the cloud computing as it is still preferred for large data storage and high end batch processing. Hence, it can be stated that both the technology are complement to each other. When the need arise for large amount of resource storage and maintenance without worrying about delay feature than cloud computing play a vital role with low cost. On the other hand, if service require immediately without any consideration of cost and less delay than fog computing comes into pictures. Thus, both co-exists, provide services for two different approaches and complementing each other whenever required.

# REFERENCES

Aazam, M., & Huh, E. N. (2015). Fog computing micro datacenter based dynamic resource estimation and pricing model for iot. *IEEE 29th International Conference on Advanced Information Networking and Applications*, 687–694.

Aazam, M., & Huh, E. N. (2014). Fog computing and smart gateway based communication for cloud of things. *Future Internet of Things and Cloud (FiCloud), 2014 International Conference on*, 464–470.

Antonić, A., Marjanović, M., Pripužić, K., & Žarko, I. P. (2016). A mobile crowd sensing ecosystem enabled by CUPUS: Cloud-based publish/subscribe middleware for the Internet of Things. *Future Generation Computer Systems*, *56*, 22–607. doi:10.1016/j.future.2015.08.005

Badger, L., Grance, T., Patt-Corner, R., & Voas, J. (2012). *NIST's cloud computing synopsis and recommendations*. Academic Press.

Bakshi, K. (2009). *Cisco cloud computing-data center strategy, architecture, and solutions*. Retrieved from http://www. cisco. com/web/strategy/docs/gov/ CiscoCloudComputing_WP. pdf

Bonomi, F., Milito, R., Natarajan, P., & Zhu, J. (2014). *Fog computing: A platform for Internet of Things and analytics. In Big Data and Internet of Things: A Roadmap for Smart Environments (Studies in Computational Intelligence)* (pp. 169–186). New York: Springer.

Cao, Y., Hou, P., Brown, D., Wang, J., & Chen, S. (2015). Distributed analytics and edge intelligence: Pervasive health monitoring at the era of fog computing. *Proc. ACM Workshop Mobile Big Data*, 43–48.

Cardellini, V., Grassi, V., Presti, F. L., & Nardelli, M. (2015). On qos-aware scheduling of data stream applications over fog computing infrastructures. *IEEE Symposium on Computers and Communication (ISCC)*, 271–276.

Charlton, S. (2008). Cloud computing and the next generation of enterprise architecture. *Cloud Computing Expo*.

Cirani, S., Ferrari, G., Iotti, N., & Picone, M. (2015). The iot hub: a fog node for seamless management of heterogeneous connected smart objects. *Sensing, Communication, and Networking- Workshops (SECONWorkshops), 2015 12th Annual IEEE International Conference on*, 1–6.

Cirani, S., Ferrari, G., Iotti, N., & Picone, M. (2015). The IoT hub: A fog node for seamless management of heterogeneous connected smart objects. *Proc. 12th Annu. IEEE Int. Conf. Sens., Commun., Netw.-Workshops (SECON Workshops)*, 1–6.

Díaz, M., Martín, C., & Rubio, B. (2016). State-of-the-art, challenges, and open issues in the integration of Internet of Things and cloud computing. *Journal of Network and Computer Applications*, *67*, 99–117. doi:10.1016/j.jnca.2016.01.010

DRAFT, F. P. (2009). *Recommended security controls for federal information systems and organizations*. NIST Special Publication, 800, 53.

Dsouza, C., Ahn, G. J., & Taguinod, M. (2014). Policy-driven security management for fog computing: Preliminary framework and a case study. *Information Reuse and Integration (IRI), 2014 IEEE 15th International Conference on*, 16–23.

Foerster, J. (2015). Towards realizing video aware wireless networks. *Intel Technol. J.*, *19*(3), 6–25.

Fog Computing and Internet of Things: Extend the Cloud to Where the Things Are. (n.d.). Available: http://www.cisco.com/ dam/en_us/solutions/trends/iot/docs/computing-overview.pdf

Gia, T. N., Jiang, M., Rahmani, A.-M., Westerlund, T., Liljeberg, P., & Tenhunen, H. (2015). Fog Computing in healthcare Internet of Things: A case study on ECG feature extraction. *Proc. IEEE Int. Conf. Comput. Inf. Technol. Ubiquitous Comput. Commun. Dependable, Auton. Secure Comput. Pervasive Intell. Comput. (CIT/IUCC/DASC/PICOM)*, 356–363.

Gu, L., Zeng, D., Guo, S., Barnawi, A., & Xiang, Y. (2015). Cost-efficient resource management in fog computing supported medical cps. *IEEE Transactions on Emerging Topics in Computing*.

Hong, K., Lillethun, D., Ramachandran, U., Ottenw¨alder, B., & Koldehofe, B. (2013). Mobile fog: A programming model for large-scale applications on the internet of things. *Proceedings of the second ACM SIGCOMM workshop on Mobile cloud computing*, 15–20. 10.1145/2491266.2491270

Hong, K., Lillethun, D., Ramachandran, U., Ottenwälder, B., & Koldehofe, B. (2013). Mobile fog: A programming model for large-scale applications on the Internet of Things. *Proc. 2nd ACM SIGCOMM Workshop Mobile Cloud Comput.*, 15–20.

Hou, X., Li, Y., Chen, M., Wu, D., Jin, D., & Chen, S. (2016). Vehicular fog computing: A viewpoint of vehicles as the infrastructures. *IEEE Transactions on Vehicular Technology, 65*(6), 3860–3873. doi:10.1109/TVT.2016.2532863

Jalali, F., Hinton, K., Ayre, R., Alpcan, T., & Tucker, R. S. (2016, May). Fog computing may help to save energy in cloud computing. *IEEE Journal on Selected Areas in Communications, 34*(5), 1728–1739. doi:10.1109/JSAC.2016.2545559

Kitchin, R. (2014). The real-time city? Big data and smart urbanism. *GeoJournal, 79*(1), 1–14. doi:10.100710708-013-9516-8

Kundra, V. (2011). *Federal cloud computing strategy*. Academic Press.

Lee, W., Nam, K., Roh, H. G., & Kim, S. H. (2016). A gateway based fog computing architecture for wireless sensors and actuator networks. *2016 18th International Conference on Advanced Communication Technology (ICACT)*, 210–213.

Magurawalage, C. S., Yang, K., & Wang, K. (2015). *Aqua computing: Coupling computing and communications*. Available: https://arxiv.org/abs/1510.07250

Mahmud, M.R., Afrin, M., Razzaque, M.A., Hassan, M.M., Alelaiwi, A., & Alrubaian, M. (2016). Maximizing quality of experience through context-aware mobile application scheduling in cloudlet infrastructure. *Software: Practice and Experience, 46*(11), 1525–1545.

Mell, P., & Grance, T. (2011). *The NIST definition of cloud computing*. Academic Press.

Nazmudeen, M. S. H., Wan, A. T., & Buhari, S. M. (2016). Improved throughput for power line communication (plc) for smart meters using fog computing based data aggregation approach. *IEEE International Smart Cities Conference (ISC2)*, 1–4.

Osanaiye, O., Chen, S., Yan, Z., Lu, R., Choo, K.-K. R., & Dlodlo, M. (2017). From cloud to fog computing: A review and a conceptual live VM migration framework. *IEEE Access: Practical Innovations, Open Solutions, 5*, 8284–8300. doi:10.1109/ACCESS.2017.2692960

Oueis, J., Strinati, E. C., Sardellitti, S., & Barbarossa, S. (2015). Small cell clustering for efficient distributed fog computing: A multi-user case. Vehicular Technology Conference (VTC Fall), 2015 IEEE 82nd, 1–5.

Popović, K., & Hocenski, Ž. (2010, May). Cloud computing security issues and challenges. In *MIPRO, 2010 proceedings of the 33rd international convention* (pp. 344-349). IEEE.

Sehgal, V. K., Patrick, A., Soni, A., & Rajput, L. (2015). *Smart human security framework using Internet of Things, cloud and fog computing. In Intelligent Distributed Computing (Advances in Intelligent Systems and Computing)* (Vol. 321, pp. 251–263). New York: Springer.

Stojmenovic, I., & Wen, S. (2014). The fog computing paradigm: Scenarios and security issues. *Proc. IEEE Federated Conf. Comput. Sci. Inf. Syst. (FedCSIS)*, 1–8.

Suciu, G., Suciu, V., Martian, A., Craciunescu, R., Vulpe, A., Marcu, I., ... Fratu, O. (2015). Big data, Internet of Things and cloud convergence— An architecture for secure E-health applications. *Journal of Medical Systems*, *39*(11), 1–8. doi:10.100710916-015-0327-y PMID:26345453

Tang, B., Chen, Z., Hefferman, G., Wei, T., He, H., & Yang, Q. (2015). A hierarchical distributed fog computing architecture for big data analysis in smart cities. *Proc. ACM ASE BigData Social Inform.*, 28.

Truong, N. B., Lee, G. M., & Ghamri-Doudane, Y. (2015). Software defined networking-based vehicular adhoc network with fog computing. *IFIP/IEEE International Symposium on Integrated Network Management (IM)*, 1202–1207. 10.1109/INM.2015.7140467

Yan, S., Peng, M., & Wang, W. (2016). User access mode selection in fog computing based radio access networks. *IEEE International Conference on Communications (ICC)*, 1–6.

Yannuzzi, M., Milito, R., Serral-Gracià, R., Montero, D., & Nemirovsky, M. (2014). Key ingredients in an IoT recipe: Fog computing, cloud computing, and more Fog computing. *Proc. 19th IEEE Int. Workshop Comput.-Aided Modeling Design Commun. Links Netw. (CAMAD)*, 325–329.

Ye, D., Wu, M., Tang, S., & Yu, R. (2016). Scalable fog computing with service offloading in bus networks. *IEEE 3rd International Conference on Cyber Security and Cloud Computing (CSCloud)*, 247–251.

Yi, S., Hao, Z., Qin, Z., & Li, Q. (2015). Fog computing: Platform and applications. *Proc. 3rd IEEE Workshop Hot Topics Web Syst. Technol. (HotWeb)*, 73–78. 10.1109/HotWeb.2015.22

Zeng, D., Gu, L., Guo, S., Cheng, Z., & Yu, S. (2016). Joint optimization of task scheduling and image placement in fog computing supported software-defined embedded system. *IEEE Transactions on Computers*.

Zhu, J., Chan, D. S., Prabhu, M. S., Natarajan, P., Hu, H., & Bonomi, F. (2013). Improving web sites performance using edge servers in fog computing architecture. *Service Oriented System Engineering (SOSE), 2013 IEEE 7th International Symposium on*, 320–323.

Zhu, X., Chan, D. S., Hu, H., Prabhu, M. S., Ganesan, E., & Bonomi, F. (2015). Improving video performance with edge servers in the fog computing architecture. *Intel Technol. J., 19*(3), 202–224.

# Chapter 6
# Comparing User Authentication Techniques for Fog Computing

**Kashif Munir**
*University of Hafr Al-Batin, Saudi Arabia*

**Lawan A. Mohammed**
*University of Hafr Al Batin, Saudi Arabia*

## ABSTRACT

*In the IoT scenario, things at the edge can create significantly large amounts of data. Fog computing has recently emerged as the paradigm to address the needs of edge computing in internet of things (IoT) and industrial internet of things (IIoT) applications. Authentication is an important issue for the security of fog computing since services are offered to massive-scale end users by front fog nodes. Fog computing faces new security and privacy challenges besides those inherited from cloud computing. Authentication helps to ensure and confirms a user's identity. The existing traditional password authentication does not provide enough security for the data, and there have been instances when the password-based authentication has been manipulated to gain access to the data. Since the conventional methods such as passwords do not serve the purpose of data security, this chapter focuses on biometric user authentication in fog computing environments. In this chapter, the authors present biometric smartcard authentication to protect the fog computing environment.*

DOI: 10.4018/978-1-5225-7149-0.ch006

## INTRODUCTION

Fog computing, also known as fogging/edge computing, is a model in which data, processing and applications are concentrated in devices at the network edge rather than existing almost entirely in the fog as per Cisco (2015). The concentration means that data can be processed locally in smart devices rather than being sent to the fog for processing. As per How to Geek (2014), Fog computing is one approach to dealing with the demands of the ever-increasing number of Internet-connected devices sometimes referred to as IoT. Cisco recently delivered the vision of fog computing to run applications on connected devices that would run directly at the network edge. Customers can develop, manage, and run software applications on the Cisco framework of the networked devices. This includes the difficult routes and switches. Cisco brought this new innovation where they combined the open source Linux and network operating system together in a single network device.

According to Bonomi et al (2012), fog computing is considered as an extension of the cloud computing to the edge of the network, which is a highly virtualized platform of resource pool that provides computation, storage, and networking services to nearby end users. As per Vaquero et al (2014), fog computing as "a scenario where a huge number of heterogeneous (wireless and sometimes autonomous) ubiquitous and decentralized devices communicate and potentially cooperate among them and with the network to perform storage and processing tasks without the intervention of third parties. These tasks can be for supporting basic network functions or new services and applications that run in a sandboxed environment. Users leasing part of their devices to host these services get incentives for doing so." Although those definitions are still debatable before, fog computing is no longer a buzzword.

Fog model provides benefits in advertising, computing, entertainment and other applications, well positioned for data analytics and distributed data collection points. End services like, set-up-boxes and access points can be easily hosted using fogging. It improves QoS and reduces latency. The main task of fogging is positioning information near to the user at the network edge. In general, some of the major benefits of fog computing are:

- The significant reduction in data movement across the network resulting in reduced congestion, cost and latency, elimination of bottlenecks resulting from centralized computing systems, improved security of encrypted data as it stays closer to the end user reducing exposure to hostile elements and improved scalability arising from virtualized systems.

- Eliminates the core computing environment, thereby reducing a major block and a point of failure.
- Improves the security, as data are encoded as it is moved towards the network edge.
- Edge Computing, in addition to providing sub-second response to end users, it also provides high levels of scalability, reliability and fault tolerance.
- Consumes less amount of band width.

The OpenFog consortium released the OpenFog reference architecture (RA) recommendations for anyone wishing to implement fog computing or any fog-based applications. The OpenFog Reference Architecture is based on eight core technical principles, termed pillars, which represent the key attributes that a system needs to encompass to be defined as "OpenFog." These pillars include security, scalability, openness, autonomy, RAS (reliability, availability, and serviceability), agility, hierarchy and programmability.

A detailed architecture stack shows the interrelationships between various hardware, software infrastructure, and application software layers, as well as various cross-cutting concerns such as security, performance, manageability, analytics and control that impact the function of all layers. As security is one of the most complex and critical aspects of IoT systems, a special appendix dives deeply into OpenFog security guidelines. The OpenFog architecture is depicted in Figure 1.

*Figure 1. The OpenFog reference architecture (https://www.openfogconsortium.org/ra/)*

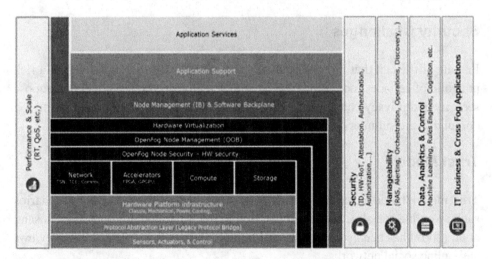

## RELATED WORK

Although there are numerous novel studies contributed to secure authentication system, recent studies have mostly considered cloud storage environments rather than fog computing. In this section, we briefly summarize some few ones among those that address fog computing and point out their limitations and difficulties in direct adoption to the fog storage architecture.

Some authentication protocols which have been proposed for fog computing systems were described in many articles. However, only a few of them can achieve privacy preservation. The first type of such authentication protocols uses symmetric key encryption algorithms (Tsai & Chang, 2006, Tsai, Chang, & Chan, 2009, He et al, 2011) due to their low computational cost. However, these protocols can be attacked by man-in-the-middle attacks, and the privacy information will inevitably be revealed. Another drawback of these protocols is the inherent scalability problem for privacy preservation, which makes them undoubtedly impractical. The second type of such authentication protocols updates an end-device's credentials regularly (Calandriello et al., 2007, Lu et al, 2010, and Zhu et al, 2008). However, during the validity period of the credential, the strong identity of an end-device can still be tracked. Furthermore, such protocols require each end-device to store a large number of certifications and pseudonyms, which means that it is difficult to remove a compromised end-device. The third type of such authentication protocols uses a delegation-based mechanism Chang & Tsai (2010). The advantage is their low computational cost, but the disadvantage is that the privacy-preserving property cannot be easily achieved. To overcome this limitation, we propose a three-factor authentication using both smart card and biometrics.

### Security Challenges

In spite of the fact that Fog Computing can play a central role in delivering a rich portfolio of services more effectively and efficiently to end users, it could impose security and privacy challenges. The major security and privacy challenges in fog computing are summarized below.

### Trust Model

Trust models based on reputation have been successfully deployed in many scenarios such as online social networks. Reputation based trust model proposed by Josang et al, (2007) has been successful in eCommerce, peer-to-peer (P2P), user reviews and online social networks.

Damiani et al.(2002) proposed a robust reputation system for resource selection in P2P networks using a distributed polling algorithm to assess the reliability of a resource before downloading. In designing a fog computing reputation-based reputation system, we may need to tackle issues such as

1.    How to achieve persistent, unique, and distinct identity,
2.    How to treat intentional and accidental misbehavior,
3.    How to conduct punishment and redemption of reputation.

There are also trusting models based on special hardware such as Secure Element (SE), Trusted Execution Environment (TEE), or Trusted Platform Module (TPM), which can provide trust utility in fog computing applications Sean & Vernon (1998).

Shanhe. Yi et al (2015) suggests that to design a trust model based on reputation in the IoT, we need to tackle how to maintain the service reliability and prevent accidental failures, handle and identify misbehavior issues, identify malicious behavior correctly, and bootstrap building a trust model based on reputation in large-scale networks.

## Rogue Fog Node

A rogue fog node would be a fog device or fog instance that pretends to be legitimate and coaxes end users to connect to it. For example, in an insider attack, a fog administrator may be authorized to manage fog instances, but may instantiate a rogue fog instance rather than a legitimate one. Stojmenovic et al (2014) has demonstrated the feasibility of man-in-the-middle attack in fog computing, before which the gateway should be either compromised or replaced by a fake one. Once connected, the adversary can manipulate the incoming and outgoing requests from end users or fog, collect or tamper user data stealthily, and easily launch further attacks. The existence of fake fog node will be a big threat to user data security and privacy. This problem is hard to address in fog computing due to several reasons

1.    Complex trust situation calls for different trust management schemes,
2.    Dynamic creating, deleting of virtual machine instance make it hard to maintain a blacklist of rogue nodes.

A rogue IoT node has the potential to misuse users' data or provide malicious data to neighboring nodes to disrupt their behaviors. Addressing this problem could be difficult in the IoT due to the complexity in trust management in various schemes. However, a trust measurement-based model could be applied to detect rogue nodes in IoT environments' which can provide limited security protection.

## User Authentication

An *identity token*, *security token*, *access token*, or simply *token*, is a physical device that performs or aids authentication. This can be a secure storage device containing passwords, such as a bankcard, remote garage door opener, or smart card. This can also be an active device that yields *one-time passcodes*, either *time-synchronous* (changing in synchrony with a master at the host) or *challenge-response* (responding to a onetime challenge). Token security defenses include tamper-resistant packaging and special hardware that disables the token if it is tampered with or if the number of failed authentication attempts exceeds a chosen threshold. When we refer to "token" in this paper, the general concept will be a portable, secure storage device accessed at the client end via a password to obtain a passcode that is transmitted to the host for authentication.

A *passcode* is a secret number like a password, except it is machine-generated and machine-stored, so it can be longer, more random, and perhaps changing. A *biometric* is a feature measured from the human body that is distinguishing enough to be used for user authentication. Biometrics include: fingerprints, eye (iris and retina), face, hand, voice, and signature, as well as other more obscure or futuristic biometrics such as gait and smell. A biometric purports to inextricably link the authenticator to its owner, something passwords and tokens cannot do, since they can be lent or stolen. When used to verify the person involved in a transaction, an inextricable link can offer the property of *non-repudiation*. (Lawrence 2003)

Biometrics are automated methods of identifying a person or verifying the identity of a person based on a physiological or behavioral characteristic (Podio and Dunn, 2001). A *biometric* typically refers to a feature or characteristic measured from a biological body. Biometric authentication systems use these features to distinguish users and for establishing establishing an identity. Some of the most common biometrics used include fingerprints, retina, iris, voice, face, hand, etc (Jain et al., 1998).

The biometrics will be compared between the enrolled data and the currently captured data. The identification mode of this technique will search for the captured data with the central database and finally the exact data of the user that has been enrolled earlier will be matched and provided using the "One-to-Many Matching" technique. The verification mode is that when the user provides the data the captured data is identified using the "One-to-One technique" matching. There are many different forms of biometric test forms available like fingerprint recognition, face recognition, voice recognition, retinal scan, signatures, Iris feature etc.

- **Fingerprint Recognition:** This is an interesting method of authentication where the user's finger print is recognized. Each and every individual had their unique finger print and this technique had followed earlier by the law and order of the government. At present they are stored using the finger print reader machines and stored electronically and used when ever needed. Each finger had different form of prints and even the difference can be found among twins and so the individual can be identified easily. This is a good replacing technique than entering the passwords (Podio and Dunn, 2001).

- **Face Recognition:** In this technique the facial image of the user is identified and accordingly the identification is obtained. The user's face has been recognized using some inexpensive cameras where the image of the face in the visible spectrum is captured. It can be done using the IR (Infrared) of facial heat image. Even though the user changed his appearance the user's hair properties and facial expressions will never change and this provides the proper identification of the user (Podio and Dunn, 2001).

- **Voice Recognition:** This is another technique to authenticate such that the user's voice is used as the identification code for verification. The user had to register the voice to the service providers while the authentication is initially made and when ever needed the user has to speak (ex: the user can say his/her name) and the voice will be matched with the voice in the database. The requirement for this system to execute is need of the system and voice recognizing software. The software calculates the user's vocal track and the characteristics that are present in the user's voice and finally it will be matched when the user used them finally. The main drawback of this process is that if the user affected with any throat related problem, the system cannot able to recognize the voice and the access cannot be provided until the reset in done.

- **Iris Recognition:** This feature provides identification using the featured iris of the eyes which is a colored portion that covers the pupil in the eyes. Each and every individual had their unique difference in their iris and this is recognized by the system and can able to identify the exact match for that iris. Both the verification and identification is done easily using this method and the increase in this type of technique is increasing at recent trends. Nowadays many users are using contact lens and eyeglasses and at present the teat of the iris can be done even with that. This system also provides good identification of the users.

- **Hand and Finger Geometry:** This is an old method for more than about twenty years and in this method the user's hand characteristics are analyzed. The characteristic includes the length, width, surface, thickness etc. The distance among the fingers are calculated and used to later idenidentification. This system is tough to handle and need more space when compared to other biometrics technique and so the usage of this technique is reducing (Podio and Dunn, 2001).

## Biometric Smartcard Authentication: A Prototype

Biometric identification is utilized to verify a person's identity by measuring digitally certain human characteristics and comparing those measurements with those that have been stored in a template for that same person. Templates can be stored at the biometric device, the institution's database, a user's smart card, or a *Trusted Third Party* service provider's database. There are two major categories of biometric techniques: *physiological* (fingerprint verification, iris analysis, hand geometry-vein patterns, ear recognition, odor detection, DNA pattern analysis and sweat pores analysis), and *behavioral* (handwritten signature verification, keystroke analysis and speech analysis). In (Dean et at., 2005), it was found that behavior based systems were perceived as less acceptable than those based on physiological characteristics. Of the physiological techniques, the most commonly utilized is that of fingerprint scanning. With biometrics, fraudulent incidents can be minimized, as an added layer of authentication is now introduced that ensures that even with the correct pin information and in possession of another person's card, the user's biometric features cannot easily be faked. The advantages of this may include: all attributes of the cards will be maintained, counterfeiting attempts are reduced due to enrolment process that verifies identity and captures biometrics, and it will be extremely high secure and excellent user-to-card authentication. These advantages are for the benefit of users as well as system administrators because the problems and costs associated with lost, reissued or temporarily issued can be avoided, thus saving some costs of the system management.

On the negative side, the major risk posed by the use of biometric systems is that a malicious subject may interfere with the communication and intercept the biometric template and use it later to obtain access (Luca et at., 2002). Likewise, an attack may be committed by generating a template from a fingerprint obtained from some surface. Although few biometric systems are fast and accurate in terms of low false acceptance rate enough to allow identification (automatically recognizing the user identity), most of current systems are suitable for the verification only, as the false acceptance rate is too high.

The propose design uses a maximum of 8 characters, numbers or mix of the both PIN and fingerprint as verification factors of the authentication process. ACOS smartcards and AET60 BioCARDKey development kit were used in the propose design. In the verification part, the users have to submit the correct PIN DES encrypted current session key to get access to the next level. Users have 3 successful attempts to enter the correct PIN, else the cards will be locked and render it to useless. Lastly, Authors use the fingerprint as the biometric identifiers as it takes shortest enrollment time. The proposed design involves two phases namely enrollment phase and verification phase. Each of the phases is briefly describe below.

*Enrollment:* Prior to an individual being identified or verified by a biometric device, the enrollment process must be completed. The objective of this enrollment process is to create a profile of the user. The process consists of the following two steps:

1.  **Sample Capture:** The user allows for a minimum of two or three biometric readings, for example: placing a finger in a fingerprint reader. The quality of the samples, together with the number of samples taken, will influence the level of accuracy at the time of validation. Not all samples are stored; the technology analyzes and measures various data points unique to each individual. The number of measured data points varies in accordance to the type of device.
2.  **Conversion and Encryption:** The individual's measurements and data points are converted to a mathematical algorithm and encrypted. These algorithms are extremely complex and cannot be reversed engineered to obtain the original image. The algorithm may then be stored as a user's template in a number of places including servers and card.

A new and blank card has to be enrolled with user details before it can be verified later. Enrollment system is usually operated by the admin to enter their user's details into the card. However, exception applies to the PIN entry where it should be entered by the user themselves and need to enter the PIN again to make sure they enter the correct ones.

*Identification and Verification:* Once the individual has been enrolled in a system, he/she can start to use biometric technology to have access the enrolled services from the fog database server.

1.  **Identification:** A one-to-many match. The user provides a biometric sample and the system looks at all user templates in the database. If there is a match, the user is granted access, otherwise, it is declined.
2.  **Verification:** A one-to-one match requiring the user provides identification such as a PIN and valid card in addition to the biometric sample. In other words, the user is establishing who he/she is and the system simply verifies if this is correct. The biometric sample with the provided identification is compared to the previously stored information in the database. If there is a match, access is provided, otherwise, it is declined.

After the card has been enrolled with user data, this particular card will be the user's ID. The PIN and fingerprint sample from the user were also encrypted and

*Figure 2. Flowchart for the enrollment process*

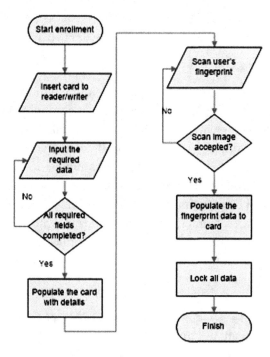

*Figure 3. Flowchart for the verification process*

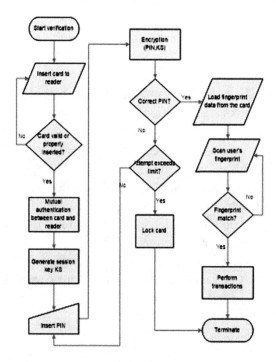

save into the card. In order to get access the fog server, the user has to present the card to the card reader, and then verify the PIN and lastly matched their fingerprint detail with the card. The sequence diagram in Figure 4 summarizes the verification process.

## FUTURE STUDY

Biometrics increasingly form the basis of identification and recognition across many sensitive applications. But as the use of biometric systems increases, so do the threats against them. The secure storage of biometric templates has therefore become a key issue in the modern era; the acceptance of biometric authentication devices by the general public is dependent on the perceived level of security of biometric information templates stored within databases.

Privacy concerns have grown because a biometric template is a unique identifier of a person. And while the template cannot be decoded back to the biometric data, it may be used to track the individual. If there is a database that ties the user to their unique biometric template, it could be used illegally to monitor the activities of the user. Such threats need to be addressed, and one potential solution is cancellable biometrics. This is a template transformation technique that uses intentional repeated distortions to provide security to biometric templates; the distortions

*Figure 4. Process for granting access to service*

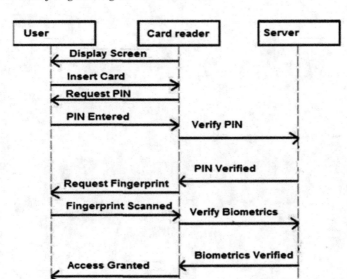

can be performed either at signal level or at feature level to achieve a transformed template. It is therefore important for further studies on cancellable biometrics and its application in IoT.

## CONCLUSION

In this paper Authors have explained the concepts of fog computing, and Authors have presented the benefits, properties and characteristics of fog computing and security issue related to it. On the other hand, Authors have explained the how to achieve the authentication of fog computing using three-factor authentication method. Authors designed the new efficient model based on fingerprint, the implemented model works on storage all the user's fingerprints with their password on fog server.

# REFERENCES

Alrawais, A., Alhothaily, A., Hu, C., & Chang, X. (2017). Fog Computing for the Internet of Things: Security and Privacy Issues. IEEE Internet Computing, 21, 34-42.

Balfanz, D., Smetters, D. K., Stewart, P., & Wong, H. C. (2002). Talking to strangers: authentication in ad-hoc wireless networks. *Network and Distributed System Security Symposium (NDSS)*.

Bonomi, F., Milito, R., Zhu, J., & Addepalli, S. (2012). Fog computing and its role in the internet of things. *Proceedings of the first edition of the MCC workshop on Mobile cloud computing*, 13-16. 10.1145/2342509.2342513

Calandriello, G., Papadimitratos, P., Hubaux, J.-P., & Lioy, A. (2007)., Efficient and robust pseudonymous authentication in VANET. *Proc. VANET*, 19–28.

Chang, C., & Tsai, H.-C. (2010). An anonymous and self-verified mobile authentication with authenticated key agreement for large-scale wireless networks. *IEEE Transactions on Wireless Communications*, 9(11), 3346–3353. doi:10.1109/TWC.2010.092410.090022

Cisco the network in review. (2015). Retrieved September 02, 2017, from http://newsroom.cisco.com/featurecontent?type=webcontent&articleId=1365576

Damiani, E., Vimercati, D. C., Paraboshi, S., Samarati, P., & Violante, F. (2002). A reputation-based approach for choosing reliable resources in peer-to-peer networks. *Proc. of the 9th ACM conference on Computer and communications security*, 207-216.

Deane, F., Barrelle, K., Henderson, R., & Mahar, D. (2005). Perceived acceptability of biometric security systems. *Computers & Security*, 14(3), 225–231. doi:10.1016/0167-4048(95)00005-S

Dsouza, C., Ahn, G. J., & Taguinod, M. (2014). Policy-driven security management for fog computing: preliminary framework and a case study. *Proceedings of the 2014 IEEE 15th International Conference on Information Reuse and Integration*. 10.1109/IRI.2014.7051866

He, D., Ma, M., Zhang, Y., Chen, C., & Bu, J. (2011). A strong user authentication scheme with smart cards for wireless communications. *Computer Communications*, 34(3), 367–374. doi:10.1016/j.comcom.2010.02.031

Jain, A., Bolle, R., & Pankanti, S. (Eds.). (1998). *Biometrics: Personal identification in networked society*. Dordrecht, The Netherlands: Kluwer.

Josang, A., Ismail, R., & Boyd, C. (2007). A survey of trust and reputation systems for online service provision. *Decision Support Systems*, *43*(2), 618–644. doi:10.1016/j.dss.2005.05.019

Lu, R., Lin, X., Liang, X., & Shen, X. (2010). FLIP: An efficient privacy-preserving protocol for finding like-minded vehicles on the road. *Proc. IEEE Globecom*, 1–5.

Luca, B., Bistarelli, S., & Vaccarelli, A. (2002). *Biometrics authentication with smartcard*. IIT TR-08/2002. Retrieved October, 9, 2017, from http://www.iat.cnr.it/attivita/progetti/parametri biomedici.html

Modi, C., Patel, D., Patel, H., Borisaniya, B., Patel, A., & Rajarajan, M. (2013). A survey of intrusion detection techniques in Cloud. *Journal of Network and Computer Applications*, *36*(1), 42–57. doi:10.1016/j.jnca.2012.05.003

O'Gorman, L. (2003). Comparing Passwords, Tokens, and Biometrics for User Authentication. *Proceedings of the IEEE*, *91*(12), 2019–2040. doi:10.1109/JPROC.2003.819605

Podio, F. L., & Dunn, J. S. (2001). *Biometric authentication technology*. Retrieved April 2010, from http://www.itl.nist.gov/div893/biometrics/Biometricsfromthemovies.pdf

Sean, W. S., & Vernon, A. (1998). Trusting Trusted Hardware: Towards a Formal Model for Programmable Secure Coprocessors. *Proceedings of the 3rd USENIX Workshop on Electronic Commerce*.

Shanhe, Y., Zhengrui, Q., & Qun, L. (2015). Security and Privacy Issues of Fog Computing: A Survey. *Proc. Int'l Conf. Wireless Algorithms Systems and Applications (WASA)*, 685–695.

Shi, Y., Abhilash, S., & Hwang, K. (2015). Cloudlet mesh for securing mobile fogs from intrusions and network attacks. *3rd IEEE International Conference on Mobile Cloud Computing, Services, and Engineering*, 1096-118.

Stojmenovic, I., & Wen, S. (2014). The fog computing paradigm: scenarios and security issues. *Proc. of the 2014 Federated Conference on Computer Science and Information Systems (FedCSIS)*, 1-8.

Tsai, H., Chang, C., & Chan, K. (2009). Roaming across wireless local area networks using SIM-based authentication protocol. *Computer Standards & Interfaces*, *31*(2), 381–389. doi:10.1016/j.csi.2008.05.002

Tsai, Y., & Chang, C. (2006). SIM-based subscriber authentication mechanism for wireless local area networks. *Computer Communications*, *29*(10), 1744–1753. doi:10.1016/j.comcom.2005.09.016

Vaquero, L. M., & Rodero-Merino, L. (2014). Finding your way in the fog: Towards a comprehensive definition of fog computing. *ACM SIGCOMM CCR*, *44*(5), 27–32. doi:10.1145/2677046.2677052

Zhu, H., Lin, X., Lu, R., Ho, P., & Shen, X. (2008). AEMA: An aggregated emergency message authentication scheme for enhancing the security of vehicular Ad Hoc networks. *Proceedings of the IEEE, ICC*, 1436–1440.

Chapter 7

# Secure Data Integrity Protocol for Fog Computing Environment

**Kashif Munir**
*University of Hafr Al-Batin, Saudi Arabia*

**Lawan Ahmed Mohammed**
*University of Hafr Al Batin, Saudi Arabia*

## ABSTRACT

*Fog computing is a distributed infrastructure in which certain application processes or services are managed at the edge of the network by a smart device. Fog systems are capable of processing large amounts of data locally, operate on-premise, are fully portable, and can be installed on heterogeneous hardware. These features make the fog platform highly suitable for time and location-sensitive applications. For example, internet of things (IoT) devices are required to quickly process a large amount of data. The significance of enterprise data and increased access rates from low-resource terminal devices demand reliable and low-cost authentication protocols. Lots of researchers have proposed authentication protocols with varied efficiencies. As a part of this chapter, the authors propose a secure authentication protocol that is strongly secure and best suited for the fog computing environment.*

DOI: 10.4018/978-1-5225-7149-0.ch007

# INTRODUCTION

Due to the significant physical distance between cloud service provider's Data Centers (2016) and End User (EU), cloud computing suffers from substantial end-to-end delay, traffic congestion, processing of huge amount of data, and communication cost. Although few companies like Apple are moving towards more environmental friendly 100 percent renewable DCs with the wind, solar, and geothermal energy, the carbon emission from DCs due to the round-the-clock operation will dominate on global carbon footprint. Fog computing emerges as an alternative to traditional cloud computing to support geographically distributed, latency sensitive, and Quality-of-Service (QoS)-aware Internet of Things (IoT) applications. Fog computing was first initiated by Cisco to extend the cloud computing to the edge of a network as per Cisco (2015). Fog computing is a highly virtualized platform [4] that provides computing, storage, and networking services between EU and DC of the traditional cloud computing. According to Bonomi et al (2012), Fog computing has the following

- Low latency and location awareness
- Supports geographic distribution
- End device mobility
- Capacity of processing high number of nodes
- Wireless access
- Real-time applications
- Heterogeneity

The OpenFog Consortium (2015), a consortium of high-tech giant companies and academic institutions across the world, aims to standardize and promote fog computing in various fields.

Many technology enablers for fog computing in various fields discussed by Chiang and Zhang (2016).Some of the examples are EU experience by GE, TOYOTA, BMW, etc., network equipment like switches, gateway by Cisco, Huawei, Ericsson, etc. The current research trends reflect the tremendous potential of fog computing towards sustainable development in global IoT market.

The term *Fog Computing* was introduced by Cisco Systems as a new model to bridge the gap between cloud computing and Internet of Things (IoT) devices (SABU, n.d.). It is a decentralized computing and it is a highly virtualized platform which provides computation, storage, and networking services between IoT devices and traditional cloud servers. Thus, the cloud-based services can be extended closer to the IoT devices (Yi, Li, & Li, 2015).

According to Bader et al (2016), fog computing extends a substantial amount of data storage, computing, communication, and networking of cloud computing near to the end devices. Due to close integration with the front-end intelligence enabled end devices, fog computing enhances the overall system efficiency, after that improving the performance of critical cyber-physical systems. An important key difference is that cloud computing tries to optimize resource in a global view, whereas fog computing organizes and manages the local virtual cluster.

According to Bonomi et al (2012), fog computing is considered as an extension of the cloud computing to the edge of the network, which is a highly virtualized platform of resource pool that provides computation, storage, and networking services to nearby end users. As per Vaquero et al (2014), fog computing as "a scenario where a huge number of heterogeneous (wireless and sometimes autonomous) ubiquitous and decentralized devices communicate and potentially cooperate among them and with the network to perform storage and processing tasks without the intervention of third parties. These tasks can be for supporting basic network functions or new services and applications that run in a sandboxed environment. Users leasing part of their devices to host these services get incentives for doing so." Although those definitions are still debatable before, fog computing is no longer a buzzword.

In this chapter, we take a close look at the secure data and authentication protocol for Fog computing paradigm. In the next section, we examine the state-of-the-art and disclose some general cryptographic algorithms in Fog computing. We further discussed some data security risks associated with fog computing. Cryptographic Parameters of Mathematical Model (TPA) and proposed TPA were also discussed in details. We finally conclude this article with discussion of future work.

## RELATED WORK

Although there are numerous novel studies contributed to secure authentication system, recent studies have mostly considered cloud storage environments rather than fog computing. In this section, we briefly summarize some few ones among those that address fog computing.

Insecure authentication protocols between Fog platforms and end-user devices have been identified as a main security concern of Fog computing by Stojmenovic et al (2015). The author's claim that the IoT devices, especially in smart grids, are prone to data tampering and spoofing attacks and can be prevented with the help of a Public Key Infrastructure (PKI), Diffie-Hellman key exchange, Intrusion detection techniques and monitoring for modified input values. Furthermore, the authors demonstrate the high importance and impact of MITM attack on Fog computing by launching a Stealth attack on video call between 3G and the WLAN users within a Fog network. Results show that the attack did not cause any visible change in memory and CPU consumption of Fog node, hence it is quite difficult to detect and mitigate. The authors recommend that the risk of such attacks can be prevented by securing communication channels between the Fog platform and the user through implementing authentication schemes.

Based on the current state of authentication in Fog platform, Fog platforms are missing rigorous authentication and secure communication protocols as per their specification and requirements. In a Fog platform both security and performance factors are considered in conjunction, and mechanisms such as the encryption methodologies known as fully homomorphic by Gentry (2009) and Fan-Vercauteren somewhat homomorphic by Bos et al (2017) can be used to secure the data. These schemes consists of a hybrid of symmetric and public-key encryption algorithms, as well as other variants of attribute-based encryption. As homomorphic encryption permits normal operations without decrypting the data, the reduction in key distribution will maintain the privacy of data. Other research work provides a similar framework to secure smart grids, regardless of Fog computing, called the Efficient and Privacy Preserving Aggregation (EPPA) scheme by Lu et al (2012). The system performs data aggregation based on the homomorphic Paillier cryptosystem. As the homomorphic ability of encryption makes it possible for local network gateways to perform an operation on cipher-text without decryption, it reduces the authentication cost (in terms of processing power) while maintaining the secrecy of data.

Security in fog computing is one of the main concerns, and without proper security and privacy preserving mechanisms, fog computing will not be adopted despite of its usefulness (Lee et al., 2015). Table 1 has been compared different cryptography algorithms which have been used to protect the user's data on fog computing. Since, we have been reviewed different papers and we didn't conduct any experiment. In this section, we will establish a pattern in reviewed work and we will compare all used techniques and cryptography algorithms. Cryptography algorithms have been compared in general and according to the reviewed papers, without comparing algorithm characteristics such as speed, key length, etc.

A general overview of fog security and privacy issues is discussed in (Stojmenovic & Wen 2014) and (S. Yi, Z. Qin, & Q. Li, 2015). However, this survey is very limited regarding open research challenges in security and privacy issues for fog computing. More recently, security and privacy preservation are discussed in (J., Ni et al., 2017). While issues related to access authorization were discussed in (M. Xiao et al., 2017). Other related works include the work by (Law et al., 2013) which elaborated public key infrastructure (PKI) based solutions which involve multicast authentication. Some authentication techniques using Diffie-Hellman key exchange

*Table 1. Existing fog computing cryptography algorithms comparison*

| Cryptography Algorithm | Strengths | Limitations |
|---|---|---|
| DES | Easy to implement (Mishra, Siddiqui & Tripathi, 2015). | DES algorithm has been cracked, it is not secure anymore (Van De Zande, 2001). It also showed slow performance on software (Mishra, Siddiqui & Tripathi, 2015). |
| 3DES | Easy and efficient (Mishra, Siddiqui & Tripathi, 2015). | 3DES algorithm has been cracked, it is not secure anymore (Makhmali & Jani, 2013). It also showed slow performance on software (Mishra, Siddiqui & Tripathi, 2015). |
| AES | It shows the best results for high processing devices. It has been Showed the best results among all symmetric key algorithms in term of security, flexibility, memory usage, and performance (Mishra, Siddiqui & Tripathi, 2015). | AES is not considered s best encryption algorithm for encrypting low processing devices (Mishra, Siddiqui & Tripathi, 2015). |
| RSA | RSA is secure cryptography algorithm. It is faster encryption than ElGamal (Mishra, Siddiqui & Tripathi, 2015). | The same security level can be obtained by ECC with less key size (Mishra, Siddiqui & Tripathi, 2015). Also, key generation step is complex (Kurumanale et al., 2017). |
| ECC | It has been provided good security with smaller key sizes than RSA, it's useful in many fog applications and it's more suitable for fog environments (Dong & Zhou, 2016). | It is much less explored and known (Sinha, Srivastava & Gupta, 2013) |
| BLOWFISH. | Appropriate in applications where the key is not changed frequently and it's more efficient in softwares (Mishra, Siddiqui & Tripathi, 2015). | BLOWFISH could be time consuming in some implementations regarding its complicated encryption functions (Makhmali & Jani, 2013). Also, once the source code have been obtained, it will be easy to hacked (Kurumanale et al., 2017). |
| RC5. | RC5 is simple, easy to implement, fast, and requires low memory(Gawali & Wadhai, 2012). | It can be broke if the used key is too short(Gawali & Wadhai, 2012). |
| ElGamal. | ElGamal showed faster decryption than RSA (Mishra, Siddiqui & Tripathi, 2015). | It's slow and needs more time in digital signature (Grewal, 2015). |
| ECDH | ECDH algorithm showed significant performance with its lightweight, robustness, and low power consumption (Goyal &. Sahula, 2016). | - |

have been discussed in (Z. Fadlullah et al., 2011). Smart meters encrypt the data and send to the Fog device, such as a home-area network (HAN) gateway. HAN then decrypts the data, aggregates the results and then passes them forward. Application and survey of intrusion detection techniques in Fog computing has been discussed in (Modi et al., 3013). Intrusion in smart grids can be detected using either a signature-based method in which the patterns of behavior are observed and checked against an already existing database of possible misbehaviors. Intrusion can also be captured by using an anomaly-based method in which an observed behavior is compared with expected behavior to check if there is a deviation. The work (Valenzuela et al., 2013) develops an algorithm that monitors power flow results and detects anomalies in the input values that could have been modified by attacks. The algorithm detects intrusion by using principal component analysis to separate power flow variability into regular and irregular subspaces.

## DATA SECURITY RISKS

Security is one of the main attributes of information technology. By access to fog services and data through the Internet, the importance of security is increased because data is at bigger amount of security risk. Within various fog service models, data responsibility is shared by more groups. Data is the most important for the organization which owns them and uses the fog services for storage. That is the reason why the organization should be aware of all risks which exist for data stored in fog environment.

### Basic Attributes of Data Security

As defined by TechTarget (2015) one of the basic data security concepts is the trio CIA shown in Figure 1. *Confidentiality, integrity* and *availability*, also known as the CIA triad, is a model designed to guide policies for information security within an organization. The model is also sometimes referred to as the AIC triad (availability, integrity and confidentiality) to avoid confusion with the Central Intelligence Agency. The elements of the triad are considered the three most crucial components of security.

As long as confidentiality is concerned it represents information protection from revealing it to unauthorized persons. A basic way how to ensure confidentiality is setting access authorization to data and introducing policies which define access right to data. The key element of confidentiality protection is cryptography. It enables that only the persons who know the key can read the information. Saved and also transmitted data can be encrypted.

*Figure 1. The security requirements triad - CIA*

Data integrity represents protection against changes by unauthorized persons. Data has value only if it is safe. Data which has been manipulated does not have any value and may cause financial waste. For example data manipulation in which information about financial accounts is stored. Similarly, cryptography plays an important role in ensuring data integrity. Frequently used methods of data integrity protection contain information about data changes and hash checksums by which data integrity is verified.

Availability concept is to make sure that the services of an organization are available for all legitimate users. This is to ensure that the system is free from DoS or DDoS attacks (denial of service or distributed denial of services). The motive behind DoS attacks is to bring down the respective services and therefore to defeat availability. Though, availability can also be defeated through some other natural causes such as disasters (flood, fire, or earthquake etc). Generally, the aim of availability is to develop systems which are fault tolerant.

## Data Encryption

One of the keys to data protection in the Fog computing is accounting for the possible states in which your data may occur, and what controls are available for that state. For the purpose of Microsoft Azure (2017), data security and encryption best practices the recommendations will be around the following data's states:

- **At-Rest:** This includes all information storage objects, containers, and types that exist statically on physical media, be it magnetic or optical disk.
- **In-Transit:** When data is being transferred between components, locations or programs, such as over the network, across a service bus (from on-premises to cloud and vice-versa, including hybrid connections such as ExpressRoute), or during an input/output process, it is thought of as being in-motion.

Some of the recommended best practices for data security and encryption are as follows:

- Enforce multi-factor authentication
- Use role based access control (RBAC)
- Encrypt virtual machines
- Use hardware security models
- Manage with Secure Workstations
- Enable SQL data encryption
- Protect data in transit
- Enforce file level data encryption

## Encryption Methods Used in Securing Data

Depending on the application domain, existing encryption algorithms can be used in securing data in fog computing. Advanced Encryption Standard (AES) is a symmetrical block encryption. It is using 128 bit blocks and key of 128, 192 and 256 bits. The algorithm AES consists of bit substitution, permutation, arithmetic operation through finite field and operation XOR with key. Another example is the Triple Data Encryption Standard (TDES or 3DES) which is a symmetrical block encryption which is based on encryption algorithm Data Encryption Standard (DES). It is applied three times in order to increase resistance against breaking. TDES is slower than AES and that is why it is replaced by AES nowadays. Data is divided into 64 bit blocks (56 randomly generated bits for encryption algorithm and 8 bits for detection).

RSA is an alternative for asymmetric encryption. It is suitable for encryption and signing. In the case of a key long enough, it is considered to be safe. RSA is built on an assumption that spreading a large number on the product of prime numbers (factorization) is a computationally demanding task. From numbers n=p*q it is computationally impossible to find out p and q in real time. Nowadays, there is no known algorithm of factorization which would work in polynomial time against the size of binary numbers n. Multiplication of two big numbers is computationally not a demanding task.

## Data Integrity Check

Data integrity check in fog computing was necessary to realise by the use of data audit model by an audit page. The audit page is a confidential entity in which the data owner and the service provider have confidence. It can be directly the owner of data or data integrity check provider.

One approach to ensure data integrity is Provable Data Possession (PDP) as described in Ateniese et al., (2007). This method enables a client to verify that the server possesses his data, without having to retrieve the entire data. The model implements a challenge/response protocol between client and server, in which the server has to deliver a so-called Proof of Possession. Instead of a deterministic proof, this proof is probabilistic, as in this protocol, it is not possible to verify every bit of data. This would require having to download the entire data set, which is undesirable for large amounts of data. Instead, random samples of blocks are verified. The goal of PDP is therefore to detect misbehavior of a server when it does not possess the complete file anymore. In contrast to some other methods, PDP requires the client to store a small and constant amount of metadata locally, to minimize network communication. This enables verifying large data sets, distributed over many storage devices. The authors propose two schemes that are supposedly more secure than previous solutions, have a constant server overhead, independent of the data size, and have a performance bounded by disk I/O and not by cryptographic computation. The size of the challenge and response are both 1 Kilobit. The method works with homomorphically verifiable tags, that enable possession verification without having to possess the files locally. For each file block, such a tag is computed. The homomorphic property enables multiple tags to be combined into one value. The file blocks, together with their tags, are stored.

Whenever the user wants to check whether the server is performing the right behavior, he can decide to send a challenge to the server. The challenge consists of the references to a random subset of file blocks. The server has to construct a proof of possession out of the blocks that are queried, and their tags, to convince the client that the server possesses the blocks, without having to send them. Note here that the server should not be able to construct a proof without possessing the queried blocks. Figure 2 clearly shows the steps.

Step (a) shows the pre-processing phase, in which the client uses the file to create the metadata, and stores this metadata locally. The client may modify the file, by appending other metadata, or encrypting the file. Next, the modified file is sent to the server, which stores it without further processing. In (b), the verification step is

*Figure 2. PDP protocol (Ateniese et al., 2007)*

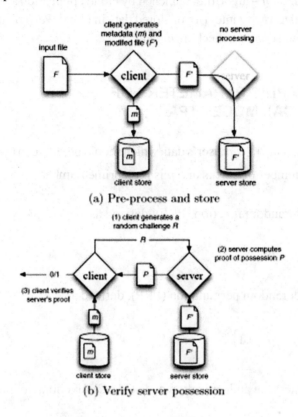

(a) Pre-process and store

(b) Verify server possession

shown. The client sends a challenge to the server. The server uses the stored file to create a proof, and sends it back to the client. The client uses the stored metadata to verify this proof.

## Data Integrity Check Model by Third Party Auditor

A mathematical model by Shacham and Waters (2007) has been chosen as a mathematical model for data audit stored on cloud which is in fact an edited model of Juels and Kaliski (2007). The same model can be applied in fog computing as well. Operation descriptions of mathematical model and formulas have been adopted from the source Cong et al., (2010). The model of public audit used four algorithms: *KeyGen* – algorithm to generate the key. *SiSSen* – algorithm used by user to generate verification metadata. Metadata contained entries needed to verify the integrity of stored data. *GenProof* – algorithm launched by cloud application server to generate metadata needed to verify integrity of stored data in cloud. *VerifyProof* – algorithm launched by audit server to check metadata.

## CRYPTOGRAPHIC PARAMETERS OF MATHEMATICAL MODEL TPA

$F = (m_1, \ldots, m_n) \in \mathbb{Z}p$ user´s data which should be stored in the server storage where $n$ is the number of blocks and $p$ is high prime number.

*fkey* $(.)$ – pseudorandom function (PRF), defined as:

$\{0,1\} * \times key \rightarrow \mathbb{Z}p$.

$\pi key (.)$ – pseudorandom permutation (PRP), defined as:

$\{0,1\}^{log2(n)} \times key \rightarrow \{0,1\}^{log2(n)}$

*MACkey* $(.)$ – message authentication code (MAC) function, defined as:

$\{0,1\} * \times key \rightarrow \{0,1\}^1$.

$H(.), h(.)$ – map-to-point hash functions, defined as: $\{0,1\} * \rightarrow G$, where $G$ is some group.

Let $G_1, G_2$ and $G_T$ to be multiplicative cyclic group of line p and e: $G_1 \times G_2 \rightarrow G_T$ was a bilinear map. Let g be the generator $G_2 . H(.)$ which was a secure map-to-point hash function: $\{0,1\} * \rightarrow G_1$ which mapped the integer (chains) uniformly into $G_1$. Hash function $h(.) : G_1 \rightarrow \mathbb{Z}p$ mapped the element groups $G_1$ into $\mathbb{Z}p$.

### Mathematical Description of TPA Model Operation

In the process of settings, the user launched the algorithm *KeyGen* and generated the public and private parameters. Randomly selected $x \leftarrow \mathbb{Z}p$, random element $u \leftarrow G_1$ and calculated $u \leftarrow g^x$ and $w \leftarrow u^x$. The private parameter was

$sk = (x)$ and the public were $vk = (v, q, g, u)$. On data $F = (m_1, \ldots, m_n)$ the user launched the algorithm *SigGen* by which he calculated the sign $\sigma_i$ for each data block mi: $\sigma_i \leftarrow (H(i) \cdot u^{mi})^x \in G_1$, for $i = (1, \ldots, n)$. Then the summary of all signs was $\Phi = \{\sigma_i\}_{1 \leq I \leq n}$ for $i = (1, \ldots, n)$. Consequently, the user sent $\{F, \Phi\}$ on a server and deleted the local copy.

During the audit, the message "*chal*" has been created. It specified the blocks' position which were needed to be checked during the audit phase. The third audit side randomly selected a subset s c elemental $I = \{S_1, \ldots, S_c\}$ sets $[1, n]$ *where* $S_q = \pi k_{prp}(q)$ where $q = (1, \ldots, c)$ and $\text{k}_{prp}$ was the third permutation key for each audit chosen by audit side. For each element $i \in I$, TAP has chosen randomly the value $v_i$. Then it has sent the message $chal = \{(i, v_i)\} i \in I$ to the server.

After receiving the the message "*chal*", the server launched the algorithm *GenProff* which generated an answer as a proof of correctness of data storage. Server selected a random element $r \leftarrow \mathbb{Z}p$ through $r = fk_{prf}(chal)$ where $\text{k}_{prf}$ was a randomly chosen key by server by the use of pseudo-random function for every unit. Then it calculated $R = (w)^r = (u^x)^r \in G_1$. Linear combinations of chosen blocks specified in the message "*chal*" was $\mu' = \Sigma v_i m_i$, for $i \in I$. For $\mu'$ and $r$ server calculated $\mu = \mu' + rh(R) \in \mathbb{Z}p$. Then server calculated aggregated signature $\sigma = \Pi_{i \in I} \sigma_i^{vi} \in G_1$, for $i \in I$. Finally, the server has sent the answer $\{\sigma, \mu, R\}$ to third audit side.

After receiving the answer from the server, TAS launched the algorithm *VerifyProof* by which it verified the accuracy of the answer by calculating in the verifying equation:

$$e(\sigma(R^{h(R)}), g) \overset{?}{=} e \; \Pi_{i=si} H(i)^{vi} \cdot u^{\mu}, \; v)$$

Random mask $R$ did not have any effect on accuracy verification. Simultaneously, the third side did not have any access to data of customer $F$, privacy has been maintained, Cong et al., (2010).

## Propose Protocol for TPA Model

The propose protocol is similar to some previously proposed schemes in the context of remote data integrity checking such as in (H. Shacham & B. Waters 2013). The protocol consists of four algorithms; *KeyGen* is run by the client and sets up the schem, *SigGen* is run by the client and generates verification metadata used for auditing, *GenProof* is run by the server and generates the proof of correctness of data, and finally *VerifyProof* which is run by the TPA and verifies the server's proof. The client first runs *KeyGen* and *SigGen*. He sends the file to the server and the metadata to the TPA. Then he deletes his local data. In the auditing phase, the TPA creates a challenge and sends it to the server. The server runs *GenProof*, sends the proof to the TPA, and the TPA runs *VerifyProof* to verify

The protocol consists of the following algorithms:

$$KeyGen\left(1^k\right) \;\rightarrow\; \left(pk,\; sk\right)$$

- Run by client. Creates a public and private key pair.

$$SigGen\left(sk,\; F\right) \;\rightarrow\; \left(\Phi,\; sig_{sk}\left(H\left(R\right)\right)\right).$$

- Run by client. Creates a set of signatures $\Phi = \{\sigma i\}$ for each block mi in file $F$, and a signature of the root $R$ (signed with the private key) of the Merkle hash tree.

$$GenProof\left(F,\; \Phi,\; chal\right) \;\rightarrow\; \left(P\right).$$

- Run by server. Constructs a proof out of file $F$, the signature set, and the challenge *chal* (created by the TPA).

$$VerifyProof\left(pk,\; chal,\; P\right) \rightarrow \{T\ RUE,\ F\ ALSE\}$$

- Run by TPA. Verifies the proof, using the public key and the corresponding challenge. Returns true or false.

$$ExecUpdate\left(F,\; \Phi,\; update\right) \;\rightarrow\; (F',\; \Phi',\; P_{update})$$

- Run by server. Performs the update on the file, and returns the new file and signatures set, as well as a proof for the update.

$$VerifyUpdate\Big(pk,\ update,\ P_{update}\Big)\ \rightarrow\ \Big\{\big(T\ RUE,\ sig_{sk}\big(H\big(R'\big)\big)\big),\ F\ ALSE\Big\}$$

- Run by client. Verifies whether the update proof is correct, meaning that the update has been performed correctly. If correct, returns a new root signature

## Securing TCP/IP Communications

There are two main subgroups of cipher suites recommended for TCP/IP transport layer security communication. RSA and ECDHE. RSA-based cipher suites use RSA as the key-exchange algorithm, while the ECDHE-based ones use an algorithm that makes use of Ephemeral Diffie–Hellman based on Elliptic Curves. The Ephemeral part means that the key is regenerated after each session, providing Perfect Forward Secrecy (PFS) in contrast to the variants based on RSA.

Figure 3 illustrates the messages exchanged during the handshake when using the cipher suite with a ECDHE key-exchange algorithm. Refers to private keys, while public keys are the ones defined as the procedure takes place as follows:

- The client sends a ClientHello specifying its supported cipher suites.
- The server responds with a ServerHello with the cipher suite selected. This is the cipher suite that is going to be used during the whole TLS session.

*Figure 3. Transport Layer Security (TLS) Handshake procedure*

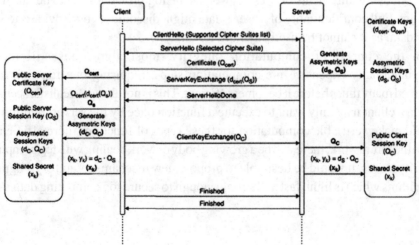

- The server sends its certificate in a Certificate message. Along with it, the public key (Qcert) of the aforementioned certificate is sent.
- The server generates a key pair $(ds, Qs)$ needed for the ECDHE algorithm and sends the public key to the client, encrypted with the private key of the certificate $(dcert(Qs)$. This corresponds to the ServerKeyExchange message.
- Once the client receives the ServerKeyExchange, it uses the certificate's public key received in the Certificate message to check the authenticity of the ECDHE public key by verifying the RSA signature $(Qcert(dcert(Qs)))$, thus obtaining the ECDHE public key $(Qs)$ of the server.
- Finally, the client generates its own ECDHE key pair $(dc, Qc)$ and sends the public key to the server.
- At this point, both server and client can obtain the Session Secret by performing an operation (ECC dot product) with one's own private key and the other party's public-key.

## CONCLUSION

This chapter has given a broad overview on data integrity-related issues in fog Computing. A distinction was made between integrity of outsourced computation, and data outsourcing. Future work should continue improving the efficiency of verification techniques, in order to achieve practical usage. Here, it is important that both the requirements of users as well as the fog provider have to be taken into account. Full confidentiality of a user's data might discourage fog providers to store their data, as it cannot be used anymore for analytics.

In the context of computation integrity, most algorithms still require computationally expensive pre-computation steps, requiring one function to be executed many times before it becomes efficient. This is not always a realistic scenario. Often, a client may only want to execute a function once by the server. Future work should make verifiable computation for these types of functions more efficient.

In the future work, there will be a growing body of work dealing with fog computing security issues. It would be desirable to propose new mechanisms and cryptography algorithms which is light, fast and strong enough to secure fog computing data. Also, integrating one or more good techniques together such as multilevel algorithm on the enhanced user behavior and decoy technology may result in secure and effective mechanism. Combining one or more techniques need more detailed experiments which focus on the algorithms performance such as robust and security.

## REFERENCES

Ateniese, G., Burns, R., Curtmola, R., Herring, J., Kissner, L., Peterson, Z., & Song, D. (2007). Provable data possession at untrusted stores. *Proc. of CCS'07*, 598–609. 10.1145/1315245.1315318

Azure. (2018). *Data Security and Encryption Best Practices*. Retrieved April 17, 2018, from https://docs.microsoft.com/en-us/azure/security/azure-security-data-encryption-best-practices

Bader, A., Ghazzai, H., Kadri, A., & Alouini, M.-S. (2016). Front-end intelligence for large-scale application-oriented Internet-of-things. *IEEE Access: Practical Innovations, Open Solutions, 4*, 3257–3272. doi:10.1109/ACCESS.2016.2580623

Bonomi, F., Milito, R., Zhu, J., & Addepalli, S. (2012). Fog computing and its role in the internet of things. *Proceedings of the first edition of the MCC workshop on Mobile cloud computing*, 13-16. 10.1145/2342509.2342513

Bos, J. W., Castryck, W., Iliashenko, I., & Vercauteren, F. (2017). Privacy-friendly forecasting for the smart grid using homomorphic encryption and the group method of data handling. *International Conference on Cryptology in Africa*, 184–201.

Chiang, M., & Zhang, T. (2016). *Fog and IoT: An overview of research opportunities*. IEEE Internet of Things Journal.

Cisco. (2015). *Cisco delivers vision of fog computing to accelerate value from billions of connected devices*. Retrieved December 02, 2017, from https://newsroom.cisco.com/press-release-content?type=webcontent&articleId=1334100

Cong, W., Qian, W., Kui, R., & Wenjing, L. (2010). Privacy-Preserving Public Auditing for Data Storage Security in Cloud Computing. *INFOCOM, 2010 Proceedings IEEE*, 1-9.

Data Center Companies. (2016). Retrieved November, 9, 2017, from https://www.datacenters.com/ directory/companies

Dong, M. T., & Zhou, X. (2016). Fog Computing. *Comprehensive Approach for Security Data Theft Attack Using Elliptic Curve Cryptography and Decoy Technology, 3*, 1–14.

Fadlullah, Z., Fouda, M., Kato, N., Takeuchi, A., Iwasaki, N., & Nozaki, Y. (2011). Toward intelligent machine-to-machine communications in smart grid. *Communications Magazine, IEEE, 49*(4), 60–65. doi:10.1109/MCOM.2011.5741147

Gentry, C. (2009). Fully homomorphic encryption using ideal lattices. *STOC*, *9*, 169–178.

Juels, A., Burton, J., & Kaliski, S. (2007). Pors: Proofs of retrievability for large files. *Proc. of CCS'07*, 584–597. 10.1145/1315245.1315317

Law, Y. W., Palaniswami, M., Kounga, G., & Lo, A. (2013). Wake: Key management scheme for wide-area measurement systems in smart grid. *Communications Magazine, IEEE*, *51*(1), 34–41. doi:10.1109/MCOM.2013.6400436

Lee, K., Kim, D., Ha, D., Rajput, U., & Oh, H. (2015). *On security and privacy issues of fog computing supported Internet of Things environment*. Academic Press. doi:10.1109/NOF.2015.7333287

Lu, R., Liang, X., Li, X., Lin, X., & Shen, X. (2012). Eppa: An efficient and privacy-preserving aggregation scheme for secure smart grid communications. *IEEE Transactions on Parallel and Distributed Systems*, *23*(9), 1621–1631. doi:10.1109/TPDS.2012.86

Mishra, N., Siddiqui, S., & Tripathi, J. P. (2015). A Compendium Over Cloud Computing Cryptographic Algorithms and Security Issues. *Int. J. Inf. Technol. Bharati Vidyapeeth's Inst. Comput. Appl. Manag.*, *7*(1), 973–5658.

Modi, C., Patel, D., Borisaniya, B., Patel, H., Patel, A., & Rajarajan, M. (2013). A survey of intrusion detection techniques in cloud. *Journal of Network and Computer Applications*, *36*(1), 42–57. doi:10.1016/j.jnca.2012.05.003

Ni, Zhang, Lin, & Shen. (2017). Security, privacy, and fairness in fog-based vehicular crowdsensing. *IEEE Commun. Mag.*, *55*(6), 146-152.

OpenFog Consortium. (2015). Retrieved December 02, 2017, from https://www.openfogconsortium.org

Polk, T., McKay, K., & Chokhani, S. (2005). *Guidelines for the Selection and Use of Transport Layer Security (TLS) Implementations. NIST Special Publication 800-52 Revision 1*. Gaithersburg, MD: NIST.

Shacham, H., & Waters, B. (2013). Compact proofs of retrievability. *Journal of Cryptology*, *26*(3), 442–483. doi:10.100700145-012-9129-2

Sinha, Srivastava, & Gupta. (2013). Performance Based Comparison Study of RSA. *International Journal of Scientific & Engineering Research*, *4*(4).

Stojmenovic, I., & Wen, S. (2014). The Fog computing paradigm: Scenarios and security issues. *Proc. Federated Conf. Comput. Sci. Inf.Syst. (FedCSIS)*, 1-8.

Stojmenovic, I., Wen, S., Huang, X., & Luan, H. (2015). An overview of fog computing and its security issues. *Concurrency and Computation.*

TechTarget. (2015). *Confidentiality, integrity, and availability (CIA triad)*. Retrieved April 02, 2018, from:https://whatis.techtarget.com/definition/Confidentiality-integrity-and-availability-CIA

Valenzuela, J., Wang, J., & Bissinger, N. (2013). Real-time intrusion detection in power system operations. *Power Systems. IEEE Transactions on*, 28(2), 1052–1062.

Xiao, M., Zhou, J., Liu, X., & Jiang, M. (2017). A hybrid scheme for fine-grained search and access authorization in fog computing environment. *Sensors (Basel)*, 17(6), 1–22. doi:10.339017061423 PMID:28629131

Yi, S., Qin, Z., & Li, Q. (2015). Security and privacy issues of fog computing: A survey. *Proc. 10th Int. Conf. Wireless Algorithms, Syst.,Appl. (WASA)*, 685-695. 10.1007/978-3-319-21837-3_67

# Chapter 8
# Unique Fog Computing Taxonomy for Evaluating Cloud Services

**Akashdeep Bhardwaj**
*University of Petroleum and Energy Studies, India*

**Sam Goundar**
*Victoria University of Wellington, New Zealand*

## ABSTRACT

*Fog computing has the potential to resolve cloud computing issues by extending the cloud service provider's reach to the edge of the cloud network model, right up to the cloud service consumer. This enables a whole new state of applications and services which increases the security, enhances the cloud experience, and keeps the data close to the user. This chapter presents a review on the academic literature research work on fog computing, introduces a novel taxonomy to classify cloud products based on fog computing elements, and then determines the best fit fog computing product to choose for the cloud service consumer.*

DOI: 10.4018/978-1-5225-7149-0.ch008

## INTRODUCTION

The primary objective of Fog computing is to ensure the user data stays as close to the user by employing geographically distributed computing infrastructure at the Edge of the cloud-user network. This involves virtualized platforms, smart devices, sensors and nodes that provide storage, computing and network services located at the Edge of the cloud network. Yet Fog computing is not a replacement for Cloud computing. Cloud Computing, Internet of Things and Fog Computing are discussed in this section.

Cloud Computing organizes a pool of shared infrastructure of hardware and software stack hosted inside a centralized data center for delivering service layers over the Internet. These performs compute, storage and networking functions to receive, process and respond to user requests. Cloud computing services are related to applications, platforms and infrastructure, delivered to the Cloud service consumers. The hosted resources are shared by the Cloud service consumers as per different commercial models. Current market examples include Google Docs, Sales Force, Microsoft Office 365 and Amazon Web Services (AWS). Internet of Things or IoT is an internetworked connection of physical devices, buildings, vehicles and smart systems. These are implanted with sensors, actuators over existing network to act as nodes for collecting and exchanging real time data. Examples of IoT include Kolibree Smart Toothbrush, Samsung Smart Things Hub, Nest Smart Thermostat and WeMo Switch Smart Plug as per Internet of Things (2018)[1].

Fog Computing refers to a distributed, decentralized system level architecture that extends the reach of Cloud computing, storage, networking and access control right up to the Edge of the network near the user and devices involved. This involves the use of smart devices, nodes, data hub and sensors configured as near to the IoT data collection point. The IoT data is processed by a smart hub locally, as close to the sensor that is generating the data, unlike Cloud architecture which is has centralized computing. Fog network works at two levels – data level and control level. The data level plans for data management, processing and configuration of the computing resource devices (nodes). The control plane decides the network overview, routing protocols and the control architecture. This leads to low latency, faster, efficient management for collaboration and accessibility with Edge node devices using wireless networks. An IDC study by Yoko Ono (2016)[2] estimates that in 2020, over 10% of the user data would be processed by smart Edge devices involving use of Fog computing.

For Computing empowers the smart hub and nodes to carry out computing and processing functions that would otherwise be performed at a far off centralized data center –

*Figure 1. Cloud Computing, Fog Computing and Internet of Things Architecture*

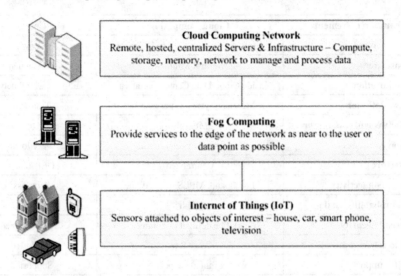

- Local data processing
- Low latency with better QoS
- Cache data management
- Edge node analytics
- Dense geographical distribution
- Local resource pool

Table 1 provides a comparison of Cloud Computing and Fog Computing from a feature requirement perspective.

## LITERATURE SURVEY

In order to understand existing solutions and research on Fog Computing product evaluation, the author surveyed several research publications and reviewed academic literature works from IEEE, ACM Science Direct, Elsevier and ACM, searching for keywords as Fog Computing, Edge Computing, Nodes, Sensors, Internet of Things and IoT.

Hofer et al. (2011)[3] described the advantage and features for Cloud computing and Fog computing from services and commercial point of view for global corporates entering the Cloud domain for the first time. The authors proposed a tree based structured Fog computing taxonomy. The primary aim of the research was to have a Fog computing taxonomy that classified the Cloud services by arranging the

*Table 1. Comparison between Cloud Computing and Fog Computing*

| Feature requirements | Cloud Computing | Fog Computing |
| --- | --- | --- |
| Latency involved | High, depends on User to DC route | Low |
| Response time | Several Minutes | Milliseconds |
| Service Location | Inside Cloud Data Center via internet | Edge of Cloud network |
| Time for data storage | Months or years as per contract | Transient |
| Hops between user & server | Multiple | One |
| Location Awareness | None, need manual routing | Very local |
| Architecture | Centralized | Distributed |
| Last mile connectivity | Broadband, MPLS, Leased line | Wireless |
| Attach probability on data | High | Low |
| End to end Security | Cannot be defined or controlled | Can be defined |
| Nodes to collect data | Very few | Unlimited |
| Mobility support | Limited support | Supported |

Fog elements in a simple and comparative manner and levels for even a layman to understand and take decisions. The proposed taxonomy levels included Main Services, License Types, and Payment Methods, Intended User groups, Formal Service Agreements, Security Measures and Standardization efforts involved. The authors also included examples and samples in the research paper for better clarity.

The achievement of the research paper by Youseff et al. (2008)[4] is being one of the first serious endeavors to establish a detailed taxonomy of Cloud computing way back in 2008. The authors proposed a detailed ontology with a thorough understanding of Cloud and its adoption with the aim to ensure Cloud domain gets established in a better manner worldwide. Various inter-relations between the Cloud components and its layers were used to establish the ontology, discussing the advantages, strength and limitations of each element in detail.

Cloud computing services have registering a huge interest among the cloud service consumers. Alan Sill (2017)[5] presented the research proposing that the communication between Cloud components including cloud applications, data center devices, humans seem to have diminished their boundaries by colluding between Cloud (centralized access over Internet), Edge Fog (distributed cloud in form of highly diffused setup) and IoT (connected and no connected components). There is hence an urgent need for developing a standard and having clear definition of the components.

Mazin Yousif (2017)[6] focused on associating Fog and distributed computing. The article centered on Fog, Edge and Distributed computing. While Fog processing was initiated in 2014, the paper proposed Edge processing attempts to accomplish a similar objective, through various methodologies. The objective was to define Fog processing moving the computing to the IoT gateways or to the client neighborhood. The paper also evaluated how Edge computing drives the data process and information to the Edge gadgets at the base of the Cloud engineering chain.

The pervasiveness and all-inclusiveness of mobile phones makes them perfect Fog gadgets to extend the Edge gadgets and the Cloud. Dantu et al. (2017)[7] proposed an architecture for enabling reliability and adaptability of smart phones running Android operating systems. The authors illustrated the software architecture, constraints faced by systems and applications and presented options to address he challenges. As a future research subject, this work on Android could be stretched to adjust for other versatile smart phone OSs.

Li et al. (2017)[8] proposed that vehicular networks when integrated with Cloud and Fog platforms can be worthy systems displaying a significant part in day to day social lives and help social marketers. Another application implementation as recommender framework to assist advertisers in enhancing and promoting marketing adequacy. The authors proposed three algorithms to increase the effectiveness of advertisers' promoting viability in view of various assessment measures. The first algorithm chooses those vehicles that can get most extreme advantages for the advertisers, in which the vehicles are chosen in view of passing locales with more advantages. This determination strategy may lose some potential markets in light of area impediments. The second algorithm chooses those vehicles that can achieve the most extreme scope proportion in the city and bring the advertisers all the more showcasing viability later on, despite the fact that the present advantages are not the best. The third algorithm joins the two earlier algorithm results, finding a tradeoff amongst scope and advantages. The viability of the proposed algorithms was assessed with real time information to demonstrate the adequacy and proficiency of selecting vehicles as recommenders for vehicular social networks.

Etemad et al. (2017)[9] proposed that with the expansion of Internet of Things (IoT), cloud and Fog computing, involving human services, administrations, sensor systems, and cell phones, a considerable measure of information is being produced at the perception layer. Cloud computing systems are the most reasonable solution for information stockpiling, computing, preparing and administration. Cloud additionally assists in the production of further service administrations tasks, which is refined by the specific situations and prerequisites. Fog computing, in form of an extended cloud existing in the vicinity of hidden nodes, moderate the issues which traditional

Clouds can't understand since they are usually independent. Fog provides fast reaction to the applications and preprocess and channels the information as indicated by the necessities. The authors proposed solutions by examining both the cloud-only and cloud-Fog situations with regards to delay in processing and power consumption issues when number of clients are increased.

Xiao et al. (2017)[10] proposed use of Fog computing to convert vehicles into mobile Fog computing nodes. The authors presented a framework and system design to utilize the mobility aspect of vehicles to provide low-cost, on-demand Fog computing for vehicular applications.

Alrawais et al (2017)[11] discussed the privacy and security issues inherent in the Internet of Things (IoT) devices. This included limited computing power, restricted storage capacity and need for new upgraded platform for handling and processing data efficiently. Fog computing on the other hand, provides variety of advantages in comparison. These include upgraded security, reduced data transfer bandwidth capacity and decreased latency. These advantages make the Fog a great fit for IoT applications. The authors also displayed potential research options for utilizing Fog computing to improve security and protection issues in IoT application environments.

Yannuzzi et al. (2017)[12] discussed the technical difficulties and issues faced by city communities when implementing smart city ideas and designs as part of Fog computing. The authors outlined standards and lessons learned from implementation activities on Fog processing in Barcelona, Spain. Specifically, Quadruple Silo (QS) issue was pointed out in the research paper that has four classifications of silos as physical (equipment) silo, information silo, administration silo and regulatory silo. The article uncovered cases in which Fog computing processing is an unquestionable requirement demonstrating the reasons behind deploying Fog computing.

In context of the growth and issues for Cloud and Fog computing, David Linthicum (2017)[13] analyzed issues for cloud data traveling from Fog devices at the user base to the data centers over the internet, growth rates and time latency issues. The devices included thermostat and wristbands among other devices. The authors proposed that alternatives to cloud need to be determined as use of public clouds in Fog scenarios is notan effective implementation and most times it proves to be not feasible.

Garcia et al. (2017)[14] introduced a framework to determine and control the commercial aspects when enabling a shared economy vision by using Edge devices for smart city scenarios. The authors contended that the use of Edge devices and cloud services is critical component of the Technology Stack for Internet of Things. While both Edge devices and cloud services are incorporated for smart city ecosystems, cloud providers do include pricing strategies in their service offerings, but the Edge devices do not reflect on the economic aspects.

Mahadev Satyanarayanan (2017)[15] presented many ideas and results from discussions and research collaborations including industry ventures and investments in the Edge processing domain. The author presented the origin and roots of Edge computing since 1990s starting with Akamai CDNs to 2012 when Flavio Bonomi introduced Fog computing. The author discussed the need for proximity location for high result intensive cloud computing services, scalability for Edge analytics using Giga Sight framework for mobile devices on real time video analytics, Privacy enforcement for cloudlets to masking Cloud outages. The results pointed out to the use of Edge and Fog computing as the technologies to go for future.

Hao et al. (2017)[16] presented a detailed narrative of research challenges and issues for Fog computing. Based upon the results, the authors proposed a detailed computing software architecture framework to customize the different designs and include user policies and then finally evaluate on the software prototype system.

Rafel et al. (2017)[17] presented a hybrid Fog and cloud framework. This interconnected framework was scalable and multi tenanted solution can be easily configured deployment over layer 2 and layer 3 networks across both Fog and Cloud infrastructures. Use of virtualization and underlying Fog and Cloud technologies was implemented as a solution for cross-site networks for Cloud and Fog computing infrastructures.

Lu et al. (2017)[18] presented a lightweight privacy preserving information aggregation model for Fog computing. The paper employed aggregating the data from all hybrid IoT devices into one based on Chinese Remainder Theorem. The three significant contributions by this paper are firstly the use of the Lightweight Privacy model for Preserving Data Aggregation, secondly the data aggregation presented was secure under the defined security model as the model mitigated and blocked differential attacks and thirdly the results indicated the proposed model as being lightweight and suitable for Fog computing.

Deng et al. (2016)[19] proposed investigated the issues related to consumption of power and delays in transmission in Fog-Cloud computing systems and proposed solutions to resolve the relationship and support between the two. The authors proposed implementing optimal workload allocation for Fog and Cloud, consuming minimum power with balanced delay in services. The authors finally concluded that by reducing unbarring computing resources, bandwidth can be saved along with reduced latency, which in turn significantly improved the Cloud computing performance.

Gu et al. (2017)[20] investigated the Quality of Service (QoS) challenges in the healthcare industry for medical cyber physical systems which sense data from medical devices. In order to resolve this issue, Fog computing is proposed as a possible solution. The authors integrated Fog computing and the medical systems and also proposed a two-phase heuristic algorithm based on linear programming.

Luiz at al. (2017)[21] analyzed the Fog computing resource management and scheduling issues by focusing on user mobility influencing application performance and using scheduling policies such as concurrent scheduling, Delay priority scheduling and first come first served scheduling

Chiang et al. (2017)[22] proposed a framework for interconnected Cloud and Fog systems. The proposed framework provided options for cross site virtual networking infrastructures comprising of Cloud and Fog with scalable, multi-tenant solution. The interface designed was simple and generic for implementing across layer 2 and layer 3 networks

While acknowledging that IoT technology is still in a nascent stage, Li et al. (2017)[23] contended that this has a high potential which can create smart, intelligent solutions. These solutions could well turn out to be more effective, easy to use, energy efficient and safe. The authors discussed the opportunities of cognitive computing on interconnected instrumented things. The paper also reviewed the out the trend for system of systems and methods for Dynamic Data Driven Application Systems. This can be used for advanced understanding, analysis and real-time decision support models.IBSS, Xi'an Jiaotong-Liverpool University, Suzhou, China

Farahani et al. (2018)24 proposed a holistic architecture of IoT eHealth ecosystem and discussed IoT application in Healthcare and Medicine. Due to increasing demands of rising aging population with chronic diseases, the global healthcare is becoming increasingly difficult to manage. This has led to insufficient and less effective healthcare service availability. This ecosystem need to have a transition from the clinic-centric treatment to patient-centric healthcare where each agent such as hospital, patient, and services are seamlessly connected to each other. This patient-centric IoT eHealth ecosystem needs a multi-layer architecture, firstly the device, secondly Fog computing and thirdly the cloud to empower handling of complex data in terms of its variety, speed, and latency. The authors cited examples of services and applications which range from mobile health, assisted living, e-medicine, implants, early warning systems, to population monitoring in smart cities. Finally the authors addressed the challenges of IoT eHealth such as data management, scalability, regulations, interoperability, device–network–human interfaces, security, and privacy.

## Proposed Taxonomy for Fog Computing

While a number of research surveys have been published on the Fog computing, this paper is different from them in the following manner:

- Most researchers focus on Fog computing for infrastructure, connectivity or data collection features. Our taxonomy focusses on classifying products based on four specific elements. Other surveys and research papers which are reviewed above have limited scope of research.
- Implementation and usage of Fog Computing against Cloud Computing environments is highlighted in some of the review papers, while our taxonomy proposes a simple hierarchical, layered model which can be extended with little or no constraints on dimensions or the feature elements, which are independent of each other.

The authors propose the below illustrated classification of Fog computing by dividing into four major elements as per Deployment model, Technical features implemented, Security architecture and Service model offered by the Cloud provider in Figure 2.

Table 2 has the summary of existing Fog Computing academic papers that have been reviewed in this research paper.

*Figure 2. Proposed Fog Computing Taxonomy Classification*

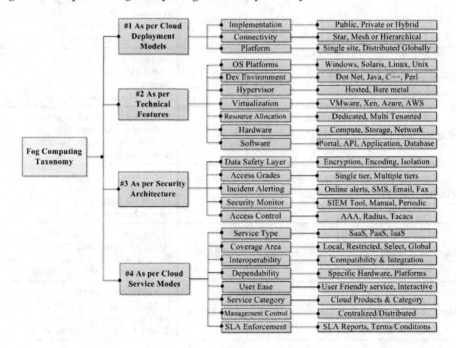

*Table 2. Summary of DDoS attack mechanism summary*

| Reference | Architecture | Deployed | Fog Element |
|---|---|---|---|
| Hofer et al. (2011)[3] | Fog Computing | Access point | Deployment → Implementation<br>Technical →Resource Allocation<br>Security → Data Safety<br>Service Mode → Dependability |
| Yousef et al. (2017)[4] | Fog Computing | Distributed | Deployment → Connectivity<br>Technical → Operating System<br>Security → Data Safety Layer<br>Service Mode → Coverage Area |
| Alan Sill (2017)[5] | Internet of Things | Access point | Deployment → Connectivity<br>Technical → Software type<br>Security → Access Control<br>Service Mode → User Ease |
| Mazin Yousif (2017)[6] | Fog Computing | Distributed | Deployment → Implementation<br>Technical → Resource allocation<br>Security → Security Monitor<br>Service Mode → Service Category |
| Dantu et al. (2017)[7] | Internet of Things | Access point | Deployment → Implementation<br>Technical → Operating System<br>Security → Access Grades<br>Service Mode → Service Type |
| Li et al. (2017)[8] | Internet of Things | Distributed | Deployment → Implementation<br>Technical → Hardware Type<br>Security → Incident Handling<br>Service Mode → Service Type |
| Etemad et al. (2017)[9] | Fog Computing | Access point | Deployment → Connectivity<br>Technical → Hardware Type<br>Security → Access Control<br>Service Mode → Service Type |
| Xiao et al. (2017)[10] | Fog Computing | Access point | Deployment → Implementation<br>Technical → Hardware Type<br>Security → Data Safety Layer<br>Service Mode → Management |
| Alrawais et al. (2017)[11] | Internet of Things | Access point | Deployment → Platform<br>Technical → Hardware Type<br>Security → Data Safety Layer<br>Service Mode → User Ease |
| Yannuzzi et al. (2017)[12] | Fog Computing | Distributed | Deployment → Implementation<br>Technical → Hardware Type<br>Security → Security Monitor<br>Service Mode → SLA Enforcement |
| David Linthicum (2017)[13] | Internet of Things | Access point | Deployment → Implementation<br>Technical → Hardware Type<br>Security → Incident Alerting<br>Service Mode → Management |

*continued on following page*

*Table 2. Continued*

| Reference | Architecture | Deployed | Fog Element |
|---|---|---|---|
| Garcia et al. (2017)[14] | Fog Computing | Access point | Deployment → Implementation<br>Technical → Hardware Type<br>Security → Access Grades<br>Service Mode → User Ease |
| Satyanarayanan Mahadev (2017)[15] | Fog Computing | Access point | Deployment → Connectivity<br>Technical → Hardware Type<br>Security → Access Control<br>Service Mode → Dependability |
| Hao et al. (2017)[16] | Fog Computing | Access point | Deployment →Connectivity<br>Technical → Hardware Type<br>Security → Access Control<br>Service Mode → Service Category |
| Rafael et al. (2017)[17] | Fog Computing | Access point | Deployment →Implementation<br>Technical → Hardware Type<br>Security → Access Grades<br>Service Mode → Service Type |
| Lu et al. (2017)[18] | Internet of Things | Distributed | Deployment →Connectivity<br>Technical → Hardware Type<br>Security → Access Grades<br>Service Mode → User Ease |
| Deng et al. (2016)[19] | Fog Computing | Access point | Deployment → Connectivity<br>Technical → Hardware Type<br>Security → Access Control<br>Service Mode → Dependability |
| Gu et al. (2017)[20] | Fog Computing | Access point | Deployment → Platform<br>Technical → Software Type<br>Security → Security Monitor<br>Service Mode → User Ease |
| Luiz at al. (2017)[21] | Fog Computing | Access point | Deployment → Platform<br>Technical → Software Type<br>Security → Security Monitor<br>Service Mode → Service Category |
| Chiang et al. (2017)[22] | Fog Computing | Access point | Deployment → Implementation<br>Technical →OS Platforms<br>Security → Data Safety Layer<br>Service Mode → Service Type |
| Li et al. (2017) 23 | | | |

## Evaluation Method Using the Proposed Taxonomy

In this section the authors present the methodology to select the best matching Fog product as per the Cloud provider and user preference and policies. Each cloud product was graded and scored based on semantic and deterministic element features and sub feature characteristics. The products are then ranked and matching percentage is calculated, based on which the best fit product can be suggested to the Cloud user. Table 3 displays the types and score ranges for features and sub features for determining the best fit value of the Fog computing product.

To determine the numeric value for each Fog element 'score', the allocated scores for 'Yes', 'No' or 'Very Low' to 'Very High' range convert into actual deterministic values for each element feature in Table 4.

*Table 3. Fog computing best fit selection model*

| Element Type | Classification | Feature | Sub Feature | Score |
|---|---|---|---|---|
| #1 Deployment Model | • Implementation<br>• Platform<br>• Connectivity | Deterministic<br>Semantic<br>Deterministic | Deterministic<br>Deterministic<br>Deterministic | Very Low – Very High<br>Very Low – High<br>Very Low – Medium |
| #2 Technical Features | • OS Platform<br>• Dev Environment<br>• Hypervisor<br>• Virtualization<br>• Resource allocation<br>• Hardware Type<br>• Software Type | Semantic<br>Semantic<br>Semantic<br>Semantic<br>Deterministic<br>Deterministic<br>Semantic | Semantic<br>Semantic<br>Deterministic<br>Semantic<br>Deterministic<br>Deterministic<br>Deterministic | Very Low – High<br>Very Low – High<br>Very Low – Very High<br>Very Low – Low<br>Yes/No<br>Yes/No<br>Yes/No<br>Yes/No |
| #3 Security Architecture | • Data Safety Layer<br>• Access Grades<br>• Incident Alerting<br>• Security Monitoring<br>• Access Control | Semantic<br>Semantic<br>Semantic<br>Deterministic<br>Semantic | Deterministic<br>Deterministic<br>Semantic<br>Deterministic<br>Deterministic | Very Low – High<br>Very Low – High<br>Low - High<br>Yes/No<br>Yes/No |
| #4 Cloud Service Model | • Service Type<br>• Coverage Area<br>• Interoperability<br>• Dependability<br>• User Ease<br>• Service Category<br>• Cloud Architecture<br>• SLA Enforcement | Semantic<br>Deterministic<br>Semantic<br>Semantic<br>Semantic<br>Semantic<br>Deterministic<br>Semantic<br>Semantic | Deterministic<br>Semantic<br>Deterministic<br>Deterministic<br>Deterministic<br>Deterministic<br>Deterministic<br>Deterministic<br>Deterministic | Very Low – Low<br>Low – High<br>Yes/No<br>Yes/No<br>Yes/No<br>Very Low – Low<br>Very Low – Low<br>Yes/No<br>Yes/No |

*Table 4. Transition from Designated to Actual Values*

| Designated Value | Numeric Value |
|---|---|
| Yes | 3 |
| No | 1 |
| Very Low | 1 |
| Low | 2 |
| Medium | 3 |
| High | 4 |
| Very High | 5 |

*Table 5. Transition from designated to actual values*

| Fog Element | Classification | Product #1 | Product#2 | Product#3 | Product#4 |
|---|---|---|---|---|---|
| **#1 Deployment Model** | Implementation | 1 | 2 | 3 | 4 |
| | Platform | 2 | 3 | 2 | 4 |
| | Connectivity | 2 | 1 | 4 | 3 |
| **#2 Technical Features** | OS Platform | 2 | 3 | 3 | 3 |
| | Dev Platform | 1 | 2 | 2 | 4 |
| | Hypervisor | 2 | 1 | 1 | 2 |
| | Virtualization | 1 | 3 | 1 | 3 |
| | Resource allocation | 1 | 3 | 3 | 3 |
| | Hardware Type | 3 | 1 | 3 | 3 |
| | Software Type | 1 | 3 | 1 | 3 |
| **#3 Security Architecture** | Data Safety layer | 2 | 1 | 2 | 4 |
| | Access Grades | 1 | 1 | 3 | 4 |
| | Incident Alerting | 2 | 2 | 4 | 4 |
| | Security Monitoring | 1 | 3 | 1 | 3 |
| | Access Control | 1 | 1 | 3 | 3 |
| **#4 Service Model** | Service Type | 1 | 1 | 1 | 2 |
| | Coverage Area | 2 | 2 | 3 | 4 |
| | Interoperability | 1 | 1 | 3 | 3 |
| | Dependability | 3 | 1 | 1 | 3 |
| | User Ease | 1 | 3 | 1 | 1 |
| | Service Category | 1 | 2 | 2 | 2 |
| | Cloud Architecture | 3 | 1 | 3 | 3 |
| | SLA enforcement | 1 | 1 | 1 | 3 |

## Experimental Results

In order to avoid favoring or infringing on any Fog vendor, four cloud products without a brand name are considered for the practical cloud product evaluation and their features are assessed for each of the proposed sub features for Fog Computing best fit methodology model. Initially numeric values are assigned to the Fog computing element classification features for each product. These values are determined by converting semantic to deterministic numeric values as shown in Table 5.

Cloud product score as per customer requirements is illustrated in the graphs below. This is calculated by the values of each element for each product. Numeric values for an ideal cloud product are also displayed, as shown in Table 6. These can help the Cloud product consumer to make calculated decision.

Figure 3 illustrates the four Cloud Fog products and the ideal Fog computing product.

From the Fog Product Score graph, Products 1, 2 and 3 score low to average on most Fog element features and hence can be rejected, while Product 4 scores relatively higher in comparison so can be a good fit as per the user requirements. Product 4 comes across as being relatively close to an ideal Cloud product score, hence can be chosen as the Fog product to deploy and implement by the user. In this manner, any product can be easily compared and an analytical judgment can be established.

## CONCLUSION

This paper presents a survey of the academic literature on Fog Computing. A new Fog computing taxonomy model is proposed to determine the best fit cloud Fog product evaluation for the cloud service consumers. The mandatory Fog elements are chosen to determine the score of Fog computing products as per four major

*Table 6. Product score calculation for fog elements*

| Element/Products | Product #1 | Product #2 | Product #3 | Product #4 | Ideal Product |
|---|---|---|---|---|---|
| #1 Deployment Model | 5 | 6 | 9 | 11 | 12 |
| #2 Technical Features | 11 | 16 | 14 | 21 | 24 |
| #3 Security Architecture | 7 | 8 | 13 | 18 | 18 |
| #4 Service model | 13 | 12 | 15 | 19 | 22 |
| Score | 36 | 42 | 51 | 69 | 76 |

*Figure 3. Fog product scores*

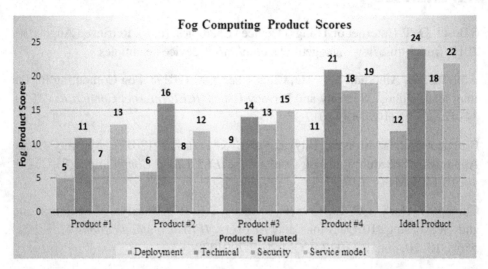

elements as Deployment models, Technical Features, Security Architecture and Service Model. The proposed Cloud product evaluation model calculates and helps decide on choosing the best fit Fog computing product. Future research can be aimed at devising a similar model suitable for evaluating Cloud computing service product offerings using Cloud feature elements and sub-features. Yet another future research area can be for real-time Cloud application services.

# REFERENCES

6 Best I. O. T. (Internet of Things) Devices Examples. (n.d.). Retrieved August 30, 2018, from https://www.gadgetranks.com/iot/iot-devices-examples

Alrawais, A., Alhothaily, A., Hu, C., & Cheng, X. (2017). Fog Computing for the Internet of Things: Security and Privacy Issues. *IEEE Internet Computing*, *21*(2), 34–42. doi:10.1109/MIC.2017.37

Bittencourt, Diaz-Montes, Buyya, Rana, & Parashar. (2017). Mobility-Aware Application Scheduling in Fog Computing. *IEEE Cloud Computing, 4*(2), 26-35. doi:10.1109/MCC.2017.27

Chiang, M., Ha, S., i, C.-L., Risso, F., & Zhang, T. (2017). Clarifying Fog Computing and Networking: 10 Questions and Answers. *IEEE Communications Magazine*, *55*(4), 18–20. doi:10.1109/MCOM.2017.7901470

Dantu, K., Ko, S., & Ziarek, S. (2017). RAINA: Reliability and Adaptability in Android for Fog Computing. *IEEE Communications Magazine*, *55*(4), 41–45. doi:10.1109/MCOM.2017.1600901

Deng, R., Lu, R., Lai, C., Luan, T. H., & Liang, H. (2016). Optimal Workload Allocation in Fog-Cloud Computing Toward Balanced Delay and Power Consumption. *IEEE Internet of Things Journal*, *3*(6), 1171–1181. doi:10.1109/JIOT.2016.2565516

Edge/Fog Computing Trends Analysis: Decentralized Cooperative and Data Centric IoT Platform by Yoko Ono. (n.d.). Retrieved June 02, 2017, from http://www.idc.com/getdoc.jsp?containerId=JPE40927316

Etemad, M., Aazam, M., & St-Hilaire, M. (2017). Using DEVS for modeling and simulating a Fog Computing environment. *IEEE International Conference on Computing, Networking and Communications (ICNC)*. doi: 10.1109/ICCNC.2017.7876242

Farahania, B., Farshad, F., Changc, V., Mustafa, B., Constante, N., & Mankodiya, K. (2018). Towards Fog-driven IoT eHealth: Promises and challenges of IoT in medicine and healthcare. *Future Generation Computer Systems*, *78*, 659–676. doi:10.1016/j.future.2017.04.036

García, M., Fernández, P., Ruiz-Cortés, A., Dustdar, S., & Toro, M. (2017). Edge and Cloud Pricing for the Sharing Economy. *IEEE Internet Computing*, *21*(2), 78–84. doi:10.1109/MIC.2017.24

Gu, L., Zeng, D., Guo, S., Barnawi, A., & Xiang, Y. (2017). Cost Efficient Resource Management in Fog Computing Supported Medical Cyber-Physical System. *IEEE Transactions on Emerging Topics in Computing*, 5(1), 108–119. doi:10.1109/TETC.2015.2508382

Hao, Z., Novak, E., Yi, S., & Li, Q. (2017). Challenges and Software Architecture for Fog Computing. *IEEE Internet Computing*, 21(2), 44–53. doi:10.1109/MIC.2017.26

Hofer, C. N., & Karagiannis, G. (2011). Cloud Computing Services: Taxonomy and Comparison. *International Journal of Internet Server Applications*, 2(2), 81–94. doi:10.100713174-011-0027-x

Li, C.-S., Darema, F., & Chang, V. (2018). Distributed behavior model orchestration in cognitive internet of things solution. *Enterprise Information Systems*, 12(4), 414–434. doi:10.1080/17517575.2017.1355984

Li, T., Zhao, M., Liu, A., & Huang, C. (2017). On Selecting Vehicles as Recommenders for Vehicular Social Networks. *IEEE Access: Practical Innovations, Open Solutions*, 5, 5539–5555. doi:10.1109/ACCESS.2017.2678512

Linthicum, D. (2017). Connecting Fog and Cloud Computing. *IEEE Cloud Computing*, 4(2), 18–20. doi:10.1109/MCC.2017.37

Lu, R., Heung, K., Lashkari, A. H., & Ghorbani, A. A. (2017). A Lightweight Privacy-Preserving Data Aggregation Scheme for Fog Computing-Enhanced IoT. *IEEE Access: Practical Innovations, Open Solutions*, 5, 3302–3312. doi:10.1109/ACCESS.2017.2677520

Moreno-Vozmediano, R., Montero, R. S., Huedo, E., & Llorente, I. M. (2017). Cross-Site Virtual Network in Cloud and Fog Computing. *IEEE Cloud Computing*, 4(2), 46–54. doi:10.1109/MCC.2017.28

Satyanarayanan, M. (2017). Emergence of Edge Computing. *IEEE Computer Communications*, 50(1), 30–39. doi:10.1109/MC.2017.9

Sill, A. (2017). Standards at the Edge of the Cloud. *IEEE Cloud Computing*, 4(2), 63–67. doi:10.1109/MCC.2017.23

Xiao, Y., & Chau, Z. (2017). Vehicular Fog Computing: Vision and challenges. *IEEE International Conference on Pervasive Computing and Communication Workshops (Percom Workshops)*. doi: 10.1109/PERCOMW.2017.7917508

Yannuzzi, M., Lingen, F., Jain, A., Parellada, O., Flores, M., & Carrera, D. (2017). A New Era for Cities with Fog Computing. *IEEE Internet Commuting, 21*(2), 54-67. doi:10.1109/MIC.2017.25

Youseff, L., Butrico, M., & Silva, D. (2008). Towards a Unified Ontology of Cloud Computing. *IEEE Grid Computing Environments Workshop (GEC 2008).* 10.1109/GCE.2008.4738443

Yousif. (2017). Cloudy, Foggy and Edgy. *IEEE Cloud Computing, 4*(2), 4-5. doi:10.1109/MCC.2017.38

# Compilation of References

6 Best I. O. T. (Internet of Things) Devices Examples. (n.d.). Retrieved August 30, 2018, from https://www.gadgetranks.com/iot/iot-devices-examples

Aazam, M., & Huh, E. N. (2014). Fog computing and smart gateway based communication for cloud of things. *Future Internet of Things and Cloud (FiCloud), 2014 International Conference on*, 464–470.

Aazam, M., & Huh, E. N. (2015). Fog computing micro datacenter based dynamic resource estimation and pricing model for iot. *IEEE 29th International Conference on Advanced Information Networking and Applications*, 687–694.

Aazam, M., & Huh, E.-N. (2015). Fog computing micro datacenter based dynamic resource estimation and pricing model for IoT. *IEEE 29th International Conference on Advanced Information Networking and Applications*, 687–694.

Alhamad, M., Dillon, T., & Chang, E. (2010, April). Conceptual SLA framework for cloud computing. In *Digital Ecosystems and Technologies (DEST), 2010 4th IEEE International Conference on* (pp. 606-610). IEEE. 10.1109/DEST.2010.5610586

AL-Hawawreh, M., Moustafa, N., & Sitnikova, E. (2018). Identification of malicious activities in industrial internet of things based on deep learning models. *Journal of Information Security and Applications*, *41*, 1–11. doi:10.1016/j.jisa.2018.05.002

Alrawais, A., Alhothaily, A., Hu, C., & Chang, X. (2017). Fog Computing for the Internet of Things: Security and Privacy Issues. IEEE Internet Computing, 21, 34-42.

Alrawais, A., Alhothaily, A., Hu, C., & Cheng, X. (2017). Fog Computing for the Internet of Things: Security and Privacy Issues. *IEEE Internet Computing*, *21*(2), 34–42. doi:10.1109/MIC.2017.37

Alturki, R., & Mehmood, R. (2012). *Using Cross-Layer Techniques for Communication Systems. Using Cross-Layer Techniques for Communication Systems*. Information Science Reference; doi:10.4018/978-1-4666-0960-0

Amanatullah, Y., Lim, C., Ipung, H., & Juliandri, A. (2011). *Toward Cloud Computing Reference Architecture*. Academic Press.

Antonić, A., Marjanović, M., Pripužić, K., & Žarko, I. P. (2016). A mobile crowd sensing ecosystem enabled by CUPUS: Cloud-based publish/subscribe middleware for the Internet of Things. *Future Generation Computer Systems*, *56*, 22–607. doi:10.1016/j.future.2015.08.005

Antunes, N., & Vieira, M. (2013). SOA-scanner: An integrated tool to detect vulnerabilities in service-based infrastructures. *Proceedings - IEEE 10th International Conference on Services Computing, SCC 2013*, 280–287. 10.1109/SCC.2013.28

Applications, F. C., Zheng, Z., Zhou, T. C., Member, S., Lyu, M. R., King, I., & Member, S. (2012). Component Ranking for. *IEEE Transactions on Services Computing*, *5*(4), 540–550.

Ateniese, G., Burns, R., Curtmola, R., Herring, J., Kissner, L., Peterson, Z., & Song, D. (2007). Provable data possession at untrusted stores. *Proc. of CCS'07*, 598–609. 10.1145/1315245.1315318

Azure. (2018). *Data Security and Encryption Best Practices*. Retrieved April 17, 2018, from https://docs.microsoft.com/en-us/azure/security/azure-security-data-encryption-best-practices

Bader, A., Ghazzai, H., Kadri, A., & Alouini, M.-S. (2016). Front-end intelligence for large-scale application-oriented Internet-of-things. *IEEE Access: Practical Innovations, Open Solutions*, *4*, 3257–3272. doi:10.1109/ACCESS.2016.2580623

Badger, L., Grance, T., Patt-Corner, R., & Voas, J. (2012). *NIST's cloud computing synopsis and recommendations*. Academic Press.

Bakshi, K. (2009). *Cisco cloud computing-data center strategy, architecture, and solutions*. Retrieved from http://www. cisco. com/web/strategy/docs/gov/ CiscoCloudComputing_WP. pdf

Balfanz, D., Smetters, D. K., Stewart, P., & Wong, H. C. (2002). Talking to strangers: authentication in ad-hoc wireless networks. *Network and Distributed System Security Symposium (NDSS)*.

Barillaud, F. (2015). *IBM cloud technologies : How they all fit together*. Retrieved April 3, 2017, from https://www.ibm.com/developerworks/cloud/library/cl-cloud-technology-basics/

Bertion, E., Paci, F., & Ferrini, R. (2009, March). Privacy-Preserving Digital Identity Management for Cloud Computing. IEEE Computer Society Data Engineering Bulletin, 1-4.

Beston, C. (2015). *What are the business impacts of cloud computing?* Retrieved April 3, 2017, from http://www.pwc.com/us/en/issues/cloud-computing/functional-changes.html

Bianco, P., Lewis, G. A., & Merson, P. (2008). *Service level agreements in service-oriented architecture environments (No. CMU/SEI-2008-TN-021)*. Carnegie-Mellon Univ Software Engineering Inst. doi:10.21236/ADA528751

Bittencourt, Diaz-Montes, Buyya, Rana, & Parashar. (2017). Mobility-Aware Application Scheduling in Fog Computing. *IEEE Cloud Computing, 4*(2), 26-35. doi:10.1109/MCC.2017.27

Blaze, M., Kannan, S., Lee, I., Sokolsky, O., Smith, J. M., Keromytis, A. D., & Lee, W. (2009). Dynamic Trust Management. *IEEE Computer, 42*(2), 44–52. doi:10.1109/MC.2009.51

Bonomi. (2011). Connected vehicles, the internet of things, and fog computing. *VANET 2011*.

Bonomi. (2012). *Fog Computing and Its Role in the Internet of Things*. ACM.

Bonomi, F., Milito, R., Natarajan, P., & Zhu, J. (2014). *Fog computing: A platform for Internet of Things and analytics. In Big Data and Internet of Things: A Roadmap for Smart Environments (Studies in Computational Intelligence)* (pp. 169–186). New York: Springer.

Bonomi, F., Milito, R., Zhu, J., & Addepalli, S. (2012). Fog computing and its role in the internet of things. *Proceedings of the first edition of the MCC workshop on Mobile cloud computing*, 13-16. 10.1145/2342509.2342513

Bos, J. W., Castryck, W., Iliashenko, I., & Vercauteren, F. (2017). Privacy-friendly forecasting for the smart grid using homomorphic encryption and the group method of data handling. *International Conference on Cryptology in Africa*, 184–201.

Boss, G. P., & Hall, H. (2008). Cloud Computing. IBM Corporation.

Bowman, M., Debray, S. K., & Peterson, L. L. (1993). Reasoning about naming systems. *ACM Transactions on Programming Languages and Systems*, *15*(5), 795–825. doi:10.1145/161468.161471

Calandriello, G., Papadimitratos, P., Hubaux, J.-P., & Lioy, A. (2007)., Efficient and robust pseudonymous authentication in VANET. *Proc. VANET*, 19–28.

Cao, Y., Hou, P., Brown, D., Wang, J., & Chen, S. (2015). Distributed analytics and edge intelligence: Pervasive health monitoring at the era of fog computing. *Proc. ACM Workshop Mobile Big Data*, 43–48.

Cardellini, V., Grassi, V., Presti, F. L., & Nardelli, M. (2015). On qos-aware scheduling of data stream applications over fog computing infrastructures. *IEEE Symposium on Computers and Communication (ISCC)*, 271–276.

Casola, V., De Benedictis, A., Erascu, M., Modic, J., & Rak, M. (2016). Automatically Enforcing Security SLAs in the Cloud. *IEEE Transactions on Services Computing, 1374*, 1–15.

Chanak, P., Banerjee, I., & Sherratt, R. S. (2016). Mobile sink based fault diagnosis scheme for wireless sensor networks. *Journal of Systems and Software*, *119*, 45–57. doi:10.1016/j.jss.2016.05.041

Chandana. (2013). *Cloud Computing Architecture*. Author.

Chang, C., & Tsai, H.-C. (2010). An anonymous and self-verified mobile authentication with authenticated key agreement for large-scale wireless networks. *IEEE Transactions on Wireless Communications*, *9*(11), 3346–3353. doi:10.1109/TWC.2010.092410.090022

Charlton, S. (2008). Cloud computing and the next generation of enterprise architecture. *Cloud Computing Expo*.

Chiang, M., Ha, S., i, C.-L., Risso, F., & Zhang, T. (2017). Clarifying Fog Computing and Networking: 10 Questions and Answers. *IEEE Communications Magazine*, *55*(4), 18–20. doi:10.1109/MCOM.2017.7901470

Chiang, M., & Zhang, T. (2016). *Fog and IoT: An overview of research opportunities*. IEEE Internet of Things Journal.

Cirani, S., Ferrari, G., Iotti, N., & Picone, M. (2015). The IoT hub: A fog node for seamless management of heterogeneous connected smart objects. *Proc. 12th Annu. IEEE Int. Conf. Sens., Commun., Netw.-Workshops (SECON Workshops)*, 1–6.

Cirani, S., Ferrari, G., Iotti, N., & Picone, M. (2015). The iot hub: a fog node for seamless management of heterogeneous connected smart objects. *Sensing, Communication, and Networking- Workshops (SECONWorkshops), 2015 12th Annual IEEE International Conference on*, 1–6.

Cisco the network in review. (2015). Retrieved September 02, 2017, from http://newsroom.cisco.com/featurecontent?type=webcontent&articleId=1365576

Cisco. (2015). *Cisco delivers vision of fog computing to accelerate value from billions of connected devices*. Retrieved December 02, 2017, from https://newsroom.cisco.com/press-release-content?type=webcontent&articleId=1334100

Cloud Computing Issues Organizations Must Consider. (n.d.). Retrieved April 3, 2017, from https://www.globaldatasentinel.com/the-latest/data-security-news/cloud-computing-issues-organizations-must-consider/

Cong, W., Qian, W., Kui, R., & Wenjing, L. (2010). Privacy-Preserving Public Auditing for Data Storage Security in Cloud Computing. *INFOCOM, 2010 Proceedings IEEE*, 1-9.

CSA. (1999). Security research alliance to promote network security. *Network Security*, (2): 3–4. doi:10.1016/S1353-4858(99)90042-9

Damiani, E., Vimercati, D. C., Paraboshi, S., Samarati, P., & Violante, F. (2002). A reputation-based approach for choosing reliable resources in peer-to-peer networks. *Proc. of the 9th ACM conference on Computer and communications security*, 207-216.

Dantu, K., Ko, S., & Ziarek, S. (2017). RAINA: Reliability and Adaptability in Android for Fog Computing. *IEEE Communications Magazine*, 55(4), 41–45. doi:10.1109/MCOM.2017.1600901

Data Center Companies. (2016). Retrieved November, 9, 2017, from https://www.datacenters.com/ directory/companies

Deane, F., Barrelle, K., Henderson, R., & Mahar, D. (2005). Perceived acceptability of biometric security systems. *Computers & Security*, 14(3), 225–231. doi:10.1016/0167-4048(95)00005-S

Deng, R., Lu, R., Lai, C., Luan, T. H., & Liang, H. (2016). Optimal Workload Allocation in Fog-Cloud Computing Toward Balanced Delay and Power Consumption. *IEEE Internet of Things Journal, 3*(6), 1171–1181. doi:10.1109/JIOT.2016.2565516

Díaz, M., Martín, C., & Rubio, B. (2016). State-of-the-art, challenges, and open issues in the integration of Internet of Things and cloud computing. *Journal of Network and Computer Applications, 67*, 99–117. doi:10.1016/j.jnca.2016.01.010

Dong, M. T., & Zhou, X. (2016). Fog Computing. *Comprehensive Approach for Security Data Theft Attack Using Elliptic Curve Cryptography and Decoy Technology, 3*, 1–14.

DRAFT, F. P. (2009). *Recommended security controls for federal information systems and organizations*. NIST Special Publication, 800, 53.

Dsouza, C., Ahn, G. J., & Taguinod, M. (2014). Policy-driven security management for fog computing: Preliminary framework and a case study. *Information Reuse and Integration (IRI), 2014 IEEE 15th International Conference on*, 16–23.

Dsouza, C., Ahn, G. J., & Taguinod, M. (2014). Policy-driven security management for fog computing: preliminary framework and a case study. *Proceedings of the 2014 IEEE 15th International Conference on Information Reuse and Integration*. 10.1109/IRI.2014.7051866

Edge/Fog Computing Trends Analysis: Decentralized Cooperative and Data Centric IoT Platform by Yoko Ono. (n.d.). Retrieved June 02, 2017, from http://www.idc.com/getdoc.jsp?containerId=JPE40927316

Etemad, M., Aazam, M., & St-Hilaire, M. (2017). Using DEVS for modeling and simulating a Fog Computing environment. *IEEE International Conference on Computing, Networking and Communications (ICNC)*. doi: 10.1109/ICCNC.2017.7876242

European Network and Information Security Agency (ENISA). (2009). *Cloud Computing: Cloud Computing: Benefits, Risks and recommendations for Information Security*. Report No: 2009. Author.

Fadlullah, Z., Fouda, M., Kato, N., Takeuchi, A., Iwasaki, N., & Nozaki, Y. (2011). Toward intelligent machine-to-machine communications in smart grid. *Communications Magazine, IEEE, 49*(4), 60–65. doi:10.1109/MCOM.2011.5741147

Farahania, B., Farshad, F., Changc, V., Mustafa, B., Constante, N., & Mankodiya, K. (2018). Towards Fog-driven IoT eHealth: Promises and challenges of IoT in medicine and healthcare. *Future Generation Computer Systems, 78*, 659–676. doi:10.1016/j.future.2017.04.036

Foerster, J. (2015). Towards realizing video aware wireless networks. *Intel Technol. J., 19*(3), 6–25.

Fog Computing and Internet of Things: Extend the Cloud to Where the Things Are. (n.d.). Available: http://www.cisco.com/ dam/en_us/solutions/trends/iot/docs/computing-overview.pdf

Freitas, A. L., Parlavantzas, N., & Pazat, J. L. (2012, June). An integrated approach for specifying and enforcing slas for cloud services. In *Cloud Computing (CLOUD), 2012 IEEE 5th International Conference on* (pp. 376-383). IEEE.

Furht, B., & Escalante, A. (2010). *Handbook of Cloud Computing*. Springer; doi:10.1007/978-1-4419-6524-0

García, M., Fernández, P., Ruiz-Cortés, A., Dustdar, S., & Toro, M. (2017). Edge and Cloud Pricing for the Sharing Economy. *IEEE Internet Computing, 21*(2), 78–84. doi:10.1109/MIC.2017.24

Gentry, C. (2009). Fully homomorphic encryption using ideal lattices. *STOC, 9*, 169–178.

Ghazizadeh, P., Olariu, S., Zadeh, A. G., & El-Tawab, S. (2015). Towards Fault-Tolerant Job Assignment in Vehicular Cloud. *Proceedings - 2015 IEEE International Conference on Services Computing, SCC 2015*, 17–24. 10.1109/SCC.2015.13

Gia, T. N., Jiang, M., Rahmani, A.-M., Westerlund, T., Liljeberg, P., & Tenhunen, H. (2015). Fog Computing in healthcare Internet of Things: A case study on ECG feature extraction. *Proc. IEEE Int. Conf. Comput. Inf. Technol. Ubiquitous Comput. Commun. Dependable, Auton. Secure Comput. Pervasive Intell. Comput. (CIT/IUCC/DASC/PICOM)*, 356–363.

Gou, Q., Yan, L., Liu, Y., & Li, Y. (2013). Construction and Strategies in IoT Security System. *IEEE International Conference on Green Computing and Communications and IEEE Internet of Things and IEEE Cyber*, 1129-1132. 10.1109/GreenCom-iThings-CPSCom.2013.195

Gu, L., Zeng, D., Guo, S., Barnawi, A., & Xiang, Y. (2015). Cost-efficient resource management in fog computing supported medical cps. *IEEE Transactions on Emerging Topics in Computing*.

Gubbi, J., Buyya, R., Marusic, S., & Palaniswami, M. (2013). Internet of Things (IoT): A Vision, Architectural Elements, and Future Directions. *Future Generation Computer Systems*, *29*(7), 1645-1660.

Gu, L., Zeng, D., Guo, S., Barnawi, A., & Xiang, Y. (2017). Cost Efficient Resource Management in Fog Computing Supported Medical Cyber-Physical System. *IEEE Transactions on Emerging Topics in Computing*, *5*(1), 108–119. doi:10.1109/TETC.2015.2508382

Hao, Z., Novak, E., Yi, S., & Li, Q. (2017). Challenges and Software Architecture for Fog Computing. *IEEE Internet Computing*, *21*(2), 44–53. doi:10.1109/MIC.2017.26

Hasselmeyer, P., Mersch, H., Koller, B., Quyen, H. N., Schubert, L., & Wieder, P. (2007, October). Implementing an SLA negotiation framework. In *Proceedings of the eChallenges Conference (e-2007)* (Vol. 4, pp. 154-161). Academic Press.

HCL. (2016). *Cloud architecture: What is cloud computing technology architecture?* HCL.

He, D., Ma, M., Zhang, Y., Chen, C., & Bu, J. (2011). A strong user authentication scheme with smart cards for wireless communications. *Computer Communications*, *34*(3), 367–374. doi:10.1016/j.comcom.2010.02.031

Hofer, C. N., & Karagiannis, G. (2011). Cloud Computing Services: Taxonomy and Comparison. *International Journal of Internet Server Applications*, *2*(2), 81–94. doi:10.100713174-011-0027-x

Hong, K., Lillethun, D., Ramachandran, U., Ottenwälder, B., & Koldehofe, B. (2013). Mobile fog: A programming model for large-scale applications on the internet of things. *Proceedings of the second ACM SIGCOMM workshop on Mobile cloud computing*, 15–20. 10.1145/2491266.2491270

Hong, K., Lillethun, D., Ramachandran, U., Ottenwälder, B., & Koldehofe, B. (2013). Mobile fog: A programming model for large-scale applications on the Internet of Things. *Proc. 2nd ACM SIGCOMM Workshop Mobile Cloud Comput.*, 15–20.

Hou, X., Li, Y., Chen, M., Wu, D., Jin, D., & Chen, S. (2016). Vehicular fog computing: A viewpoint of vehicles as the infrastructures. *IEEE Transactions on Vehicular Technology*, *65*(6), 3860–3873. doi:10.1109/TVT.2016.2532863

Huang, Z., Lin, K. J., Zhang, J., Nie, W., & Han, L. (2013). Performance diagnosis for SOA on hybrid cloud using the Markov network model. *Proceedings - IEEE 6th International Conference on Service-Oriented Computing and Applications, SOCA 2013*, 17–24. 10.1109/SOCA.2013.55

Ismail, A., Yan, J., & Shen, J. (2011). Analyzing fault-impact region of composite service for supporting fault handling process. *Proceedings - 2011 IEEE International Conference on Services Computing, SCC 2011*, 290–297. 10.1109/SCC.2011.51

Jain, A., Bolle, R., & Pankanti, S. (Eds.). (1998). *Biometrics: Personal identification in networked society*. Dordrecht, The Netherlands: Kluwer.

Jalali, F., Hinton, K., Ayre, R., Alpcan, T., & Tucker, R. S. (2016, May). Fog computing may help to save energy in cloud computing. *IEEE Journal on Selected Areas in Communications*, *34*(5), 1728–1739. doi:10.1109/JSAC.2016.2545559

Josang, A., Ismail, R., & Boyd, C. (2007). A survey of trust and reputation systems for online service provision. *Decision Support Systems*, *43*(2), 618–644. doi:10.1016/j.dss.2005.05.019

Joshi, J. B. D., Bhatti, R., Bertino, E., & Ghafoor, A. (2004). Access Control Language for Multi-domain Environments. *IEEE Internet Computing*, *8*(6), 40–50. doi:10.1109/MIC.2004.53

Juels, A., Burton, J., & Kaliski, S. (2007). Pors: Proofs of retrievability for large files. *Proc. of CCS'07*, 584–597. 10.1145/1315245.1315317

Kamalinejad, P., Mahapatra, C., Sheng, Z., Mirabbasi, S., Leung, V. C., & Guan, Y. L. (2015). Wireless energy harvesting for the Internet of Things. *IEEE Communications Magazine*, *53*(6), 102–108. doi:10.1109/MCOM.2015.7120024

Keller, A., & Ludwig, H. (2003). The WSLA framework: Specifying and monitoring service level agreements for web services. *Journal of Network and Systems Management*, *11*(1), 57–81. doi:10.1023/A:1022445108617

Kepes, B. (2011b). Revoution Not Evolution How Cloud computing differs from traditional IT and why it matters. *Diversity Limited.* Retrieved from https://docs. google.com/viewer?a=v&q=cache:2Y0nj1_GULMJ:broadcast.rackspace.com/ hosting_knowledge/whitepapers/Revolution_Not_Evolution-Whitepaper.pdf+rev olution+not+evolution+how+cloud+computing+differs+from+traditional+it+a nd+why+it+matters&hl=en&gl=us&p

Kepes, B. (2013). *Understanding the Cloud Computing Stack SaaS, Paas, IaaS.* Retrieved April 3, 2017, from https://www.rackspace.com/knowledge_center/sites/ default/files/whitepaper_pdf/Understanding-the-Cloud-Computing-Stack.pdf

Kepes, B. (2011a). A Primer for "The Cloud.". *Cloud University, 53*(11), 43.

Khajeh-Hosseini, A., Greenwood, D., Smith, J. W., & Sommerville, I. (2012). The Cloud Adoption Toolkit: Supporting cloud adoption decisions in the enterprise. *Software, Practice & Experience, 42*(4), 447–465. doi:10.1002pe.1072

Khan, R., & Hasan, R. (2015). Fuzzy Authentication Using Interaction Provenance in Service Oriented Computing. *Proceedings - 2015 IEEE International Conference on Services Computing, SCC 2015,* 170–177. 10.1109/SCC.2015.32

Kim, W. (2013). *Cloud computing architecture.* Academic Press. doi:10.1504/ IJWGS.2013.055724

Kitchin, R. (2014). The real-time city? Big data and smart urbanism. *GeoJournal, 79*(1), 1–14. doi:10.100710708-013-9516-8

Ko, M., Ahn, G.-J., & Shehab, M. (2009). Privacy-Enhanced User-Centric Identity Management. *Proceedings of IEEE International Conference on Communications,* 998-1002.

Kundra, V. (2011). *Federal cloud computing strategy.* Academic Press.

Law, Y. W., Palaniswami, M., Kounga, G., & Lo, A. (2013). Wake: Key management scheme for wide-area measurement systems in smart grid. *Communications Magazine, IEEE, 51*(1), 34–41. doi:10.1109/MCOM.2013.6400436

Lee, K., Kim, D., Ha, D., Rajput, U., & Oh, H. (2015). *On security and privacy issues of fog computing supported Internet of Things environment.* Academic Press. doi:10.1109/NOF.2015.7333287

Lee, W., Nam, K., Roh, H. G., & Kim, S. H. (2016). A gateway based fog computing architecture for wireless sensors and actuator networks. *2016 18th International Conference on Advanced Communication Technology (ICACT)*, 210–213.

Li, C.-S., Darema, F., & Chang, V. (2018). Distributed behavior model orchestration in cognitive internet of things solution. *Enterprise Information Systems*, *12*(4), 414–434. doi:10.1080/17517575.2017.1355984

Li, L. (2012). Study on Security Architecture in the Internet of Things. *International Conference on Measurement Information and Control*, *1*, 374–377.

Linthicum, D. (2017). Connecting Fog and Cloud Computing. *IEEE Cloud Computing*, *4*(2), 18–20. doi:10.1109/MCC.2017.37

Li, T., Zhao, M., Liu, A., & Huang, C. (2017). On Selecting Vehicles as Recommenders for Vehicular Social Networks. *IEEE Access: Practical Innovations, Open Solutions*, *5*, 5539–5555. doi:10.1109/ACCESS.2017.2678512

Liu, F., Tong, J., Mao, J., Bohn, R., Messina, J., Badger, L., & Leaf, D. (2011). NIST Cloud Computing Reference Architecture. *National Institute of Standards and Technology Special Publication*, *500*(292), 35.

Lopez, P. G., Montresor, A., Epema, D., Iamnitchi, A., & Felber, P. (2015). Edge-centric Computing : Vision and Challenges. *Computer Communication Review*, *45*(5), 37–42. doi:10.1145/2831347.2831354

Luca, B., Bistarelli, S., & Vaccarelli, A. (2002). *Biometrics authentication with smartcard*. IIT TR-08/2002. Retrieved October, 9, 2017, from http://www.iat.cnr.it/attivita/progetti/parametri biomedici.html

Lu, R., Heung, K., Lashkari, A. H., & Ghorbani, A. A. (2017). A Lightweight Privacy-Preserving Data Aggregation Scheme for Fog Computing-Enhanced IoT. *IEEE Access: Practical Innovations, Open Solutions*, *5*, 3302–3312. doi:10.1109/ACCESS.2017.2677520

Lu, R., Liang, X., Li, X., Lin, X., & Shen, X. (2012). Eppa: An efficient and privacy-preserving aggregation scheme for secure smart grid communications. *IEEE Transactions on Parallel and Distributed Systems*, *23*(9), 1621–1631. doi:10.1109/TPDS.2012.86

Lu, R., Lin, X., Liang, X., & Shen, X. (2010). FLIP: An efficient privacy-preserving protocol for finding like-minded vehicles on the road. *Proc. IEEE Globecom*, 1–5.

Magurawalage, C. S., Yang, K., & Wang, K. (2015). *Aqua computing: Coupling computing and communications*. Available: https://arxiv.org/abs/1510.07250

Mahmud, M.R., Afrin, M., Razzaque, M.A., Hassan, M.M., Alelaiwi, A., & Alrubaian, M. (2016). Maximizing quality of experience through context-aware mobile application scheduling in cloudlet infrastructure. *Software: Practice and Experience, 46*(11), 1525–1545.

Manikandakumar, M., & Ramanujam, E. (2018). Security and Privacy Challenges in Big Data Environment. In *Handbook of Research on Network Forensics and Analysis Techniques* (pp. 315–325). IGI Global. doi:10.4018/978-1-5225-4100-4.ch017

Maple, C. (2017). Security and privacy in the internet of things. *Journal of Cyber Policy, 2*(2), 155–184. doi:10.1080/23738871.2017.1366536

Marilly, E., Martinot, O., Betgé-Brezetz, S., & Delègue, G. (2002). Requirements for service level agreement management. In *IP Operations and Management, 2002 IEEE Workshop on* (pp. 57-62). IEEE. 10.1109/IPOM.2002.1045756

Mell, P., & Grance, T. (2011). *The NIST definition of cloud computing*. Academic Press.

Mell, P., Grance, T., & Grance, T. (2011). The NIST Definition of Cloud Computing Recommendations of the National Institute of Standards and Technology. *National Institute of Standards and Technology Special Publication 800-145, 2*, 7. Retrieved from http://scholar.google.com/scholar?hl=en&btnG=Search&q=intitle:The+NIST+Definition+of+Cloud+Computing+Recommendations+of+the+National+Institute+of+Standards+and+Technology#6

Miller, M. (2009). *Cloud Computing: Web-Based Applications That Change the Way You Work and Collaborate Online*. Que Publishing Company; doi:10.1109/CLOUD.2009.53

Mishra, N., Siddiqui, S., & Tripathi, J. P. (2015). A Compendium Over Cloud Computing Cryptographic Algorithms and Security Issues. *Int. J. Inf. Technol. Bharati Vidyapeeth's Inst. Comput. Appl. Manag., 7*(1), 973–5658.

Modi, C., Patel, D., Patel, H., Borisaniya, B., Patel, A., & Rajarajan, M. (2013). A survey of intrusion detection techniques in Cloud. *Journal of Network and Computer Applications*, *36*(1), 42–57. doi:10.1016/j.jnca.2012.05.003

Mohamed, M., Anya, O., Sakairi, T., Tata, S., Mandagere, N., & Ludwig, H. (2016). The rSLA framework: Monitoring and enforcement of service level agreements for cloud services. *Proceedings - 2016 IEEE International Conference on Services Computing, SCC 2016*, 625–632. 10.1109/SCC.2016.87

Mondal, S. K., Yin, X., Muppala, J. K., Alonso Lopez, J., & Trivedi, K. S. (2015). Defects per million computation in service-oriented environments. *IEEE Transactions on Services Computing*, *8*(1), 32–46. doi:10.1109/TSC.2013.52

Moreno-Vozmediano, R., Montero, R. S., Huedo, E., & Llorente, I. M. (2017). Cross-Site Virtual Network in Cloud and Fog Computing. *IEEE Cloud Computing*, *4*(2), 46–54. doi:10.1109/MCC.2017.28

Nazmudeen, M. S. H., Wan, A. T., & Buhari, S. M. (2016). Improved throughput for power line communication (plc) for smart meters using fog computing based data aggregation approach. *IEEE International Smart Cities Conference (ISC2)*, 1–4.

Ni, Zhang, Lin, & Shen. (2017). Security, privacy, and fairness infog-based vehicular crowdsensing. *IEEE Commun. Mag.*, *55*(6), 146-152.

NIST. (2016). *Cloud Computing*. NIST.

O'Gorman, L. (2003). Comparing Passwords, Tokens, and Biometrics for User Authentication. *Proceedings of the IEEE*, *91*(12), 2019–2040. doi:10.1109/JPROC.2003.819605

OpenFog Consortium. (2015). Retrieved December 02, 2017, from https://www.openfogconsortium.org

Oracle, A., Paper, W., Enterprise, O., & Solutions, T. (2012). *Cloud Reference Architecture*. Oracle Enterprise Transformation Solutions Series Cloud- An Oracle White Paper.

Osanaiye, O., Chen, S., Yan, Z., Lu, R., Choo, K.-K. R., & Dlodlo, M. (2017). From cloud to fog computing: A review and a conceptual live VM migration framework. *IEEE Access: Practical Innovations, Open Solutions*, *5*, 8284–8300. doi:10.1109/ACCESS.2017.2692960

Oueis, J., Strinati, E. C., Sardellitti, S., & Barbarossa, S. (2015). Small cell clustering for efficient distributed fog computing: A multi-user case. Vehicular Technology Conference (VTC Fall), 2015 IEEE 82nd, 1–5.

Pearson, S. (2013). *Privacy and Security for Cloud Computing*. Academic Press. doi:10.1007/978-1-4471-4189-1

Podio, F. L., & Dunn, J. S. (2001). *Biometric authentication technology*. Retrieved April 2010, from http://www.itl.nist.gov/div893/biometrics/Biometricsfromthemovies.pdf

Polk, T., McKay, K., & Chokhani, S. (2005). *Guidelines for the Selection and Use of Transport Layer Security (TLS) Implementations. NIST Special Publication 800-52 Revision 1*. Gaithersburg, MD: NIST.

Popović, K., & Hocenski, Ž. (2010, May). Cloud computing security issues and challenges. In *MIPRO, 2010 proceedings of the 33rd international convention* (pp. 344-349). IEEE.

Raza, M. (2014). Article. *Analysis of Cloud Computing and Security Challenges*, *1*(6), 104–107.

Rhodes, S. M., & Collins, S. K. (2015). *The organizational impact of presenteeism*. Retrieved April 3, 2017, from https://www.wired.com/insights/2012/11/the-organizational-impact-of-the-cloud/

Rosa, N. S., Cunha, P. R. F., & Justo, G. R. R. (2004). An approach for reasoning and refining non-functional requirements. *Journal of the Brazilian Computer Society*, *10*(1), 59–81. doi:10.1590/S0104-65002004000200006

Sahai, A., Graupner, S., Machiraju, V., & van Moorsel, A. (2003, May). Specifying and monitoring guarantees in commercial grids through SLA. In *Cluster Computing and the Grid, 2003. Proceedings. CCGrid 2003. 3rd IEEE/ACM International Symposium on* (pp. 292-299). IEEE.

Satyanarayanan, M. (2017). Emergence of Edge Computing. *IEEE Computer Communications*, *50*(1), 30–39. doi:10.1109/MC.2017.9

Satyanarayanan, M., Bahl, P., Cáceres, R., & Davies, N. (2009). The case for VM-based cloudlets in mobile computing. *IEEE Pervasive Computing*, *8*(4), 14–23. doi:10.1109/MPRV.2009.82

Sean, W. S., & Vernon, A. (1998). Trusting Trusted Hardware: Towards a Formal Model for Programmable Secure Coprocessors. *Proceedings of the 3rd USENIX Workshop on Electronic Commerce*.

Sehgal, V. K., Patrick, A., Soni, A., & Rajput, L. (2015). *Smart human security framework using Internet of Things, cloud and fog computing. In Intelligent Distributed Computing (Advances in Intelligent Systems and Computing)* (Vol. 321, pp. 251–263). New York: Springer.

Sen, J., & Sengupta, I. (2005). Autonomous Agent-Based Distributed Fault-Tolerant Intrusion Detection System. In *Proceedings of the 2nd International Conference on Distributed Computing and Internet Technology (ICDCIT'05)* (pp. 125-131). Springer. 10.1007/11604655_16

Sen, J. (2010a, August). An Agent-Based Intrusion Detection System for Local Area Networks. *International Journal of Communication Networks and Information Security*, 2(2), 128–140.

Sen, J. (2010b). An Intrusion Detection Architecture for Clustered Wireless Ad Hoc Networks. *Proceedings of the 2nd IEEE International Conference on Intelligence in Communication Systems and Networks (CICSyN'10)*, 202-207.

Sen, J. (2010c). A Robust and Fault-Tolerant Distributed Intrusion Detection System. *Proceedings of the 1st International Conference on Parallel, Distributed and Grid Computing (PDGC'10)*, 123-128.

Sen, J., Sengupta, I., & Chowdhury, P. R. (2006b). An Architecture of a Distributed Intrusion Detection System Using Cooperating Agents. *Proceedings of the International Conference on Computing and Informatics (ICOCI'06)*, 1-6.

Sen, J., Ukil, A., Bera, D., & Pal, A. (2008). A Distributed Intrusion Detection System for Wireless Ad Hoc Networks. *Proceedings of the 16th IEEE International Conference on Networking (ICON'08)*, 1-5.

Seshachala, S. (2015). *Cloud Computing Architecture: an overview*. Academic Press.

Shacham, H., & Waters, B. (2013). Compact proofs of retrievability. *Journal of Cryptology*, 26(3), 442–483. doi:10.100700145-012-9129-2

Shahzad, A., Kim, Y. G., & Elgamoudi, A. (2017). Secure IoT Platform for Industrial Control Systems. In *International Conference on Platform Technology and Service (PlatCon)* (pp. 1-6). IEEE.

Shanhe, Y., Zhengrui, Q., & Qun, L. (2015). Security and Privacy Issues of Fog Computing: A Survey. *Proc. Int'l Conf. Wireless Algorithms Systems and Applications (WASA)*, 685–695.

Sheng, Yang, Yu, & Vasilakos. (2014). A Survey on the IETF Protocol Suite for the Internet of Things: Standards, Challenges, and Opportunities. *Wireless Communications, IEEE, 20*(6), 91-98.

She, W., Yen, I. L., Thuraisingham, B., & Bertino, E. (2013). Security-aware service composition with fine-grained information flow control. *IEEE Transactions on Services Computing, 6*(3), 330–343. doi:10.1109/TSC.2012.3

Shin, D., & Ahn, G.-J. (2005). Role-Based Privilege and Trust Management. *Computer Systems Science and Engineering, 20*(6), 401–410.

Shi, W., Cao, J., Zhang, Q., Li, Y., & Xu, L. (2016). Edge Computing: Vision and Challenges. *IEEE Internet of Things Journal, 3*(5), 637–646. doi:10.1109/JIOT.2016.2579198

Shi, Y., Abhilash, S., & Hwang, K. (2015). Cloudlet mesh for securing mobile fogs from intrusions and network attacks. *3rd IEEE International Conference on Mobile Cloud Computing, Services, and Engineering*, 1096-118.

Sill, A. (2017). Standards at the Edge of the Cloud. *IEEE Cloud Computing, 4*(2), 63–67. doi:10.1109/MCC.2017.23

Sinha, Srivastava, & Gupta. (2013). Performance Based Comparison Study of RSA. *International Journal of Scientific & Engineering Research, 4*(4).

Stojmenovic, I., & Wen, S. (2014). The fog computing paradigm: Scenarios and security issues. *Proc. IEEE Federated Conf. Comput. Sci. Inf. Syst. (FedCSIS)*, 1–8.

Stojmenovic, I., & Wen, S. (2014). The fog computing paradigm: scenarios and security issues. *Proc. of the 2014 Federated Conference on Computer Science and Information Systems (FedCSIS)*, 1-8.

Stojmenovic, I., & Wen, S. (2014). The Fog computing paradigm: Scenarios and security issues. *Proc. Federated Conf. Comput. Sci. Inf.Syst. (FedCSIS)*, 1-8.

Stojmenovic, I., Wen, S., Huang, X., & Luan, H. (2015). An overview of fog computing and its security issues. *Concurrency and Computation*.

Suciu, G., Suciu, V., Martian, A., Craciunescu, R., Vulpe, A., Marcu, I., ... Fratu, O. (2015). Big data, Internet of Things and cloud convergence—An architecture for secure E-health applications. *Journal of Medical Systems, 39*(11), 1–8. doi:10.100710916-015-0327-y PMID:26345453

Tahir, A., Tosi, D., & Morasca, S. (2013). A systematic review on the functional testing of semantic web services. *Journal of Systems and Software, 86*(11), 2877–2889. doi:10.1016/j.jss.2013.06.064

Tan, C., Liu, K., & Sun, L. (2013). A design of evaluation method for SaaS in cloud computing. *Journal of Industrial Engineering and Management, 6*(1), 50–72. doi:10.3926/jiem.661

Tang, B., Chen, Z., Hefferman, G., Wei, T., He, H., & Yang, Q. (2015). A hierarchical distributed fog computing architecture for big data analysis in smart cities. *Proc. ACM ASE BigData Social Inform.*, 28.

TechTarget. (2015). *Confidentiality, integrity, and availability (CIA triad)*. Retrieved April 02, 2018, from:https://whatis.techtarget.com/definition/Confidentiality-integrity-and-availability-CIA

The difference between IaaS and PaaS. (n.d.). Retrieved April 3, 2017, from http://www.qrimp.com/blog/blog.The-Difference-between-IaaS-and-PaaS.html

Tripathi, M. (2015). *Cloud Computing Concepts: IaaS*. Retrieved April 2, 2017, from https://www.mindstick.com/Blog/799/cloud-computing-concepts-iaas

Truong, N. B., Lee, G. M., & Ghamri-Doudane, Y. (2015). Software defined networking-based vehicular adhoc network with fog computing. *IFIP/IEEE International Symposium on Integrated Network Management (IM)*, 1202–1207. 10.1109/INM.2015.7140467

Trusted Computing Group (TCG)'s White Paper. (2010). *Cloud Computing and Security- A Natural Match*. Available online at: http://www.trustedcomputinggroup.org

Tsai, H., Chang, C., & Chan, K. (2009). Roaming across wireless local area networks using SIM-based authentication protocol. *Computer Standards & Interfaces, 31*(2), 381–389. doi:10.1016/j.csi.2008.05.002

Tsai, Y., & Chang, C. (2006). SIM-based subscriber authentication mechanism for wireless local area networks. *Computer Communications*, *29*(10), 1744–1753. doi:10.1016/j.comcom.2005.09.016

Valenzuela, J., Wang, J., & Bissinger, N. (2013). Real-time intrusion detection in power system operations. *Power Systems. IEEE Transactions on*, *28*(2), 1052–1062.

Vaquero, L. M., & Rodero-Merino, L. (2014). Finding your way in the fog: Towards a comprehensive definition of fog computing. *ACM SIGCOMM CCR*, *44*(5), 27–32. doi:10.1145/2677046.2677052

Varghese, B., Wang, N., Barbhuiya, S., Kilpatrick, P., & Nikolopoulos, D. S. (2016). Challenges and Opportunities in Edge Computing. *Proceedings - 2016 IEEE International Conference on Smart Cloud, SmartCloud 2016*, 20–26. 10.1109/SmartCloud.2016.18

Wang, L., Wombacher, A., Pires, L. F., Van Sinderen, M. J., & Chi, C. (2013). Robust client/server shared state interactions of collaborative process with system crash and network failures. *Proceedings - IEEE 10th International Conference on Services Computing, SCC 2013*, 192–199. 10.1109/SCC.2013.39

Wu, L., & Buyya, R. (2012). Service level agreement (SLA) in utility computing systems. IGI Global.

Wu, Z., & Chu, N. (2013). Efficient service re-composition using semantic augmentation for fast cloud fault recovery. *Proceedings - IEEE 10th International Conference on Services Computing, SCC 2013*, 176–183. 10.1109/SCC.2013.78

Wustenhoff, E., & BluePrints, S. (2002). *Service level agreement in the data center*. Sun Microsystems Professional.

Xiao, Y., & Chau, Z. (2017). Vehicular Fog Computing: Vision and challenges. *IEEE International Conference on Pervasive Computing and Communication Workshops (Percom Workshops)*. doi: 10.1109/PERCOMW.2017.7917508

Xiao, M., Zhou, J., Liu, X., & Jiang, M. (2017). A hybrid scheme for fine-grained search and access authorization in fog computing environment. *Sensors (Basel)*, *17*(6), 1–22. doi:10.339017061423 PMID:28629131

Yannuzzi, M., Lingen, F., Jain, A., Parellada, O., Flores, M., & Carrera, D. (2017). A New Era for Cities with Fog Computing. *IEEE Internet Commuting, 21*(2), 54-67. doi:10.1109/MIC.2017.25

Yannuzzi, M., Milito, R., Serral-Gracià, R., Montero, D., & Nemirovsky, M. (2014). Key ingredients in an IoT recipe: Fog computing, cloud computing, and more Fog computing. *Proc. 19th IEEE Int. Workshop Comput.-Aided Modeling Design Commun. Links Netw. (CAMAD)*, 325–329.

Yan, S., Peng, M., & Wang, W. (2016). User access mode selection in fog computing based radio access networks. *IEEE International Conference on Communications (ICC)*, 1–6.

Ye, D., Wu, M., Tang, S., & Yu, R. (2016). Scalable fog computing with service offloading in bus networks. *IEEE 3rd International Conference on Cyber Security and Cloud Computing (CSCloud)*, 247–251.

Yeo, C. S., Buyya, R., de Assuncao, M. D., Yu, J., Sulistio, A., Venugopal, S., & Placek, M. (2007). Utility computing on global grids. *Handbook of Computer Networks*, 110-130.

Yi, S., Hao, Z., Qin, Z., & Li, Q. (2015). Fog computing: Platform and applications. *Proc. 3rd IEEE Workshop Hot Topics Web Syst. Technol. (HotWeb)*, 73–78. 10.1109/HotWeb.2015.22

Yi, S., Qin, Z., & Li, Q. (2015). Security and privacy issues of fog computing: A survey. *Proc. 10th Int. Conf. Wireless Algorithms, Syst.,Appl. (WASA)*, 685-695. 10.1007/978-3-319-21837-3_67

Youseff, L., Butrico, M., & Silva, D. (2008). Towards a Unified Ontology of Cloud Computing. *IEEE Grid Computing Environments Workshop (GEC 2008)*. 10.1109/GCE.2008.4738443

Yousif. (2017). Cloudy, Foggy and Edgy. *IEEE Cloud Computing, 4*(2), 4-5. doi:10.1109/MCC.2017.38

Zeng, D., Gu, L., Guo, S., Cheng, Z., & Yu, S. (2016). Joint optimization of task scheduling and image placement in fog computing supported software-defined embedded system. *IEEE Transactions on Computers*.

Zhai, K., Jiang, B., & Chan, W. K. (2014). Prioritizing test cases for regression testing of location-based services: Metrics, techniques, and case study. *IEEE Transactions on Services Computing*, 7(1), 54–67. doi:10.1109/TSC.2012.40

Zhang, Z. K., Cho, M. C. Y., Wang, C. W., Hsu, C. W., Chen, C. K., & Shieh, S. (2014). IoT security: ongoing challenges and research opportunities. In *Service-Oriented Computing and Applications (SOCA), IEEE 7th International Conference on* (pp. 230-234). IEEE.

Zhang, Y., & Joshi, J. (2009). *Access Control and Trust Management for Emerging Multidomain Environments*. In S. Upadhyay & R. O. Rao (Eds.), *Annals of Emerging Research in Information Assurance, Security and Privacy Services* (pp. 421–452). Emerald Group Publishing.

Zhu, J., Chan, D. S., Prabhu, M. S., Natarajan, P., Hu, H., & Bonomi, F. (2013). Improving web sites performance using edge servers in fog computing architecture. *Service Oriented System Engineering (SOSE), 2013 IEEE 7th International Symposium on*, 320–323.

Zhu, H., Lin, X., Lu, R., Ho, P., & Shen, X. (2008). AEMA: An aggregated emergency message authentication scheme for enhancing the security of vehicular Ad Hoc networks. *Proceedings of the IEEE, ICC*, 1436–1440.

Zhu, X., Chan, D. S., Hu, H., Prabhu, M. S., Ganesan, E., & Bonomi, F. (2015). Improving video performance with edge servers in the fog computing architecture. *Intel Technol. J.*, 19(3), 202–224.

# Related References

To continue our tradition of advancing information science and technology research, we have compiled a list of recommended IGI Global readings. These references will provide additional information and guidance to further enrich your knowledge and assist you with your own research and future publications.

Aasi, P., Rusu, L., & Vieru, D. (2017). The Role of Culture in IT Governance Five Focus Areas: A Literature Review. *International Journal of IT/Business Alignment and Governance, 8*(2), 42-61. doi:10.4018/IJITBAG.2017070103

Abdrabo, A. A. (2018). Egypt's Knowledge-Based Development: Opportunities, Challenges, and Future Possibilities. In A. Alraouf (Ed.), *Knowledge-Based Urban Development in the Middle East* (pp. 80–101). Hershey, PA: IGI Global. doi:10.4018/978-1-5225-3734-2.ch005

Abu Doush, I., & Alhami, I. (2018). Evaluating the Accessibility of Computer Laboratories, Libraries, and Websites in Jordanian Universities and Colleges. *International Journal of Information Systems and Social Change, 9*(2), 44–60. doi:10.4018/IJISSC.2018040104

Adeboye, A. (2016). Perceived Use and Acceptance of Cloud Enterprise Resource Planning (ERP) Implementation in the Manufacturing Industries. *International Journal of Strategic Information Technology and Applications, 7*(3), 24–40. doi:10.4018/IJSITA.2016070102

Adegbore, A. M., Quadri, M. O., & Oyewo, O. R. (2018). A Theoretical Approach to the Adoption of Electronic Resource Management Systems (ERMS) in Nigerian University Libraries. In A. Tella & T. Kwanya (Eds.), *Handbook of Research on Managing Intellectual Property in Digital Libraries* (pp. 292–311). Hershey, PA: IGI Global. doi:10.4018/978-1-5225-3093-0.ch015

Adhikari, M., & Roy, D. (2016). Green Computing. In G. Deka, G. Siddesh, K. Srinivasa, & L. Patnaik (Eds.), *Emerging Research Surrounding Power Consumption and Performance Issues in Utility Computing* (pp. 84–108). Hershey, PA: IGI Global. doi:10.4018/978-1-4666-8853-7.ch005

Afolabi, O. A. (2018). Myths and Challenges of Building an Effective Digital Library in Developing Nations: An African Perspective. In A. Tella & T. Kwanya (Eds.), *Handbook of Research on Managing Intellectual Property in Digital Libraries* (pp. 51–79). Hershey, PA: IGI Global. doi:10.4018/978-1-5225-3093-0.ch004

Agarwal, R., Singh, A., & Sen, S. (2016). Role of Molecular Docking in Computer-Aided Drug Design and Development. In S. Dastmalchi, M. Hamzeh-Mivehroud, & B. Sokouti (Eds.), *Applied Case Studies and Solutions in Molecular Docking-Based Drug Design* (pp. 1–28). Hershey, PA: IGI Global. doi:10.4018/978-1-5225-0362-0.ch001

Ali, O., & Soar, J. (2016). Technology Innovation Adoption Theories. In L. Al-Hakim, X. Wu, A. Koronios, & Y. Shou (Eds.), *Handbook of Research on Driving Competitive Advantage through Sustainable, Lean, and Disruptive Innovation* (pp. 1–38). Hershey, PA: IGI Global. doi:10.4018/978-1-5225-0135-0.ch001

Alsharo, M. (2017). Attitudes Towards Cloud Computing Adoption in Emerging Economies. *International Journal of Cloud Applications and Computing*, 7(3), 44–58. doi:10.4018/IJCAC.2017070102

Amer, T. S., & Johnson, T. L. (2016). Information Technology Progress Indicators: Temporal Expectancy, User Preference, and the Perception of Process Duration. *International Journal of Technology and Human Interaction*, 12(4), 1–14. doi:10.4018/IJTHI.2016100101

Amer, T. S., & Johnson, T. L. (2017). Information Technology Progress Indicators: Research Employing Psychological Frameworks. In A. Mesquita (Ed.), *Research Paradigms and Contemporary Perspectives on Human-Technology Interaction* (pp. 168–186). Hershey, PA: IGI Global. doi:10.4018/978-1-5225-1868-6.ch008

*Related References*

Anchugam, C. V., & Thangadurai, K. (2016). Introduction to Network Security. In D. G., M. Singh, & M. Jayanthi (Eds.), Network Security Attacks and Countermeasures (pp. 1-48). Hershey, PA: IGI Global. doi:10.4018/978-1-4666-8761-5.ch001

Anchugam, C. V., & Thangadurai, K. (2016). Classification of Network Attacks and Countermeasures of Different Attacks. In D. G., M. Singh, & M. Jayanthi (Eds.), Network Security Attacks and Countermeasures (pp. 115-156). Hershey, PA: IGI Global. doi:10.4018/978-1-4666-8761-5.ch004

Anohah, E. (2016). Pedagogy and Design of Online Learning Environment in Computer Science Education for High Schools. *International Journal of Online Pedagogy and Course Design*, 6(3), 39–51. doi:10.4018/IJOPCD.2016070104

Anohah, E. (2017). Paradigm and Architecture of Computing Augmented Learning Management System for Computer Science Education. *International Journal of Online Pedagogy and Course Design*, 7(2), 60–70. doi:10.4018/IJOPCD.2017040105

Anohah, E., & Suhonen, J. (2017). Trends of Mobile Learning in Computing Education from 2006 to 2014: A Systematic Review of Research Publications. *International Journal of Mobile and Blended Learning*, 9(1), 16–33. doi:10.4018/IJMBL.2017010102

Assis-Hassid, S., Heart, T., Reychav, I., & Pliskin, J. S. (2016). Modelling Factors Affecting Patient-Doctor-Computer Communication in Primary Care. *International Journal of Reliable and Quality E-Healthcare*, 5(1), 1–17. doi:10.4018/IJRQEH.2016010101

Bailey, E. K. (2017). Applying Learning Theories to Computer Technology Supported Instruction. In M. Grassetti & S. Brookby (Eds.), *Advancing Next-Generation Teacher Education through Digital Tools and Applications* (pp. 61–81). Hershey, PA: IGI Global. doi:10.4018/978-1-5225-0965-3.ch004

Balasubramanian, K. (2016). Attacks on Online Banking and Commerce. In K. Balasubramanian, K. Mala, & M. Rajakani (Eds.), *Cryptographic Solutions for Secure Online Banking and Commerce* (pp. 1–19). Hershey, PA: IGI Global. doi:10.4018/978-1-5225-0273-9.ch001

Baldwin, S., Opoku-Agyemang, K., & Roy, D. (2016). Games People Play: A Trilateral Collaboration Researching Computer Gaming across Cultures. In K. Valentine & L. Jensen (Eds.), *Examining the Evolution of Gaming and Its Impact on Social, Cultural, and Political Perspectives* (pp. 364–376). Hershey, PA: IGI Global. doi:10.4018/978-1-5225-0261-6.ch017

Banerjee, S., Sing, T. Y., Chowdhury, A. R., & Anwar, H. (2018). Let's Go Green: Towards a Taxonomy of Green Computing Enablers for Business Sustainability. In M. Khosrow-Pour (Ed.), *Green Computing Strategies for Competitive Advantage and Business Sustainability* (pp. 89–109). Hershey, PA: IGI Global. doi:10.4018/978-1-5225-5017-4.ch005

Basham, R. (2018). Information Science and Technology in Crisis Response and Management. In M. Khosrow-Pour, D.B.A. (Ed.), Encyclopedia of Information Science and Technology, Fourth Edition (pp. 1407-1418). Hershey, PA: IGI Global. doi:10.4018/978-1-5225-2255-3.ch121

Batyashe, T., & Iyamu, T. (2018). Architectural Framework for the Implementation of Information Technology Governance in Organisations. In M. Khosrow-Pour, D.B.A. (Ed.), Encyclopedia of Information Science and Technology, Fourth Edition (pp. 810-819). Hershey, PA: IGI Global. doi:10.4018/978-1-5225-2255-3.ch070

Bekleyen, N., & Çelik, S. (2017). Attitudes of Adult EFL Learners towards Preparing for a Language Test via CALL. In D. Tafazoli & M. Romero (Eds.), *Multiculturalism and Technology-Enhanced Language Learning* (pp. 214–229). Hershey, PA: IGI Global. doi:10.4018/978-1-5225-1882-2.ch013

Bennett, A., Eglash, R., Lachney, M., & Babbitt, W. (2016). Design Agency: Diversifying Computer Science at the Intersections of Creativity and Culture. In M. Raisinghani (Ed.), *Revolutionizing Education through Web-Based Instruction* (pp. 35–56). Hershey, PA: IGI Global. doi:10.4018/978-1-4666-9932-8.ch003

Bergeron, F., Croteau, A., Uwizeyemungu, S., & Raymond, L. (2017). A Framework for Research on Information Technology Governance in SMEs. In S. De Haes & W. Van Grembergen (Eds.), *Strategic IT Governance and Alignment in Business Settings* (pp. 53–81). Hershey, PA: IGI Global. doi:10.4018/978-1-5225-0861-8.ch003

Bhatt, G. D., Wang, Z., & Rodger, J. A. (2017). Information Systems Capabilities and Their Effects on Competitive Advantages: A Study of Chinese Companies. *Information Resources Management Journal, 30*(3), 41–57. doi:10.4018/IRMJ.2017070103

*Related References*

Bogdanoski, M., Stoilkovski, M., & Risteski, A. (2016). Novel First Responder Digital Forensics Tool as a Support to Law Enforcement. In M. Hadji-Janev & M. Bogdanoski (Eds.), *Handbook of Research on Civil Society and National Security in the Era of Cyber Warfare* (pp. 352–376). Hershey, PA: IGI Global. doi:10.4018/978-1-4666-8793-6.ch016

Boontarig, W., Papasratorn, B., & Chutimaskul, W. (2016). The Unified Model for Acceptance and Use of Health Information on Online Social Networks: Evidence from Thailand. *International Journal of E-Health and Medical Communications*, 7(1), 31–47. doi:10.4018/IJEHMC.2016010102

Brown, S., & Yuan, X. (2016). Techniques for Retaining Computer Science Students at Historical Black Colleges and Universities. In C. Prince & R. Ford (Eds.), *Setting a New Agenda for Student Engagement and Retention in Historically Black Colleges and Universities* (pp. 251–268). Hershey, PA: IGI Global. doi:10.4018/978-1-5225-0308-8.ch014

Burcoff, A., & Shamir, L. (2017). Computer Analysis of Pablo Picasso's Artistic Style. *International Journal of Art, Culture and Design Technologies*, 6(1), 1–18. doi:10.4018/IJACDT.2017010101

Byker, E. J. (2017). I Play I Learn: Introducing Technological Play Theory. In C. Martin & D. Polly (Eds.), *Handbook of Research on Teacher Education and Professional Development* (pp. 297–306). Hershey, PA: IGI Global. doi:10.4018/978-1-5225-1067-3.ch016

Calongne, C. M., Stricker, A. G., Truman, B., & Arenas, F. J. (2017). Cognitive Apprenticeship and Computer Science Education in Cyberspace: Reimagining the Past. In A. Stricker, C. Calongne, B. Truman, & F. Arenas (Eds.), *Integrating an Awareness of Selfhood and Society into Virtual Learning* (pp. 180–197). Hershey, PA: IGI Global. doi:10.4018/978-1-5225-2182-2.ch013

Carlton, E. L., Holsinger, J. W. Jr, & Anunobi, N. (2016). Physician Engagement with Health Information Technology: Implications for Practice and Professionalism. *International Journal of Computers in Clinical Practice*, 1(2), 51–73. doi:10.4018/IJCCP.2016070103

Carneiro, A. D. (2017). Defending Information Networks in Cyberspace: Some Notes on Security Needs. In M. Dawson, D. Kisku, P. Gupta, J. Sing, & W. Li (Eds.), Developing Next-Generation Countermeasures for Homeland Security Threat Prevention (pp. 354-375). Hershey, PA: IGI Global. doi:10.4018/978-1-5225-0703-1.ch016

Cavalcanti, J. C. (2016). The New "ABC" of ICTs (Analytics + Big Data + Cloud Computing): A Complex Trade-Off between IT and CT Costs. In J. Martins & A. Molnar (Eds.), *Handbook of Research on Innovations in Information Retrieval, Analysis, and Management* (pp. 152–186). Hershey, PA: IGI Global. doi:10.4018/978-1-4666-8833-9.ch006

Chase, J. P., & Yan, Z. (2017). Affect in Statistics Cognition. In *Assessing and Measuring Statistics Cognition in Higher Education Online Environments: Emerging Research and Opportunities* (pp. 144–187). Hershey, PA: IGI Global. doi:10.4018/978-1-5225-2420-5.ch005

Chen, C. (2016). Effective Learning Strategies for the 21st Century: Implications for the E-Learning. In M. Anderson & C. Gavan (Eds.), *Developing Effective Educational Experiences through Learning Analytics* (pp. 143–169). Hershey, PA: IGI Global. doi:10.4018/978-1-4666-9983-0.ch006

Chen, E. T. (2016). Examining the Influence of Information Technology on Modern Health Care. In P. Manolitzas, E. Grigoroudis, N. Matsatsinis, & D. Yannacopoulos (Eds.), *Effective Methods for Modern Healthcare Service Quality and Evaluation* (pp. 110–136). Hershey, PA: IGI Global. doi:10.4018/978-1-4666-9961-8.ch006

Cimermanova, I. (2017). Computer-Assisted Learning in Slovakia. In D. Tafazoli & M. Romero (Eds.), *Multiculturalism and Technology-Enhanced Language Learning* (pp. 252–270). Hershey, PA: IGI Global. doi:10.4018/978-1-5225-1882-2.ch015

Cipolla-Ficarra, F. V., & Cipolla-Ficarra, M. (2018). Computer Animation for Ingenious Revival. In F. Cipolla-Ficarra, M. Ficarra, M. Cipolla-Ficarra, A. Quiroga, J. Alma, & J. Carré (Eds.), *Technology-Enhanced Human Interaction in Modern Society* (pp. 159–181). Hershey, PA: IGI Global. doi:10.4018/978-1-5225-3437-2.ch008

Cockrell, S., Damron, T. S., Melton, A. M., & Smith, A. D. (2018). Offshoring IT. In M. Khosrow-Pour, D.B.A. (Ed.), Encyclopedia of Information Science and Technology, Fourth Edition (pp. 5476-5489). Hershey, PA: IGI Global. doi:10.4018/978-1-5225-2255-3.ch476

Coffey, J. W. (2018). Logic and Proof in Computer Science: Categories and Limits of Proof Techniques. In J. Horne (Ed.), *Philosophical Perceptions on Logic and Order* (pp. 218–240). Hershey, PA: IGI Global. doi:10.4018/978-1-5225-2443-4.ch007

Dale, M. (2017). Re-Thinking the Challenges of Enterprise Architecture Implementation. In M. Tavana (Ed.), *Enterprise Information Systems and the Digitalization of Business Functions* (pp. 205–221). Hershey, PA: IGI Global. doi:10.4018/978-1-5225-2382-6.ch009

Das, A., Dasgupta, R., & Bagchi, A. (2016). Overview of Cellular Computing-Basic Principles and Applications. In J. Mandal, S. Mukhopadhyay, & T. Pal (Eds.), *Handbook of Research on Natural Computing for Optimization Problems* (pp. 637–662). Hershey, PA: IGI Global. doi:10.4018/978-1-5225-0058-2.ch026

De Maere, K., De Haes, S., & von Kutzschenbach, M. (2017). CIO Perspectives on Organizational Learning within the Context of IT Governance. *International Journal of IT/Business Alignment and Governance, 8*(1), 32-47. doi:10.4018/IJITBAG.2017010103

Demir, K., Çaka, C., Yaman, N. D., İslamoğlu, H., & Kuzu, A. (2018). Examining the Current Definitions of Computational Thinking. In H. Ozcinar, G. Wong, & H. Ozturk (Eds.), *Teaching Computational Thinking in Primary Education* (pp. 36–64). Hershey, PA: IGI Global. doi:10.4018/978-1-5225-3200-2.ch003

Deng, X., Hung, Y., & Lin, C. D. (2017). Design and Analysis of Computer Experiments. In S. Saha, A. Mandal, A. Narasimhamurthy, S. V, & S. Sangam (Eds.), Handbook of Research on Applied Cybernetics and Systems Science (pp. 264-279). Hershey, PA: IGI Global. doi:10.4018/978-1-5225-2498-4.ch013

Denner, J., Martinez, J., & Thiry, H. (2017). Strategies for Engaging Hispanic/Latino Youth in the US in Computer Science. In Y. Rankin & J. Thomas (Eds.), *Moving Students of Color from Consumers to Producers of Technology* (pp. 24–48). Hershey, PA: IGI Global. doi:10.4018/978-1-5225-2005-4.ch002

Devi, A. (2017). Cyber Crime and Cyber Security: A Quick Glance. In R. Kumar, P. Pattnaik, & P. Pandey (Eds.), *Detecting and Mitigating Robotic Cyber Security Risks* (pp. 160–171). Hershey, PA: IGI Global. doi:10.4018/978-1-5225-2154-9.ch011

Dores, A. R., Barbosa, F., Guerreiro, S., Almeida, I., & Carvalho, I. P. (2016). Computer-Based Neuropsychological Rehabilitation: Virtual Reality and Serious Games. In M. Cruz-Cunha, I. Miranda, R. Martinho, & R. Rijo (Eds.), *Encyclopedia of E-Health and Telemedicine* (pp. 473–485). Hershey, PA: IGI Global. doi:10.4018/978-1-4666-9978-6.ch037

Doshi, N., & Schaefer, G. (2016). Computer-Aided Analysis of Nailfold Capillaroscopy Images. In D. Fotiadis (Ed.), *Handbook of Research on Trends in the Diagnosis and Treatment of Chronic Conditions* (pp. 146–158). Hershey, PA: IGI Global. doi:10.4018/978-1-4666-8828-5.ch007

Doyle, D. J., & Fahy, P. J. (2018). Interactivity in Distance Education and Computer-Aided Learning, With Medical Education Examples. In M. Khosrow-Pour, D.B.A. (Ed.), Encyclopedia of Information Science and Technology, Fourth Edition (pp. 5829-5840). Hershey, PA: IGI Global. doi:10.4018/978-1-5225-2255-3.ch507

Elias, N. I., & Walker, T. W. (2017). Factors that Contribute to Continued Use of E-Training among Healthcare Professionals. In F. Topor (Ed.), *Handbook of Research on Individualism and Identity in the Globalized Digital Age* (pp. 403–429). Hershey, PA: IGI Global. doi:10.4018/978-1-5225-0522-8.ch018

Eloy, S., Dias, M. S., Lopes, P. F., & Vilar, E. (2016). Digital Technologies in Architecture and Engineering: Exploring an Engaged Interaction within Curricula. In D. Fonseca & E. Redondo (Eds.), *Handbook of Research on Applied E-Learning in Engineering and Architecture Education* (pp. 368–402). Hershey, PA: IGI Global. doi:10.4018/978-1-4666-8803-2.ch017

Estrela, V. V., Magalhães, H. A., & Saotome, O. (2016). Total Variation Applications in Computer Vision. In N. Kamila (Ed.), *Handbook of Research on Emerging Perspectives in Intelligent Pattern Recognition, Analysis, and Image Processing* (pp. 41–64). Hershey, PA: IGI Global. doi:10.4018/978-1-4666-8654-0.ch002

Filipovic, N., Radovic, M., Nikolic, D. D., Saveljic, I., Milosevic, Z., Exarchos, T. P., ... Parodi, O. (2016). Computer Predictive Model for Plaque Formation and Progression in the Artery. In D. Fotiadis (Ed.), *Handbook of Research on Trends in the Diagnosis and Treatment of Chronic Conditions* (pp. 279–300). Hershey, PA: IGI Global. doi:10.4018/978-1-4666-8828-5.ch013

Fisher, R. L. (2018). Computer-Assisted Indian Matrimonial Services. In M. Khosrow-Pour, D.B.A. (Ed.), Encyclopedia of Information Science and Technology, Fourth Edition (pp. 4136-4145). Hershey, PA: IGI Global. doi:10.4018/978-1-5225-2255-3.ch358

Fleenor, H. G., & Hodhod, R. (2016). Assessment of Learning and Technology: Computer Science Education. In V. Wang (Ed.), *Handbook of Research on Learning Outcomes and Opportunities in the Digital Age* (pp. 51–78). Hershey, PA: IGI Global. doi:10.4018/978-1-4666-9577-1.ch003

García-Valcárcel, A., & Mena, J. (2016). Information Technology as a Way To Support Collaborative Learning: What In-Service Teachers Think, Know and Do. *Journal of Information Technology Research*, *9*(1), 1–17. doi:10.4018/JITR.2016010101

Gardner-McCune, C., & Jimenez, Y. (2017). Historical App Developers: Integrating CS into K-12 through Cross-Disciplinary Projects. In Y. Rankin & J. Thomas (Eds.), *Moving Students of Color from Consumers to Producers of Technology* (pp. 85–112). Hershey, PA: IGI Global. doi:10.4018/978-1-5225-2005-4.ch005

Garvey, G. P. (2016). Exploring Perception, Cognition, and Neural Pathways of Stereo Vision and the Split–Brain Human Computer Interface. In A. Ursyn (Ed.), *Knowledge Visualization and Visual Literacy in Science Education* (pp. 28–76). Hershey, PA: IGI Global. doi:10.4018/978-1-5225-0480-1.ch002

Ghafele, R., & Gibert, B. (2018). Open Growth: The Economic Impact of Open Source Software in the USA. In M. Khosrow-Pour (Ed.), *Optimizing Contemporary Application and Processes in Open Source Software* (pp. 164–197). Hershey, PA: IGI Global. doi:10.4018/978-1-5225-5314-4.ch007

Ghobakhloo, M., & Azar, A. (2018). Information Technology Resources, the Organizational Capability of Lean-Agile Manufacturing, and Business Performance. *Information Resources Management Journal*, *31*(2), 47–74. doi:10.4018/IRMJ.2018040103

Gianni, M., & Gotzamani, K. (2016). Integrated Management Systems and Information Management Systems: Common Threads. In P. Papajorgji, F. Pinet, A. Guimarães, & J. Papathanasiou (Eds.), *Automated Enterprise Systems for Maximizing Business Performance* (pp. 195–214). Hershey, PA: IGI Global. doi:10.4018/978-1-4666-8841-4.ch011

Gikandi, J. W. (2017). Computer-Supported Collaborative Learning and Assessment: A Strategy for Developing Online Learning Communities in Continuing Education. In J. Keengwe & G. Onchwari (Eds.), *Handbook of Research on Learner-Centered Pedagogy in Teacher Education and Professional Development* (pp. 309–333). Hershey, PA: IGI Global. doi:10.4018/978-1-5225-0892-2.ch017

Gokhale, A. A., & Machina, K. F. (2017). Development of a Scale to Measure Attitudes toward Information Technology. In L. Tomei (Ed.), *Exploring the New Era of Technology-Infused Education* (pp. 49–64). Hershey, PA: IGI Global. doi:10.4018/978-1-5225-1709-2.ch004

Grace, A., O'Donoghue, J., Mahony, C., Heffernan, T., Molony, D., & Carroll, T. (2016). Computerized Decision Support Systems for Multimorbidity Care: An Urgent Call for Research and Development. In M. Cruz-Cunha, I. Miranda, R. Martinho, & R. Rijo (Eds.), *Encyclopedia of E-Health and Telemedicine* (pp. 486–494). Hershey, PA: IGI Global. doi:10.4018/978-1-4666-9978-6.ch038

Gupta, A., & Singh, O. (2016). Computer Aided Modeling and Finite Element Analysis of Human Elbow. *International Journal of Biomedical and Clinical Engineering*, *5*(1), 31–38. doi:10.4018/IJBCE.2016010104

H., S. K. (2016). Classification of Cybercrimes and Punishments under the Information Technology Act, 2000. In S. Geetha, & A. Phamila (Eds.), *Combating Security Breaches and Criminal Activity in the Digital Sphere* (pp. 57-66). Hershey, PA: IGI Global. doi:10.4018/978-1-5225-0193-0.ch004

Hafeez-Baig, A., Gururajan, R., & Wickramasinghe, N. (2017). Readiness as a Novel Construct of Readiness Acceptance Model (RAM) for the Wireless Handheld Technology. In N. Wickramasinghe (Ed.), *Handbook of Research on Healthcare Administration and Management* (pp. 578–595). Hershey, PA: IGI Global. doi:10.4018/978-1-5225-0920-2.ch035

Hanafizadeh, P., Ghandchi, S., & Asgarimehr, M. (2017). Impact of Information Technology on Lifestyle: A Literature Review and Classification. *International Journal of Virtual Communities and Social Networking*, *9*(2), 1–23. doi:10.4018/IJVCSN.2017040101

*Related References*

Harlow, D. B., Dwyer, H., Hansen, A. K., Hill, C., Iveland, A., Leak, A. E., & Franklin, D. M. (2016). Computer Programming in Elementary and Middle School: Connections across Content. In M. Urban & D. Falvo (Eds.), *Improving K-12 STEM Education Outcomes through Technological Integration* (pp. 337–361). Hershey, PA: IGI Global. doi:10.4018/978-1-4666-9616-7.ch015

Haseski, H. İ., Ilic, U., & Tuğtekin, U. (2018). Computational Thinking in Educational Digital Games: An Assessment Tool Proposal. In H. Ozcinar, G. Wong, & H. Ozturk (Eds.), *Teaching Computational Thinking in Primary Education* (pp. 256–287). Hershey, PA: IGI Global. doi:10.4018/978-1-5225-3200-2.ch013

Hee, W. J., Jalleh, G., Lai, H., & Lin, C. (2017). E-Commerce and IT Projects: Evaluation and Management Issues in Australian and Taiwanese Hospitals. *International Journal of Public Health Management and Ethics*, 2(1), 69–90. doi:10.4018/IJPHME.2017010104

Hernandez, A. A. (2017). Green Information Technology Usage: Awareness and Practices of Philippine IT Professionals. *International Journal of Enterprise Information Systems*, 13(4), 90–103. doi:10.4018/IJEIS.2017100106

Hernandez, A. A., & Ona, S. E. (2016). Green IT Adoption: Lessons from the Philippines Business Process Outsourcing Industry. *International Journal of Social Ecology and Sustainable Development*, 7(1), 1–34. doi:10.4018/IJSESD.2016010101

Hernandez, M. A., Marin, E. C., Garcia-Rodriguez, J., Azorin-Lopez, J., & Cazorla, M. (2017). Automatic Learning Improves Human-Robot Interaction in Productive Environments: A Review. *International Journal of Computer Vision and Image Processing*, 7(3), 65–75. doi:10.4018/IJCVIP.2017070106

Horne-Popp, L. M., Tessone, E. B., & Welker, J. (2018). If You Build It, They Will Come: Creating a Library Statistics Dashboard for Decision-Making. In L. Costello & M. Powers (Eds.), *Developing In-House Digital Tools in Library Spaces* (pp. 177–203). Hershey, PA: IGI Global. doi:10.4018/978-1-5225-2676-6.ch009

Hossan, C. G., & Ryan, J. C. (2016). Factors Affecting e-Government Technology Adoption Behaviour in a Voluntary Environment. *International Journal of Electronic Government Research*, 12(1), 24–49. doi:10.4018/IJEGR.2016010102

Hu, H., Hu, P. J., & Al-Gahtani, S. S. (2017). User Acceptance of Computer Technology at Work in Arabian Culture: A Model Comparison Approach. In M. Khosrow-Pour (Ed.), *Handbook of Research on Technology Adoption, Social Policy, and Global Integration* (pp. 205–228). Hershey, PA: IGI Global. doi:10.4018/978-1-5225-2668-1.ch011

Huie, C. P. (2016). Perceptions of Business Intelligence Professionals about Factors Related to Business Intelligence input in Decision Making. *International Journal of Business Analytics*, *3*(3), 1–24. doi:10.4018/IJBAN.2016070101

Hung, S., Huang, W., Yen, D. C., Chang, S., & Lu, C. (2016). Effect of Information Service Competence and Contextual Factors on the Effectiveness of Strategic Information Systems Planning in Hospitals. *Journal of Global Information Management*, *24*(1), 14–36. doi:10.4018/JGIM.2016010102

Ifinedo, P. (2017). Using an Extended Theory of Planned Behavior to Study Nurses' Adoption of Healthcare Information Systems in Nova Scotia. *International Journal of Technology Diffusion*, *8*(1), 1–17. doi:10.4018/IJTD.2017010101

Ilie, V., & Sneha, S. (2018). A Three Country Study for Understanding Physicians' Engagement With Electronic Information Resources Pre and Post System Implementation. *Journal of Global Information Management*, *26*(2), 48–73. doi:10.4018/JGIM.2018040103

Inoue-Smith, Y. (2017). Perceived Ease in Using Technology Predicts Teacher Candidates' Preferences for Online Resources. *International Journal of Online Pedagogy and Course Design*, *7*(3), 17–28. doi:10.4018/IJOPCD.2017070102

Islam, A. A. (2016). Development and Validation of the Technology Adoption and Gratification (TAG) Model in Higher Education: A Cross-Cultural Study Between Malaysia and China. *International Journal of Technology and Human Interaction*, *12*(3), 78–105. doi:10.4018/IJTHI.2016070106

Islam, A. Y. (2017). Technology Satisfaction in an Academic Context: Moderating Effect of Gender. In A. Mesquita (Ed.), *Research Paradigms and Contemporary Perspectives on Human-Technology Interaction* (pp. 187–211). Hershey, PA: IGI Global. doi:10.4018/978-1-5225-1868-6.ch009

Jamil, G. L., & Jamil, C. C. (2017). Information and Knowledge Management Perspective Contributions for Fashion Studies: Observing Logistics and Supply Chain Management Processes. In G. Jamil, A. Soares, & C. Pessoa (Eds.), *Handbook of Research on Information Management for Effective Logistics and Supply Chains* (pp. 199–221). Hershey, PA: IGI Global. doi:10.4018/978-1-5225-0973-8.ch011

Jamil, G. L., Jamil, L. C., Vieira, A. A., & Xavier, A. J. (2016). Challenges in Modelling Healthcare Services: A Study Case of Information Architecture Perspectives. In G. Jamil, J. Poças Rascão, F. Ribeiro, & A. Malheiro da Silva (Eds.), *Handbook of Research on Information Architecture and Management in Modern Organizations* (pp. 1–23). Hershey, PA: IGI Global. doi:10.4018/978-1-4666-8637-3.ch001

Janakova, M. (2018). Big Data and Simulations for the Solution of Controversies in Small Businesses. In M. Khosrow-Pour, D.B.A. (Ed.), Encyclopedia of Information Science and Technology, Fourth Edition (pp. 6907-6915). Hershey, PA: IGI Global. doi:10.4018/978-1-5225-2255-3.ch598

Jha, D. G. (2016). Preparing for Information Technology Driven Changes. In S. Tiwari & L. Nafees (Eds.), *Innovative Management Education Pedagogies for Preparing Next-Generation Leaders* (pp. 258–274). Hershey, PA: IGI Global. doi:10.4018/978-1-4666-9691-4.ch015

Jhawar, A., & Garg, S. K. (2018). Logistics Improvement by Investment in Information Technology Using System Dynamics. In A. Azar & S. Vaidyanathan (Eds.), *Advances in System Dynamics and Control* (pp. 528–567). Hershey, PA: IGI Global. doi:10.4018/978-1-5225-4077-9.ch017

Kalelioğlu, F., Gülbahar, Y., & Doğan, D. (2018). Teaching How to Think Like a Programmer: Emerging Insights. In H. Ozcinar, G. Wong, & H. Ozturk (Eds.), *Teaching Computational Thinking in Primary Education* (pp. 18–35). Hershey, PA: IGI Global. doi:10.4018/978-1-5225-3200-2.ch002

Kamberi, S. (2017). A Girls-Only Online Virtual World Environment and its Implications for Game-Based Learning. In A. Stricker, C. Calongne, B. Truman, & F. Arenas (Eds.), *Integrating an Awareness of Selfhood and Society into Virtual Learning* (pp. 74–95). Hershey, PA: IGI Global. doi:10.4018/978-1-5225-2182-2.ch006

Kamel, S., & Rizk, N. (2017). ICT Strategy Development: From Design to Implementation – Case of Egypt. In C. Howard & K. Hargiss (Eds.), *Strategic Information Systems and Technologies in Modern Organizations* (pp. 239–257). Hershey, PA: IGI Global. doi:10.4018/978-1-5225-1680-4.ch010

Kamel, S. H. (2018). The Potential Role of the Software Industry in Supporting Economic Development. In M. Khosrow-Pour, D.B.A. (Ed.), Encyclopedia of Information Science and Technology, Fourth Edition (pp. 7259-7269). Hershey, PA: IGI Global. doi:10.4018/978-1-5225-2255-3.ch631

Karon, R. (2016). Utilisation of Health Information Systems for Service Delivery in the Namibian Environment. In T. Iyamu & A. Tatnall (Eds.), *Maximizing Healthcare Delivery and Management through Technology Integration* (pp. 169–183). Hershey, PA: IGI Global. doi:10.4018/978-1-4666-9446-0.ch011

Kawata, S. (2018). Computer-Assisted Parallel Program Generation. In M. Khosrow-Pour, D.B.A. (Ed.), Encyclopedia of Information Science and Technology, Fourth Edition (pp. 4583-4593). Hershey, PA: IGI Global. doi:10.4018/978-1-5225-2255-3.ch398

Khanam, S., Siddiqui, J., & Talib, F. (2016). A DEMATEL Approach for Prioritizing the TQM Enablers and IT Resources in the Indian ICT Industry. *International Journal of Applied Management Sciences and Engineering, 3*(1), 11–29. doi:10.4018/IJAMSE.2016010102

Khari, M., Shrivastava, G., Gupta, S., & Gupta, R. (2017). Role of Cyber Security in Today's Scenario. In R. Kumar, P. Pattnaik, & P. Pandey (Eds.), *Detecting and Mitigating Robotic Cyber Security Risks* (pp. 177–191). Hershey, PA: IGI Global. doi:10.4018/978-1-5225-2154-9.ch013

Khouja, M., Rodriguez, I. B., Ben Halima, Y., & Moalla, S. (2018). IT Governance in Higher Education Institutions: A Systematic Literature Review. *International Journal of Human Capital and Information Technology Professionals, 9*(2), 52–67. doi:10.4018/IJHCITP.2018040104

Kim, S., Chang, M., Choi, N., Park, J., & Kim, H. (2016). The Direct and Indirect Effects of Computer Uses on Student Success in Math. *International Journal of Cyber Behavior, Psychology and Learning, 6*(3), 48–64. doi:10.4018/IJCBPL.2016070104

Kiourt, C., Pavlidis, G., Koutsoudis, A., & Kalles, D. (2017). Realistic Simulation of Cultural Heritage. *International Journal of Computational Methods in Heritage Science, 1*(1), 10–40. doi:10.4018/IJCMHS.2017010102

Korikov, A., & Krivtsov, O. (2016). System of People-Computer: On the Way of Creation of Human-Oriented Interface. In V. Mkrttchian, A. Bershadsky, A. Bozhday, M. Kataev, & S. Kataev (Eds.), *Handbook of Research on Estimation and Control Techniques in E-Learning Systems* (pp. 458–470). Hershey, PA: IGI Global. doi:10.4018/978-1-4666-9489-7.ch032

Köse, U. (2017). An Augmented-Reality-Based Intelligent Mobile Application for Open Computer Education. In G. Kurubacak & H. Altinpulluk (Eds.), *Mobile Technologies and Augmented Reality in Open Education* (pp. 154–174). Hershey, PA: IGI Global. doi:10.4018/978-1-5225-2110-5.ch008

Lahmiri, S. (2018). Information Technology Outsourcing Risk Factors and Provider Selection. In M. Gupta, R. Sharman, J. Walp, & P. Mulgund (Eds.), *Information Technology Risk Management and Compliance in Modern Organizations* (pp. 214–228). Hershey, PA: IGI Global. doi:10.4018/978-1-5225-2604-9.ch008

Landriscina, F. (2017). Computer-Supported Imagination: The Interplay Between Computer and Mental Simulation in Understanding Scientific Concepts. In I. Levin & D. Tsybulsky (Eds.), *Digital Tools and Solutions for Inquiry-Based STEM Learning* (pp. 33–60). Hershey, PA: IGI Global. doi:10.4018/978-1-5225-2525-7.ch002

Lau, S. K., Winley, G. K., Leung, N. K., Tsang, N., & Lau, S. Y. (2016). An Exploratory Study of Expectation in IT Skills in a Developing Nation: Vietnam. *Journal of Global Information Management*, *24*(1), 1–13. doi:10.4018/JGIM.2016010101

Lavranos, C., Kostagiolas, P., & Papadatos, J. (2016). Information Retrieval Technologies and the "Realities" of Music Information Seeking. In I. Deliyannis, P. Kostagiolas, & C. Banou (Eds.), *Experimental Multimedia Systems for Interactivity and Strategic Innovation* (pp. 102–121). Hershey, PA: IGI Global. doi:10.4018/978-1-4666-8659-5.ch005

Lee, W. W. (2018). Ethical Computing Continues From Problem to Solution. In M. Khosrow-Pour, D.B.A. (Ed.), Encyclopedia of Information Science and Technology, Fourth Edition (pp. 4884-4897). Hershey, PA: IGI Global. doi:10.4018/978-1-5225-2255-3.ch423

Lehto, M. (2016). Cyber Security Education and Research in the Finland's Universities and Universities of Applied Sciences. *International Journal of Cyber Warfare & Terrorism*, *6*(2), 15–31. doi:10.4018/IJCWT.2016040102

Lin, C., Jalleh, G., & Huang, Y. (2016). Evaluating and Managing Electronic Commerce and Outsourcing Projects in Hospitals. In A. Dwivedi (Ed.), *Reshaping Medical Practice and Care with Health Information Systems* (pp. 132–172). Hershey, PA: IGI Global. doi:10.4018/978-1-4666-9870-3.ch005

Lin, S., Chen, S., & Chuang, S. (2017). Perceived Innovation and Quick Response Codes in an Online-to-Offline E-Commerce Service Model. *International Journal of E-Adoption*, *9*(2), 1–16. doi:10.4018/IJEA.2017070101

Liu, M., Wang, Y., Xu, W., & Liu, L. (2017). Automated Scoring of Chinese Engineering Students' English Essays. *International Journal of Distance Education Technologies*, *15*(1), 52–68. doi:10.4018/IJDET.2017010104

Luciano, E. M., Wiedenhöft, G. C., Macadar, M. A., & Pinheiro dos Santos, F. (2016). Information Technology Governance Adoption: Understanding its Expectations Through the Lens of Organizational Citizenship. *International Journal of IT/Business Alignment and Governance, 7*(2), 22-32. doi:10.4018/IJITBAG.2016070102

Mabe, L. K., & Oladele, O. I. (2017). Application of Information Communication Technologies for Agricultural Development through Extension Services: A Review. In T. Tossy (Ed.), *Information Technology Integration for Socio-Economic Development* (pp. 52–101). Hershey, PA: IGI Global. doi:10.4018/978-1-5225-0539-6.ch003

Manogaran, G., Thota, C., & Lopez, D. (2018). Human-Computer Interaction With Big Data Analytics. In D. Lopez & M. Durai (Eds.), *HCI Challenges and Privacy Preservation in Big Data Security* (pp. 1–22). Hershey, PA: IGI Global. doi:10.4018/978-1-5225-2863-0.ch001

Margolis, J., Goode, J., & Flapan, J. (2017). A Critical Crossroads for Computer Science for All: "Identifying Talent" or "Building Talent," and What Difference Does It Make? In Y. Rankin & J. Thomas (Eds.), *Moving Students of Color from Consumers to Producers of Technology* (pp. 1–23). Hershey, PA: IGI Global. doi:10.4018/978-1-5225-2005-4.ch001

Mbale, J. (2018). Computer Centres Resource Cloud Elasticity-Scalability (CRECES): Copperbelt University Case Study. In S. Aljawarneh & M. Malhotra (Eds.), *Critical Research on Scalability and Security Issues in Virtual Cloud Environments* (pp. 48–70). Hershey, PA: IGI Global. doi:10.4018/978-1-5225-3029-9.ch003

McKee, J. (2018). The Right Information: The Key to Effective Business Planning. In *Business Architectures for Risk Assessment and Strategic Planning: Emerging Research and Opportunities* (pp. 38–52). Hershey, PA: IGI Global. doi:10.4018/978-1-5225-3392-4.ch003

Mensah, I. K., & Mi, J. (2018). Determinants of Intention to Use Local E-Government Services in Ghana: The Perspective of Local Government Workers. *International Journal of Technology Diffusion*, 9(2), 41–60. doi:10.4018/IJTD.2018040103

Mohamed, J. H. (2018). Scientograph-Based Visualization of Computer Forensics Research Literature. In J. Jeyasekar & P. Saravanan (Eds.), *Innovations in Measuring and Evaluating Scientific Information* (pp. 148–162). Hershey, PA: IGI Global. doi:10.4018/978-1-5225-3457-0.ch010

Moore, R. L., & Johnson, N. (2017). Earning a Seat at the Table: How IT Departments Can Partner in Organizational Change and Innovation. *International Journal of Knowledge-Based Organizations*, 7(2), 1–12. doi:10.4018/IJKBO.2017040101

Mtebe, J. S., & Kissaka, M. M. (2016). Enhancing the Quality of Computer Science Education with MOOCs in Sub-Saharan Africa. In J. Keengwe & G. Onchwari (Eds.), *Handbook of Research on Active Learning and the Flipped Classroom Model in the Digital Age* (pp. 366–377). Hershey, PA: IGI Global. doi:10.4018/978-1-4666-9680-8.ch019

Mukul, M. K., & Bhattaharyya, S. (2017). Brain-Machine Interface: Human-Computer Interaction. In E. Noughabi, B. Raahemi, A. Albadvi, & B. Far (Eds.), *Handbook of Research on Data Science for Effective Healthcare Practice and Administration* (pp. 417–443). Hershey, PA: IGI Global. doi:10.4018/978-1-5225-2515-8.ch018

Na, L. (2017). Library and Information Science Education and Graduate Programs in Academic Libraries. In L. Ruan, Q. Zhu, & Y. Ye (Eds.), *Academic Library Development and Administration in China* (pp. 218–229). Hershey, PA: IGI Global. doi:10.4018/978-1-5225-0550-1.ch013

Nabavi, A., Taghavi-Fard, M. T., Hanafizadeh, P., & Taghva, M. R. (2016). Information Technology Continuance Intention: A Systematic Literature Review. *International Journal of E-Business Research*, 12(1), 58–95. doi:10.4018/IJEBR.2016010104

Nath, R., & Murthy, V. N. (2018). What Accounts for the Differences in Internet Diffusion Rates Around the World? In M. Khosrow-Pour, D.B.A. (Ed.), Encyclopedia of Information Science and Technology, Fourth Edition (pp. 8095-8104). Hershey, PA: IGI Global. doi:10.4018/978-1-5225-2255-3.ch705

Nedelko, Z., & Potocan, V. (2018). The Role of Emerging Information Technologies for Supporting Supply Chain Management. In M. Khosrow-Pour, D.B.A. (Ed.), Encyclopedia of Information Science and Technology, Fourth Edition (pp. 5559-5569). Hershey, PA: IGI Global. doi:10.4018/978-1-5225-2255-3.ch483

Ngafeeson, M. N. (2018). User Resistance to Health Information Technology. In M. Khosrow-Pour, D.B.A. (Ed.), Encyclopedia of Information Science and Technology, Fourth Edition (pp. 3816-3825). Hershey, PA: IGI Global. doi:10.4018/978-1-5225-2255-3.ch331

Nozari, H., Najafi, S. E., Jafari-Eskandari, M., & Aliahmadi, A. (2016). Providing a Model for Virtual Project Management with an Emphasis on IT Projects. In C. Graham (Ed.), *Strategic Management and Leadership for Systems Development in Virtual Spaces* (pp. 43–63). Hershey, PA: IGI Global. doi:10.4018/978-1-4666-9688-4.ch003

Nurdin, N., Stockdale, R., & Scheepers, H. (2016). Influence of Organizational Factors in the Sustainability of E-Government: A Case Study of Local E-Government in Indonesia. In I. Sodhi (Ed.), *Trends, Prospects, and Challenges in Asian E-Governance* (pp. 281–323). Hershey, PA: IGI Global. doi:10.4018/978-1-4666-9536-8.ch014

Odagiri, K. (2017). Introduction of Individual Technology to Constitute the Current Internet. In *Strategic Policy-Based Network Management in Contemporary Organizations* (pp. 20–96). Hershey, PA: IGI Global. doi:10.4018/978-1-68318-003-6.ch003

Okike, E. U. (2018). Computer Science and Prison Education. In I. Biao (Ed.), *Strategic Learning Ideologies in Prison Education Programs* (pp. 246–264). Hershey, PA: IGI Global. doi:10.4018/978-1-5225-2909-5.ch012

Olelewe, C. J., & Nwafor, I. P. (2017). Level of Computer Appreciation Skills Acquired for Sustainable Development by Secondary School Students in Nsukka LGA of Enugu State, Nigeria. In C. Ayo & V. Mbarika (Eds.), *Sustainable ICT Adoption and Integration for Socio-Economic Development* (pp. 214–233). Hershey, PA: IGI Global. doi:10.4018/978-1-5225-2565-3.ch010

*Related References*

Oliveira, M., Maçada, A. C., Curado, C., & Nodari, F. (2017). Infrastructure Profiles and Knowledge Sharing. *International Journal of Technology and Human Interaction, 13*(3), 1–12. doi:10.4018/IJTHI.2017070101

Otarkhani, A., Shokouhyar, S., & Pour, S. S. (2017). Analyzing the Impact of Governance of Enterprise IT on Hospital Performance: Tehran's (Iran) Hospitals – A Case Study. *International Journal of Healthcare Information Systems and Informatics, 12*(3), 1–20. doi:10.4018/IJHISI.2017070101

Otunla, A. O., & Amuda, C. O. (2018). Nigerian Undergraduate Students' Computer Competencies and Use of Information Technology Tools and Resources for Study Skills and Habits' Enhancement. In M. Khosrow-Pour, D.B.A. (Ed.), Encyclopedia of Information Science and Technology, Fourth Edition (pp. 2303-2313). Hershey, PA: IGI Global. doi:10.4018/978-1-5225-2255-3.ch200

Özçınar, H. (2018). A Brief Discussion on Incentives and Barriers to Computational Thinking Education. In H. Ozcinar, G. Wong, & H. Ozturk (Eds.), *Teaching Computational Thinking in Primary Education* (pp. 1–17). Hershey, PA: IGI Global. doi:10.4018/978-1-5225-3200-2.ch001

Pandey, J. M., Garg, S., Mishra, P., & Mishra, B. P. (2017). Computer Based Psychological Interventions: Subject to the Efficacy of Psychological Services. *International Journal of Computers in Clinical Practice, 2*(1), 25–33. doi:10.4018/IJCCP.2017010102

Parry, V. K., & Lind, M. L. (2016). Alignment of Business Strategy and Information Technology Considering Information Technology Governance, Project Portfolio Control, and Risk Management. *International Journal of Information Technology Project Management, 7*(4), 21–37. doi:10.4018/IJITPM.2016100102

Patro, C. (2017). Impulsion of Information Technology on Human Resource Practices. In P. Ordóñez de Pablos (Ed.), *Managerial Strategies and Solutions for Business Success in Asia* (pp. 231–254). Hershey, PA: IGI Global. doi:10.4018/978-1-5225-1886-0.ch013

Patro, C. S., & Raghunath, K. M. (2017). Information Technology Paraphernalia for Supply Chain Management Decisions. In M. Tavana (Ed.), *Enterprise Information Systems and the Digitalization of Business Functions* (pp. 294–320). Hershey, PA: IGI Global. doi:10.4018/978-1-5225-2382-6.ch014

Paul, P. K. (2016). Cloud Computing: An Agent of Promoting Interdisciplinary Sciences, Especially Information Science and I-Schools – Emerging Techno-Educational Scenario. In L. Chao (Ed.), *Handbook of Research on Cloud-Based STEM Education for Improved Learning Outcomes* (pp. 247–258). Hershey, PA: IGI Global. doi:10.4018/978-1-4666-9924-3.ch016

Paul, P. K. (2018). The Context of IST for Solid Information Retrieval and Infrastructure Building: Study of Developing Country. *International Journal of Information Retrieval Research*, 8(1), 86–100. doi:10.4018/IJIRR.2018010106

Paul, P. K., & Chatterjee, D. (2018). iSchools Promoting "Information Science and Technology" (IST) Domain Towards Community, Business, and Society With Contemporary Worldwide Trend and Emerging Potentialities in India. In M. Khosrow-Pour, D.B.A. (Ed.), Encyclopedia of Information Science and Technology, Fourth Edition (pp. 4723-4735). Hershey, PA: IGI Global. doi:10.4018/978-1-5225-2255-3.ch410

Pessoa, C. R., & Marques, M. E. (2017). Information Technology and Communication Management in Supply Chain Management. In G. Jamil, A. Soares, & C. Pessoa (Eds.), *Handbook of Research on Information Management for Effective Logistics and Supply Chains* (pp. 23–33). Hershey, PA: IGI Global. doi:10.4018/978-1-5225-0973-8.ch002

Pineda, R. G. (2016). Where the Interaction Is Not: Reflections on the Philosophy of Human-Computer Interaction. *International Journal of Art, Culture and Design Technologies*, 5(1), 1–12. doi:10.4018/IJACDT.2016010101

Pineda, R. G. (2018). Remediating Interaction: Towards a Philosophy of Human-Computer Relationship. In M. Khosrow-Pour (Ed.), *Enhancing Art, Culture, and Design With Technological Integration* (pp. 75–98). Hershey, PA: IGI Global. doi:10.4018/978-1-5225-5023-5.ch004

Poikela, P., & Vuojärvi, H. (2016). Learning ICT-Mediated Communication through Computer-Based Simulations. In M. Cruz-Cunha, I. Miranda, R. Martinho, & R. Rijo (Eds.), *Encyclopedia of E-Health and Telemedicine* (pp. 674–687). Hershey, PA: IGI Global. doi:10.4018/978-1-4666-9978-6.ch052

Qian, Y. (2017). Computer Simulation in Higher Education: Affordances, Opportunities, and Outcomes. In P. Vu, S. Fredrickson, & C. Moore (Eds.), *Handbook of Research on Innovative Pedagogies and Technologies for Online Learning in Higher Education* (pp. 236–262). Hershey, PA: IGI Global. doi:10.4018/978-1-5225-1851-8.ch011

Radant, O., Colomo-Palacios, R., & Stantchev, V. (2016). Factors for the Management of Scarce Human Resources and Highly Skilled Employees in IT-Departments: A Systematic Review. *Journal of Information Technology Research*, *9*(1), 65–82. doi:10.4018/JITR.2016010105

Rahman, N. (2016). Toward Achieving Environmental Sustainability in the Computer Industry. *International Journal of Green Computing*, *7*(1), 37–54. doi:10.4018/IJGC.2016010103

Rahman, N. (2017). Lessons from a Successful Data Warehousing Project Management. *International Journal of Information Technology Project Management*, *8*(4), 30–45. doi:10.4018/IJITPM.2017100103

Rahman, N. (2018). Environmental Sustainability in the Computer Industry for Competitive Advantage. In M. Khosrow-Pour (Ed.), *Green Computing Strategies for Competitive Advantage and Business Sustainability* (pp. 110–130). Hershey, PA: IGI Global. doi:10.4018/978-1-5225-5017-4.ch006

Rajh, A., & Pavetic, T. (2017). Computer Generated Description as the Required Digital Competence in Archival Profession. *International Journal of Digital Literacy and Digital Competence*, *8*(1), 36–49. doi:10.4018/IJDLDC.2017010103

Raman, A., & Goyal, D. P. (2017). Extending IMPLEMENT Framework for Enterprise Information Systems Implementation to Information System Innovation. In M. Tavana (Ed.), *Enterprise Information Systems and the Digitalization of Business Functions* (pp. 137–177). Hershey, PA: IGI Global. doi:10.4018/978-1-5225-2382-6.ch007

Rao, Y. S., Rauta, A. K., Saini, H., & Panda, T. C. (2017). Mathematical Model for Cyber Attack in Computer Network. *International Journal of Business Data Communications and Networking*, *13*(1), 58–65. doi:10.4018/IJBDCN.2017010105

Rapaport, W. J. (2018). Syntactic Semantics and the Proper Treatment of Computationalism. In M. Danesi (Ed.), *Empirical Research on Semiotics and Visual Rhetoric* (pp. 128–176). Hershey, PA: IGI Global. doi:10.4018/978-1-5225-5622-0. ch007

Raut, R., Priyadarshinee, P., & Jha, M. (2017). Understanding the Mediation Effect of Cloud Computing Adoption in Indian Organization: Integrating TAM-TOE- Risk Model. *International Journal of Service Science, Management, Engineering, and Technology*, 8(3), 40–59. doi:10.4018/IJSSMET.2017070103

Regan, E. A., & Wang, J. (2016). Realizing the Value of EHR Systems Critical Success Factors. *International Journal of Healthcare Information Systems and Informatics*, 11(3), 1–18. doi:10.4018/IJHISI.2016070101

Rezaie, S., Mirabedini, S. J., & Abtahi, A. (2018). Designing a Model for Implementation of Business Intelligence in the Banking Industry. *International Journal of Enterprise Information Systems*, 14(1), 77–103. doi:10.4018/IJEIS.2018010105

Rezende, D. A. (2016). Digital City Projects: Information and Public Services Offered by Chicago (USA) and Curitiba (Brazil). *International Journal of Knowledge Society Research*, 7(3), 16–30. doi:10.4018/IJKSR.2016070102

Rezende, D. A. (2018). Strategic Digital City Projects: Innovative Information and Public Services Offered by Chicago (USA) and Curitiba (Brazil). In M. Lytras, L. Daniela, & A. Visvizi (Eds.), *Enhancing Knowledge Discovery and Innovation in the Digital Era* (pp. 204–223). Hershey, PA: IGI Global. doi:10.4018/978-1-5225-4191-2.ch012

Riabov, V. V. (2016). Teaching Online Computer-Science Courses in LMS and Cloud Environment. *International Journal of Quality Assurance in Engineering and Technology Education*, 5(4), 12–41. doi:10.4018/IJQAETE.2016100102

Ricordel, V., Wang, J., Da Silva, M. P., & Le Callet, P. (2016). 2D and 3D Visual Attention for Computer Vision: Concepts, Measurement, and Modeling. In R. Pal (Ed.), *Innovative Research in Attention Modeling and Computer Vision Applications* (pp. 1–44). Hershey, PA: IGI Global. doi:10.4018/978-1-4666-8723-3.ch001

Rodriguez, A., Rico-Diaz, A. J., Rabuñal, J. R., & Gestal, M. (2017). Fish Tracking with Computer Vision Techniques: An Application to Vertical Slot Fishways. In M. S., & V. V. (Eds.), Multi-Core Computer Vision and Image Processing for Intelligent Applications (pp. 74-104). Hershey, PA: IGI Global. doi:10.4018/978-1-5225-0889-2.ch003

Romero, J. A. (2018). Sustainable Advantages of Business Value of Information Technology. In M. Khosrow-Pour, D.B.A. (Ed.), Encyclopedia of Information Science and Technology, Fourth Edition (pp. 923-929). Hershey, PA: IGI Global. doi:10.4018/978-1-5225-2255-3.ch079

Romero, J. A. (2018). The Always-On Business Model and Competitive Advantage. In N. Bajgoric (Ed.), *Always-On Enterprise Information Systems for Modern Organizations* (pp. 23–40). Hershey, PA: IGI Global. doi:10.4018/978-1-5225-3704-5.ch002

Rosen, Y. (2018). Computer Agent Technologies in Collaborative Learning and Assessment. In M. Khosrow-Pour, D.B.A. (Ed.), Encyclopedia of Information Science and Technology, Fourth Edition (pp. 2402-2410). Hershey, PA: IGI Global. doi:10.4018/978-1-5225-2255-3.ch209

Rosen, Y., & Mosharraf, M. (2016). Computer Agent Technologies in Collaborative Assessments. In Y. Rosen, S. Ferrara, & M. Mosharraf (Eds.), *Handbook of Research on Technology Tools for Real-World Skill Development* (pp. 319–343). Hershey, PA: IGI Global. doi:10.4018/978-1-4666-9441-5.ch012

Roy, D. (2018). Success Factors of Adoption of Mobile Applications in Rural India: Effect of Service Characteristics on Conceptual Model. In M. Khosrow-Pour (Ed.), *Green Computing Strategies for Competitive Advantage and Business Sustainability* (pp. 211–238). Hershey, PA: IGI Global. doi:10.4018/978-1-5225-5017-4.ch010

Ruffin, T. R. (2016). Health Information Technology and Change. In V. Wang (Ed.), *Handbook of Research on Advancing Health Education through Technology* (pp. 259–285). Hershey, PA: IGI Global. doi:10.4018/978-1-4666-9494-1.ch012

Ruffin, T. R. (2016). Health Information Technology and Quality Management. *International Journal of Information Communication Technologies and Human Development*, 8(4), 56–72. doi:10.4018/IJICTHD.2016100105

Ruffin, T. R., & Hawkins, D. P. (2018). Trends in Health Care Information Technology and Informatics. In M. Khosrow-Pour, D.B.A. (Ed.), Encyclopedia of Information Science and Technology, Fourth Edition (pp. 3805-3815). Hershey, PA: IGI Global. doi:10.4018/978-1-5225-2255-3.ch330

Safari, M. R., & Jiang, Q. (2018). The Theory and Practice of IT Governance Maturity and Strategies Alignment: Evidence From Banking Industry. *Journal of Global Information Management*, 26(2), 127–146. doi:10.4018/JGIM.2018040106

Sahin, H. B., & Anagun, S. S. (2018). Educational Computer Games in Math Teaching: A Learning Culture. In E. Toprak & E. Kumtepe (Eds.), *Supporting Multiculturalism in Open and Distance Learning Spaces* (pp. 249–280). Hershey, PA: IGI Global. doi:10.4018/978-1-5225-3076-3.ch013

Sanna, A., & Valpreda, F. (2017). An Assessment of the Impact of a Collaborative Didactic Approach and Students' Background in Teaching Computer Animation. *International Journal of Information and Communication Technology Education*, 13(4), 1–16. doi:10.4018/IJICTE.2017100101

Savita, K., Dominic, P., & Ramayah, T. (2016). The Drivers, Practices and Outcomes of Green Supply Chain Management: Insights from ISO14001 Manufacturing Firms in Malaysia. *International Journal of Information Systems and Supply Chain Management*, 9(2), 35–60. doi:10.4018/IJISSCM.2016040103

Scott, A., Martin, A., & McAlear, F. (2017). Enhancing Participation in Computer Science among Girls of Color: An Examination of a Preparatory AP Computer Science Intervention. In Y. Rankin & J. Thomas (Eds.), *Moving Students of Color from Consumers to Producers of Technology* (pp. 62–84). Hershey, PA: IGI Global. doi:10.4018/978-1-5225-2005-4.ch004

Shahsavandi, E., Mayah, G., & Rahbari, H. (2016). Impact of E-Government on Transparency and Corruption in Iran. In I. Sodhi (Ed.), *Trends, Prospects, and Challenges in Asian E-Governance* (pp. 75–94). Hershey, PA: IGI Global. doi:10.4018/978-1-4666-9536-8.ch004

Siddoo, V., & Wongsai, N. (2017). Factors Influencing the Adoption of ISO/IEC 29110 in Thai Government Projects: A Case Study. *International Journal of Information Technologies and Systems Approach, 10*(1), 22–44. doi:10.4018/IJITSA.2017010102

Sidorkina, I., & Rybakov, A. (2016). Computer-Aided Design as Carrier of Set Development Changes System in E-Course Engineering. In V. Mkrttchian, A. Bershadsky, A. Bozhday, M. Kataev, & S. Kataev (Eds.), *Handbook of Research on Estimation and Control Techniques in E-Learning Systems* (pp. 500–515). Hershey, PA: IGI Global. doi:10.4018/978-1-4666-9489-7.ch035

Sidorkina, I., & Rybakov, A. (2016). Creating Model of E-Course: As an Object of Computer-Aided Design. In V. Mkrttchian, A. Bershadsky, A. Bozhday, M. Kataev, & S. Kataev (Eds.), *Handbook of Research on Estimation and Control Techniques in E-Learning Systems* (pp. 286–297). Hershey, PA: IGI Global. doi:10.4018/978-1-4666-9489-7.ch019

Simões, A. (2017). Using Game Frameworks to Teach Computer Programming. In R. Alexandre Peixoto de Queirós & M. Pinto (Eds.), *Gamification-Based E-Learning Strategies for Computer Programming Education* (pp. 221–236). Hershey, PA: IGI Global. doi:10.4018/978-1-5225-1034-5.ch010

Sllame, A. M. (2017). Integrating LAB Work With Classes in Computer Network Courses. In H. Alphin Jr, R. Chan, & J. Lavine (Eds.), *The Future of Accessibility in International Higher Education* (pp. 253–275). Hershey, PA: IGI Global. doi:10.4018/978-1-5225-2560-8.ch015

Smirnov, A., Ponomarev, A., Shilov, N., Kashevnik, A., & Teslya, N. (2018). Ontology-Based Human-Computer Cloud for Decision Support: Architecture and Applications in Tourism. *International Journal of Embedded and Real-Time Communication Systems, 9*(1), 1–19. doi:10.4018/IJERTCS.2018010101

Smith-Ditizio, A. A., & Smith, A. D. (2018). Computer Fraud Challenges and Its Legal Implications. In M. Khosrow-Pour, D.B.A. (Ed.), Encyclopedia of Information Science and Technology, Fourth Edition (pp. 4837-4848). Hershey, PA: IGI Global. doi:10.4018/978-1-5225-2255-3.ch419

Sohani, S. S. (2016). Job Shadowing in Information Technology Projects: A Source of Competitive Advantage. *International Journal of Information Technology Project Management, 7*(1), 47–57. doi:10.4018/IJITPM.2016010104

Sosnin, P. (2018). Figuratively Semantic Support of Human-Computer Interactions. In *Experience-Based Human-Computer Interactions: Emerging Research and Opportunities* (pp. 244–272). Hershey, PA: IGI Global. doi:10.4018/978-1-5225-2987-3.ch008

Spinelli, R., & Benevolo, C. (2016). From Healthcare Services to E-Health Applications: A Delivery System-Based Taxonomy. In A. Dwivedi (Ed.), *Reshaping Medical Practice and Care with Health Information Systems* (pp. 205–245). Hershey, PA: IGI Global. doi:10.4018/978-1-4666-9870-3.ch007

Srinivasan, S. (2016). Overview of Clinical Trial and Pharmacovigilance Process and Areas of Application of Computer System. In P. Chakraborty & A. Nagal (Eds.), *Software Innovations in Clinical Drug Development and Safety* (pp. 1–13). Hershey, PA: IGI Global. doi:10.4018/978-1-4666-8726-4.ch001

Srisawasdi, N. (2016). Motivating Inquiry-Based Learning Through a Combination of Physical and Virtual Computer-Based Laboratory Experiments in High School Science. In M. Urban & D. Falvo (Eds.), *Improving K-12 STEM Education Outcomes through Technological Integration* (pp. 108–134). Hershey, PA: IGI Global. doi:10.4018/978-1-4666-9616-7.ch006

Stavridi, S. V., & Hamada, D. R. (2016). Children and Youth Librarians: Competencies Required in Technology-Based Environment. In J. Yap, M. Perez, M. Ayson, & G. Entico (Eds.), *Special Library Administration, Standardization and Technological Integration* (pp. 25–50). Hershey, PA: IGI Global. doi:10.4018/978-1-4666-9542-9.ch002

Sung, W., Ahn, J., Kai, S. M., Choi, A., & Black, J. B. (2016). Incorporating Touch-Based Tablets into Classroom Activities: Fostering Children's Computational Thinking through iPad Integrated Instruction. In D. Mentor (Ed.), *Handbook of Research on Mobile Learning in Contemporary Classrooms* (pp. 378–406). Hershey, PA: IGI Global. doi:10.4018/978-1-5225-0251-7.ch019

Syväjärvi, A., Leinonen, J., Kivivirta, V., & Kesti, M. (2017). The Latitude of Information Management in Local Government: Views of Local Government Managers. *International Journal of Electronic Government Research*, *13*(1), 69–85. doi:10.4018/IJEGR.2017010105

*Related References*

Tanque, M., & Foxwell, H. J. (2018). Big Data and Cloud Computing: A Review of Supply Chain Capabilities and Challenges. In A. Prasad (Ed.), *Exploring the Convergence of Big Data and the Internet of Things* (pp. 1–28). Hershey, PA: IGI Global. doi:10.4018/978-1-5225-2947-7.ch001

Teixeira, A., Gomes, A., & Orvalho, J. G. (2017). Auditory Feedback in a Computer Game for Blind People. In T. Issa, P. Kommers, T. Issa, P. Isaías, & T. Issa (Eds.), *Smart Technology Applications in Business Environments* (pp. 134–158). Hershey, PA: IGI Global. doi:10.4018/978-1-5225-2492-2.ch007

Thompson, N., McGill, T., & Murray, D. (2018). Affect-Sensitive Computer Systems. In M. Khosrow-Pour, D.B.A. (Ed.), Encyclopedia of Information Science and Technology, Fourth Edition (pp. 4124-4135). Hershey, PA: IGI Global. doi:10.4018/978-1-5225-2255-3.ch357

Trad, A., & Kalpić, D. (2016). The E-Business Transformation Framework for E-Commerce Control and Monitoring Pattern. In I. Lee (Ed.), *Encyclopedia of E-Commerce Development, Implementation, and Management* (pp. 754–777). Hershey, PA: IGI Global. doi:10.4018/978-1-4666-9787-4.ch053

Triberti, S., Brivio, E., & Galimberti, C. (2018). On Social Presence: Theories, Methodologies, and Guidelines for the Innovative Contexts of Computer-Mediated Learning. In M. Marmon (Ed.), *Enhancing Social Presence in Online Learning Environments* (pp. 20–41). Hershey, PA: IGI Global. doi:10.4018/978-1-5225-3229-3.ch002

Tripathy, B. K. T. R., S., & Mohanty, R. K. (2018). Memetic Algorithms and Their Applications in Computer Science. In S. Dash, B. Tripathy, & A. Rahman (Eds.), Handbook of Research on Modeling, Analysis, and Application of Nature-Inspired Metaheuristic Algorithms (pp. 73-93). Hershey, PA: IGI Global. doi:10.4018/978-1-5225-2857-9.ch004

Turulja, L., & Bajgoric, N. (2017). Human Resource Management IT and Global Economy Perspective: Global Human Resource Information Systems. In M. Khosrow-Pour (Ed.), *Handbook of Research on Technology Adoption, Social Policy, and Global Integration* (pp. 377–394). Hershey, PA: IGI Global. doi:10.4018/978-1-5225-2668-1.ch018

Unwin, D. W., Sanzogni, L., & Sandhu, K. (2017). Developing and Measuring the Business Case for Health Information Technology. In K. Moahi, K. Bwalya, & P. Sebina (Eds.), *Health Information Systems and the Advancement of Medical Practice in Developing Countries* (pp. 262–290). Hershey, PA: IGI Global. doi:10.4018/978-1-5225-2262-1.ch015

Vadhanam, B. R. S., M., Sugumaran, V., V., V., & Ramalingam, V. V. (2017). Computer Vision Based Classification on Commercial Videos. In M. S., & V. V. (Eds.), *Multi-Core Computer Vision and Image Processing for Intelligent Applications* (pp. 105-135). Hershey, PA: IGI Global. doi:10.4018/978-1-5225-0889-2.ch004

Valverde, R., Torres, B., & Motaghi, H. (2018). A Quantum NeuroIS Data Analytics Architecture for the Usability Evaluation of Learning Management Systems. In S. Bhattacharyya (Ed.), *Quantum-Inspired Intelligent Systems for Multimedia Data Analysis* (pp. 277–299). Hershey, PA: IGI Global. doi:10.4018/978-1-5225-5219-2.ch009

Vassilis, E. (2018). Learning and Teaching Methodology: "1:1 Educational Computing. In K. Koutsopoulos, K. Doukas, & Y. Kotsanis (Eds.), *Handbook of Research on Educational Design and Cloud Computing in Modern Classroom Settings* (pp. 122–155). Hershey, PA: IGI Global. doi:10.4018/978-1-5225-3053-4.ch007

Wadhwani, A. K., Wadhwani, S., & Singh, T. (2016). Computer Aided Diagnosis System for Breast Cancer Detection. In Y. Morsi, A. Shukla, & C. Rathore (Eds.), *Optimizing Assistive Technologies for Aging Populations* (pp. 378–395). Hershey, PA: IGI Global. doi:10.4018/978-1-4666-9530-6.ch015

Wang, L., Wu, Y., & Hu, C. (2016). English Teachers' Practice and Perspectives on Using Educational Computer Games in EIL Context. *International Journal of Technology and Human Interaction, 12*(3), 33–46. doi:10.4018/IJTHI.2016070103

Watfa, M. K., Majeed, H., & Salahuddin, T. (2016). Computer Based E-Healthcare Clinical Systems: A Comprehensive Survey. *International Journal of Privacy and Health Information Management, 4*(1), 50–69. doi:10.4018/IJPHIM.2016010104

Weeger, A., & Haase, U. (2016). Taking up Three Challenges to Business-IT Alignment Research by the Use of Activity Theory. *International Journal of IT/Business Alignment and Governance, 7*(2), 1-21. doi:10.4018/IJITBAG.2016070101

Wexler, B. E. (2017). Computer-Presented and Physical Brain-Training Exercises for School Children: Improving Executive Functions and Learning. In B. Dubbels (Ed.), *Transforming Gaming and Computer Simulation Technologies across Industries* (pp. 206–224). Hershey, PA: IGI Global. doi:10.4018/978-1-5225-1817-4.ch012

Williams, D. M., Gani, M. O., Addo, I. D., Majumder, A. J., Tamma, C. P., Wang, M., ... Chu, C. (2016). Challenges in Developing Applications for Aging Populations. In Y. Morsi, A. Shukla, & C. Rathore (Eds.), *Optimizing Assistive Technologies for Aging Populations* (pp. 1–21). Hershey, PA: IGI Global. doi:10.4018/978-1-4666-9530-6.ch001

Wimble, M., Singh, H., & Phillips, B. (2018). Understanding Cross-Level Interactions of Firm-Level Information Technology and Industry Environment: A Multilevel Model of Business Value. *Information Resources Management Journal, 31*(1), 1–20. doi:10.4018/IRMJ.2018010101

Wimmer, H., Powell, L., Kilgus, L., & Force, C. (2017). Improving Course Assessment via Web-based Homework. *International Journal of Online Pedagogy and Course Design, 7*(2), 1–19. doi:10.4018/IJOPCD.2017040101

Wong, Y. L., & Siu, K. W. (2018). Assessing Computer-Aided Design Skills. In M. Khosrow-Pour, D.B.A. (Ed.), Encyclopedia of Information Science and Technology, Fourth Edition (pp. 7382-7391). Hershey, PA: IGI Global. doi:10.4018/978-1-5225-2255-3.ch642

Wongsurawat, W., & Shrestha, V. (2018). Information Technology, Globalization, and Local Conditions: Implications for Entrepreneurs in Southeast Asia. In P. Ordóñez de Pablos (Ed.), *Management Strategies and Technology Fluidity in the Asian Business Sector* (pp. 163–176). Hershey, PA: IGI Global. doi:10.4018/978-1-5225-4056-4.ch010

Yang, Y., Zhu, X., Jin, C., & Li, J. J. (2018). Reforming Classroom Education Through a QQ Group: A Pilot Experiment at a Primary School in Shanghai. In H. Spires (Ed.), *Digital Transformation and Innovation in Chinese Education* (pp. 211–231). Hershey, PA: IGI Global. doi:10.4018/978-1-5225-2924-8.ch012

Yilmaz, R., Sezgin, A., Kurnaz, S., & Arslan, Y. Z. (2018). Object-Oriented Programming in Computer Science. In M. Khosrow-Pour, D.B.A. (Ed.), Encyclopedia of Information Science and Technology, Fourth Edition (pp. 7470-7480). Hershey, PA: IGI Global. doi:10.4018/978-1-5225-2255-3.ch650

Yu, L. (2018). From Teaching Software Engineering Locally and Globally to Devising an Internationalized Computer Science Curriculum. In S. Dikli, B. Etheridge, & R. Rawls (Eds.), *Curriculum Internationalization and the Future of Education* (pp. 293–320). Hershey, PA: IGI Global. doi:10.4018/978-1-5225-2791-6.ch016

Yuhua, F. (2018). Computer Information Library Clusters. In M. Khosrow-Pour, D.B.A. (Ed.), Encyclopedia of Information Science and Technology, Fourth Edition (pp. 4399-4403). Hershey, PA: IGI Global. doi:10.4018/978-1-5225-2255-3.ch382

Zare, M. A., Taghavi Fard, M. T., & Hanafizadeh, P. (2016). The Assessment of Outsourcing IT Services using DEA Technique: A Study of Application Outsourcing in Research Centers. *International Journal of Operations Research and Information Systems*, 7(1), 45–57. doi:10.4018/IJORIS.2016010104

Zhao, J., Wang, Q., Guo, J., Gao, L., & Yang, F. (2016). An Overview on Passive Image Forensics Technology for Automatic Computer Forgery. *International Journal of Digital Crime and Forensics*, 8(4), 14–25. doi:10.4018/IJDCF.2016100102

Zimeras, S. (2016). Computer Virus Models and Analysis in M-Health IT Systems: Computer Virus Models. In A. Moumtzoglou (Ed.), *M-Health Innovations for Patient-Centered Care* (pp. 284–297). Hershey, PA: IGI Global. doi:10.4018/978-1-4666-9861-1.ch014

Zlatanovska, K. (2016). Hacking and Hacktivism as an Information Communication System Threat. In M. Hadji-Janev & M. Bogdanoski (Eds.), *Handbook of Research on Civil Society and National Security in the Era of Cyber Warfare* (pp. 68–101). Hershey, PA: IGI Global. doi:10.4018/978-1-4666-8793-6.ch004

# About the Contributors

**Kashif Munir** received his BSc degree in Mathematics and Physics from Islamia University Bahawalpur, Pakistan in 1999. He received his MSc degree in Information Technology from University Sains Malaysia in 2001. He also obtained another MS degree in Software Engineering from University of Malaya, Malaysia in 2005. He completed his PhD in Informatics from Malaysia University of Science and Technology, Malaysia. His research interests are in the areas of Cloud Computing Security, Software Engineering, and Project Management. He has published journal, conference papers and book chapters. Kashif Munir has been in the field of higher education since 2002. After an initial teaching experience with courses in Stamford College, Malaysia for around four years, he later relocated to Saudi Arabia. He worked with King Fahd University of Petroleum and Minerals, KSA from September 2006 till December 2014. He moved into University of Hafr Al-Batin, KSA in January 2015.

\* \* \*

**Guru Prasad Bhandari** received his BCA (Bachelor of Computer Application) degree from Pokhara University, Nepal in 2011 and MCA (Master of Computer Applications) degree from the Department of Computer Science, Institute of Science, Banaras Hindu University, India in 2015. He is currently pursuing Ph.D. in Computer Applications from DST-CIMS, Banaras Hindu University. His research interests cover Cloud Computing, Edge Computing, Service-Oriented Computing, Fault Tolerance and Security. He is currently working on 'Fault Diagnosis of Service-oriented Computing'.

**Nisha Angeline C. V.** is an Assistant Professor in the Dept of Information Technology, Thiagarajar College of Engineering, Madurai.

**Raja Lavanya Chakkaravarthy** is an Assistant Professor of the Department of Computer Science and Engineering, Thiagarajar College of Engineering, Madurai.

**Ratneshwer Gupta** did his Ph.D. in Component Based Software Engineering from Indian Institute of Technology, Banaras Hindu University, Varanasi (IIT-BHU), India. His research area is CBSE and SOA. He is serving as an Assistant Professor in School of Computer & Systems Sciences, JNU, New Delhi – 110067, India. He is actively involved in teaching and research for last 8 years. He has 16 research papers in International Journals and 16 research papers in international/national conference proceedings in his credit.

# Index

## A

Agreement 23, 38, 45-46
Analytics 64-67, 76, 94, 112-113, 140, 151
Apple 127
Architecture 1-5, 7, 10, 12-14, 21-22, 24-
29, 31-32, 53, 65, 70, 73-74, 76, 85,
87-90, 94-96, 113-114, 146-147, 149,
151-153, 159
Authentication 28-29, 51-52, 77, 81, 95,
111, 114, 116, 118, 121-122, 126,
128-129

## B

Biometric Authentication 116, 121
Biometrics 114, 116, 118, 121-122

## C

carbon emission 127
centralized data 146
client senses 100
Cloud Computing 1-7, 10-12, 14, 21-25,
27-32, 38-42, 44-45, 50-52, 55-56,
59, 63-66, 69, 87-90, 94, 103, 105,
111-112, 127-128, 145-149, 151, 159
cloud computing architecture 1-5, 7, 21-22,
24, 27, 29, 31-32, 87, 90
Cloud Environment 45, 50, 52-53, 91
Cloud processing worldview 97

Cloud Security 53
cloud service 23-24, 26-27, 38-39, 41, 44-
45, 51-52, 95, 127, 145-146, 148, 158
cloud-user network 146
commercial models 146
communication cost 127
Composition 8, 28, 38, 44-45
cyber-physical systems 64, 128

## D

Distributed Denial-of-Service (DDOS) 72,
79-80, 132

## E

Edge Computing 1-2, 27, 32, 65, 68-69,
111-112, 147, 149, 151
end-device's credentials 114
end-to-end delay, 127

## F

Fog Computing 63-66, 68-70, 87, 94-98,
100, 103, 105, 111-115, 122, 126-129,
131-135, 140, 145-147, 149-153, 156,
158-159
fog computing architecture 65, 94-96
Fog Computing product 145, 147, 156,
158-159
front-end intelligence 64, 128

# G

geo-distribution 64, 66
geothermal energy 127

# H

highly virtualized platform 112, 127-128

# I

Identification 50, 74, 116, 118-119, 121
information handling 31, 100
infrastructure 2-4, 7-8, 10, 12-16, 20, 22-25, 30, 39, 42, 66, 70, 76-78, 80, 83, 87, 89, 91, 95, 113, 126, 128-129, 146
Internet of Things (IoT) 2, 63-66, 72-81, 83-85, 87, 95, 97, 103, 105, 111-113, 115, 122, 126-128, 146-152
IoT applications 103, 150
IoT architecture 73-74, 76, 85
IoT security 74, 77

# L

Latency 63-66, 68, 87, 94, 112, 127, 146, 150-152
Linux 65, 75, 112
location awareness 63-64, 66

# M

Microsoft Office 365 146
Mirai attack 80
mobile device 2

# N

network edge 112
network resources 2, 66, 91
networked devices 112

# O

OpenFog 113, 127
operating system 14, 21, 67, 79, 112

# P

physical constraints 41-42
Platform-as-a-Service (PaaS) 5, 65
Privacy 10, 27-28, 38, 50-51, 56, 59, 68, 72, 77-78, 81, 85, 92, 111, 114-115, 121, 129, 137, 150-152
Private cloud 7-10
processed locally 112
Protocol 66, 76-77, 126, 128, 134-135, 138

# R

RDoS 80
reduces latency 112
Reference Architecture 24-26, 89, 113
Resource management 51, 66, 70, 95, 152
RFID 73, 75
round-the-clock operation 127

# S

Scalability 19, 24-25, 27-28, 30, 38, 41-44, 59, 68, 77, 103, 113-114, 151-152
Security 5, 10, 13, 20, 22-23, 27-29, 38, 50-53, 55-57, 59, 64-65, 69, 72-74, 76-81, 83-85, 91-93, 97-98, 103, 111, 113-116, 121-122, 128-129, 131-133, 139-141, 145, 148, 150-153, 159
Service 1-3, 5, 8, 10, 13, 15-16, 18-19, 21-24, 26-31, 38-39, 41-42, 44, 46-47, 50-52, 59, 65, 68, 78-81, 87, 89, 91-92, 94-95, 98, 105, 115, 118, 121, 127, 131-132, 134, 145-146, 148-153, 158-159
smart card 114, 116, 118

Software Defined Networks 66
sustainable development 127

transport data 73
Trust 29, 38, 50-51, 56, 59, 114-115

## T

## W

traditional techniques 41-42
traffic congestion 127

wireless nodes 73

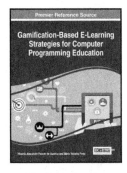
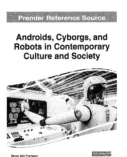

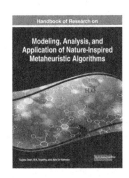

Ensure Quality Research is Introduced to the Academic Community

# Become an IGI Global Reviewer for Authored Book Projects

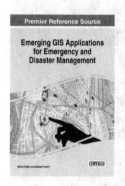

## The overall success of an authored book project is dependent on quality and timely reviews.

In this competitive age of scholarly publishing, constructive and timely feedback significantly expedites the turnaround time of manuscripts from submission to acceptance, allowing the publication and discovery of forward-thinking research at a much more expeditious rate. Several IGI Global authored book projects are currently seeking highly qualified experts in the field to fill vacancies on their respective editorial review boards:

### Applications may be sent to:
development@igi-global.com

Applicants must have a doctorate (or an equivalent degree) as well as publishing and reviewing experience. Reviewers are asked to write reviews in a timely, collegial, and constructive manner. All reviewers will begin their role on an ad-hoc basis for a period of one year, and upon successful completion of this term can be considered for full editorial review board status, with the potential for a subsequent promotion to Associate Editor.

If you have a colleague that may be interested in this opportunity, we encourage you to share this information with them.

Printed in the United States
By Bookmasters